Nelles
Guides

ROME

First Edition
1994

TABLE OF CONTENTS

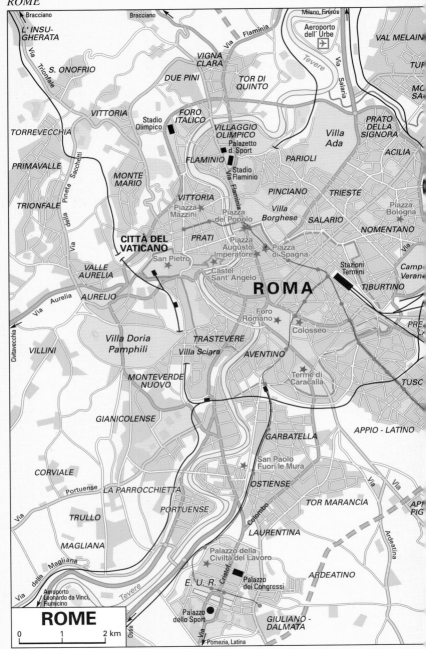

ROME

0   1   2 km

LIST OF MAPS

Nelles Guides

... get you going.

AVAIABLE TITLES

Australia
Bali - Lombok
Berlin *and Potsdam*
Brittany
California
   Las Vegas, Reno, Baja California
Cambodia - Laos
Caribbean
   The Greater Antilles, Bermuda,
   Bahamas
Caribbean
   The Lesser Antilles
China
Crete
Cyprus
Egypt
Florida
Hawaii
Hungary
India
   Northern, Northeastern
   and Central India
India
   Southern India
Indonesia *West*

Kenya
Malaysia
Mexico
Morocco
Moscow - St. Petersburg
Munich *and Surroundings*
Nepal
New York *City and State*
New Zealand
Paris
Philippines
Provence
Rome
Spain *North*
Spain *South*
Thailand
Turkey

IN PREPARATION

Canada (East)
Greece *The Mainland*
Ireland
Vietnam

ROME
© Nelles Verlag GmbH, 80935 Munich
   All rights reserved

First Edition 1994
ISBN 3-88618-391-2
Printed in Slovenia

Publisher:	Günter Nelles	**English Editor:**	Angus McGeoch
Managing Editor:	Dr. Heinz Vestner	**Color separations:**	Reproline, Munich
Project Editor:	Ulrike Bossert	**Cartography:**	Nelles Verlag GmbH
Translation:	A. Midgette, K. Lewis,		by kind permission of
	A. McGeoch,		RV-Verlag, Munich
	R. Sawers	**Printing:**	Gorenjski Tisk, Kranj

- 02 -

ROME –
THE ETERNAL CITY

On 5th November, 1786, Johann Wolfgang von Goethe wrote in his *Travels in Italy*: "Seeing such a city, aged 2000 years and more, which has changed so much and so fundamentally over the years, and yet is still the same soil, the same hill, even the same column or wall, and whose people still bear traces of the ancient Latin character, you become party to some of the great decrees of destiny. And thus, at first, it is hard for the observer to make out the way in which one Rome follows from another: not only chronologically, with the new following upon the old, but all of the different epochs, old and new, overlapping and enriching one another."

Why is it that Rome has always held such a fascination through the ages? Every fan of the city probably has a different answer to this question: Rome's southern flair, its pleasant climate, its cultural treasures...

But you can find these things in other Italian cities, as well: cities which may even be more beautiful, cleaner and better cared for. What makes Rome so fascinating is that its history has remained alive, a self-evident part of the daily life of its citizens, who live matter-of-factly before and within its thousand-year-old walls.

This nonchalant behavior toward the past conveys a sense of security, of continuity, and appeals to a secret yearning inside each one of us. In what other city can you find a mass of silent ruins, populated by countless cats, in the eye of a veritable tornado of traffic; a main thoroughfare built on top of important archaeological excavations, or a building such as the Porta Magica, unique witness to the heyday of 17th century occultism, crumbling away behind piles of garbage from a street market?

We may find these things incomprehensible, but they're merely proof that the Romans don't need to turn every ancient stone into a shrine – they have too many of them. To them, it is a matter of course that centuries overlap in their city and their houses; they take it in stride. And we may be righteously indignant at their indifference, which has allowed a cultural heritage which has survived for more than two thousand years to suffer irreparable damage in the last twenty. Yet secretly we envy the Romans their self-confidence, which is born of the knowledge of their own historical roots, visible all round them.

Rome is not only a city with a city's beauty and blemishes; it is also the inhabitants, who endow the relics of the past with a unique and vibrant life.

Classical antiquity

Every year on 21st April, Rome celebrates its birthday. According to calculations made by the chronicler Varro, the city was founded on that day in the year 753 BC. Although more recent research has proved that much earlier settlements existed, this date, and the legend that goes with it, is held in such affection and honor by the Romans that they continue to celebrate their city's fictitious anniversary with speeches, processions, fanfares and festive illuminations, and many cultural events.

The legend of the foundation of Rome

The romantic legend of Rome's founding, so memorably recounted by Virgil in his epic poem *The Aeneid* (around 20 BC), reaches back to the age

Previous pages: In the Vatican museums. On the Ponte dei Angeli. The Fountains of Trevi. View of Rome with the National Monument. St Peter's Square. Left: St Peter watches over his city.

of the Trojan War. According to Graeco-Roman mythology, Aeneas was the son of the Trojan Anchises and the goddess Aphrodite. After the Greeks sacked Troy (in about 1184 BC), Aeneas's mother ordered him to leave the burning city. Carrying his crippled father on his shoulders, and leading his small son Iulus Ascanius by the hand, he set out to find Italy, the home of his ancestors.

Aeneas's protracted wanderings led him to Sicily, where Anchises died, and to Carthage, where the beautiful Queen Dido fell in love with him and vainly tried to stop him from sailing away. Aeneas finally reached the coast of Latium, where he married Lavinia, the daughter of King Latinus, and succeeded to the throne upon the death of the king. This made him the legendary founder of the Julian dynasty (named after his son Iulus).

Above: The she-wolf with Romulus and Remus. Right: The rape of the Sabine women, painted by J. L. David (1799).

In later years, Julius Caesar and his adopted son, Augustus, claimed to descend from this line, in order to use their supposedly divine ancestry to further their political ambitions.

But to return to the story of the foundation of Rome: Iulus, the son of Aeneas, founded a city called *Alba Longa* in the Alban Hills near the present-day town of Albano. The city blossomed into the capital and cultural center of early Italy. Amulius, a descendant of Iulus, toppled his brother Numitor from the throne. To secure his reign, he made Numitor's daughter, Rhea Silvia, a vestal virgin or a priestess of Vesta, thus preventing her from marrying or bearing children.

However, Mars, the god of war, foiled Amulius's plans by fathering Rhea's twin sons, Romulus and Remus. Amulius ordered that these unwelcome rival heirs be cast into the river Tiber. But the twins were washed up on to the bank, suckled by a she-wolf and eventually found by a shepherd, Faustulus, who raised them together with his wife, Acca Larentia. After growing up to become fine warriors, the twins killed the usurper Amulius and restored their grandfather Numitor to the throne.

The brothers decided to build a new city in the place where they had grown up. As they were twins, neither of them could claim the first-born's right to rule. The gods, therefore, determined which of them could name, and later rule the city, by means of a flight of birds.

The auspices named Romulus, who founded the city of Rome on 21st April, 753 BC by drawing a line in the dust on the Palatine Hill to mark out the area. Remus, however, feeling he had been wronged, scornfully leapt over the city boundary, thus infringing Romulus' authority. This resulted in a fierce quarrel between the brothers in the course of which Romulus killed Remus.

This fratricide became the symbol for the long series of civil wars that were to

mark the coming centuries. For those trying to resist Roman domination, Romulus was seen as the embodiment of the Romans' desire for violent conquest.

According to tradition, Romulus became the first of seven legendary kings who ruled Rome until the advent of the republic. Under his rule the city grew quickly and prospered, but, so the legend goes, the settlement lacked the women who would ensure the continued existence of the new state.

This led to the fabled episode of the Rape of the Sabines: the king arranged a great feast in honor of the god Neptune and invited the men of the neighboring Sabine tribe to come and join the feast with their families. At the height of the festivities the Roman warriors carried off the daughters of their guests, who left in a great fury, vowing revenge. However, the Romans proved to be such loving and attentive husbands that the Sabine women pleaded with their menfolk on their behalf, and the feud between the two tribes was settled amicably.

So much for the legend of Romulus, which admittedly, in recent times, has been lent a certain degree of historical credence through archaeological finds.

There are a number of other stories, of various degrees of credibility, regarding the city of Rome's origins and its name. Various accounts have it that the city was founded by a certain *Romo*, who was either of Greek or Trojan descent; by a local settler called *Romi*; or by various women called *Roma* who hailed from Troy or Latium. "Rome" could also mean "city on the river," from *Rumon*, which is the archaic name for the Tiber, or simply the town of the Etruscan tribe of the *Ruma*. Last but not least it's also possible that the settlement on the Palatine Hill was named from the Etruscan word for breast, *ruma*, because this gently rounded hill is reminiscent of that part of the female anatomy.

Even in Antiquity, many authors debated the question of who founded Rome and how the city was named. Most, however, adhere to Varro's official version.

17

What may really have happened

Like most legends, the Romulus myth probably has some basis in fact, although the real story is much more complex and has to be seen in the context of various cultural phenomena which were affecting the Italian peninsula around the 8th century BC.

It is certain that during this period the powerful Etruscans exercised considerable influence, politically and culturally, on neighboring tribes. The same period saw the first flowering of the extended Greek empire (*Magna Graecia*) in southern Italy. A fragment of Greek pottery dating from the 8th century BC, which was recently found in the Forum Boarium – an ancient marketplace which existed before the foundation of Rome – proves that the newly founded city of Rome already had close trading links with these colonies.

Excavations on the Palatine Hill which revealed the remains of a village (dating from the 8th century BC) also demonstrate that the Palatine, Capitoline and Esquiline Hills, as well as the Quirinal, were settled as early as the 10th century BC. The farmers and shepherds who lived on the hills so as to remain safe from the Tiber's regular floods, from malaria and from enemy attack, probably belonged to the Latin or Sabine tribes. As their villages continued to grow, they quite naturally coalesced to form a larger community, in which the Sabines accepted a subordinate role to the Latins, who lived on the Palatine Hill in what was the most important of these early settlements.

This is the origin of the first city of Rome (*Roma quadrata*). The political and cultural influence of the Greeks and Etruscans played a decisive role in this early settlement.

Right: Roman history encapsulated in stone on the Via Appia.

The Etruscan kings

Rome's favorable position near the sea and at the mouth of the Tiber contributed much to the city's rapid political and economic rise. Under the legendary seven Etruscan kings, Romulus, Numa Pompilius, Tullius Hostilius, Ancus Martius, Tarquinius Priscus, Severius Tullius and Tarquinius Superbus, the city rapidly became rich and powerful.

Most important of the many religious sites built during this period is that of Jupiter Capitolinus, which includes the largest Etruscan temple yet discovered. Under Tarquinius Priscus (616-578 BC) the malaria-infested marshes between the hills were drained, the sewers built (the Cloaca Maxima is still in use even today), and the foundations laid for the Forum Romanum, the focus of public life. The somewhat later Servian Wall also dates back in its earliest form to the time of the monarchy, and gives an impression of the size of the city in those days. It covered 1.6 sq. miles (4 sq. km) and was larger than any other town on the Italian peninsula.

The century under Etruscan rule saw the birth of the most important symbols and traditions of the Roman state, and without giving up their Latin character or culture, the Romans adopted religious customs and institutions of the Etruscans which survived throughout the Roman republic.

The early republic

Around 509 BC, the people revolted against the tyrant Tarquinius Superbus, and ousted him from power. This ended the Etruscan monarchy and ushered in the age of the Roman republic. The supreme authority in the state was the Senate, which consisted of the patricians or nobles, in which two elected Consuls held the reins of government. Then there were the plebeians or common people,

who struggled for years to gain important political rights such as an assembly and the appointment of spokesmen called Tribunes of the People. In the middle of the 5th century BC the Twelve Tables were passed, which empowered the upper class of plebeians to hold office, and generally equalized plebeians' rights with those of patricians. Around 300 BC a new upper stratum emerged from the class struggle: the *nobilitas*, to which any Roman belonged provided he or one of his ancestors had held high office.

As far as foreign policy was concerned, Rome started by limiting itself to forming alliances with neighboring peoples against Etruscan tribes. The city suffered a severe setback in 387 BC, when the Gauls attacked and left it in smouldering ruins. It is said that most of the documents from the city's early history were destroyed in this fire, but it is more likely that the scant knowledge we have of these early centuries is due to the fact that written documents were rare at that early date.

Even after the end of the monarchy, building activity had continued at a rapid pace: this period saw the construction of temples to Saturn, the Dioscuri (Castor and Pollux), and Ceres. After the Gallic invasion, there was a new surge of building. The city walls, which had failed to withstand the enemy attack, were rebuilt as the Servian Wall with massive blocks of volcanic stone. The new city rose gradually from the ruins, shattered temples were rebuilt or altered and new ones erected. Under the Censor Claudius Caecus the first aqueduct for the city's water supply was constructed; wide roads, such as the Via Appia, were built to link the city with the recently conquered regions beyond Latium.

One by one, the towns of Italy were subjugated or forced into alliances; in the north the Samnites and the Gauls were conquered, and after three defeats at the hands of Pyrrhus, whom the Greek city of Tarentum in Apulia had summoned for assistance, Rome finally overcame its last adversary in southern Italy. The entire

peninsula was now in the hands of the Romans, who, to satisfy their thirst for territorial expansion, now turned their gaze to regions beyond Italy.

The expansion of the empire

Between 264 and 146 BC the three Punic Wars, waged against Carthage, Rome's former ally in North Africa, laid the foundations of the Roman Empire. The great Carthaginian commander, Hannibal, brought Rome to the brink of defeat, but eventually Rome's most powerful trading rival in the western Mediterranean was destroyed, just as Marcus Porcius Cato had been demanding at the end of every speech: "*Et ceterum censeo Carthaginem esse delendam.*" ("and furthermore I say that Carthage must be destroyed.") Rome thus gained the province of Africa and made Sicily, Sardinia, Corsica and Spain into its first colonies.

Above: Roman soldiers depicted in a mosaic in Palestrina. Right: Remains of a Roman aqueduct.

The Romans also waged war in the Balkans, against the Illyrians (229-228 BC and 219 BC) and the Macedonians (215-205 BC; 200-197 BC; 171-68 BC). After the important victories in Greece and Asia Minor over Antiochus III, Perseus and the Achaean League, Rome had absolute political and military control over the whole Mediterranean area.

From the conquered lands to the east — but mainly from Greece — Hellenistic culture found its way to Rome. Important artists and writers influenced literature and the theater, producing a first flowering of cultural brilliance.

Greek architecture was favored by the nobility and by the self-made men who had profited from the many wars. They built luxurious villas with marble and mosaic floors, wall-paintings and richly gilded and decorated ceilings. Remains of these villas can still be admired today, especially on the Palatine and Esquiline Hills. Wonderful gardens and magnificent villas like Nero's Domus Aurea gave the city its characteristic stamp.

Many new temples and stately public buildings bear witness to the great wealth of Rome, which had developed into a hub of world commerce. Ostia was developed into a port, and goods from Greece and Asia Minor were transported up the Tiber into the city and then sold in the great markets. The network of roads was extended, and work pushed ahead with the construction of aqueducts, to provide sufficient food and water for the rapidly growing city.

On a social level, however, the military victories gave rise to all sorts of problems. The peasants, who formed the bulk of the army but had no share in the booty, could no longer tend their fields and became increasingly impoverished. They moved into the city and established a kind of sub-class which lived off the rest of society. The deserted fields were bought up cheaply by war profiteers, and tilled with the help of slaves who were brought back in thousands from the conquered territories. And slaves weren't only used for agricultural purposes. In city workshops and quarries, mines and domestic service, slaves furnished the manpower and became the basis for the production and economy of the ancient world. Defined as "things with feet like a person" slaves were treated as objects which were only useful as long as they continued to function. If a slave died and therefore became "useless," he was thrown into a huge mass grave and left to rot with other corpses under the open sky. At some point between 40 and 35 BC, Maecenas, the wealthy friend of the emperor Augusts and famous patron of Virgil and Propertius, had he burial ground levelled and beautiful gardens laid out over it.

In addition to the construction of stately public buildings and edifices including colonnades, temples, baths, theaters and amphitheaters, private housing construction was also booming. The large number of poor migrants created a need for space-saving accommodation, which is how the first multi-storey tenements came to be built, the so-called *insulae*, which could be provided quickly

21

and cheaply by building speculators. Unfortunately, the walls of these quickly-built structures were unstable, and the houses, up to five stories high, kept collapsing and killing their numerous occupants. Another scourge was fire. As open fires were used for cooking and heating, and candles and oil-lamps for light, it was only too easy for wooden beams and floorboards to catch alight. Naturally there was no running water in these houses; it had to be laboriously carried from the nearest fountain, which meant it was hardly possible to fight a fire that had broken out. The very poorest people, who dwelt in the topmost storeys, had to live with the permanent fear of being burnt alive. For the owners, the high fire-risk cancelled out the advantage of profitable revenues from the building, and rents were therefore exorbitant.

Gradually the fact that political power was concentrated in the hands of a wealthy

Above: The murder of Julius Caesar (painting by J. L. Gerôme, 1867).

few, while the masses lived in abject poverty, led to a mood of rebellion in the city. The tribunes Tiberius and Caius Gracchus tried to pacify the people by distributing property to landless citizens and cheap grain to the needy. Both brothers paid for their enlightened ideas on social reform with their lives: Tiberius was murdered by patrician senators and Caius slain during the riots in 121 BC.

The era of the Civil Wars

These outbreaks of social unrest culminated in a long period of civil war. The Italian allies were demanding Roman citizenship, Spartacus was organizing an uprising of the slaves, and the coasts of Italy were threatened by pirates. Within the Roman ruling classes there was rivalry between the *Optimates* led by Sulla and the *Populares* under Caius Marius. In 105 BC Marius reorganized the Roman militia into a standing professional army with which he waged war against Jugurtha, King of Numidia, in North Africa, and against the Cimbri and Teutones in northern Europe. After his death in 86 BC the leadership of the *Populares* was taken over by Cnaeus Pompeius (generally known in history as Pompey). Together with Caius Julius Caesar and Crassus, he formed the First Triumvirate (60 BC), which was in fact an alliance against the aristocratic opposition.

The next civil war (49-45 BC) focused on nothing less than leadership of the Roman state. Caesar emerged triumphant. Abroad, he conquered Gaul and invaded Britain domestically, he was a clever enough politician to amass so much power that he ultimately declared himself dictator for life. Fearing that Caesar might have ambitions of founding an imperial dynasty, Cassius and Brutus formed their famous conspiracy against him, and Caesar was assassinated on the Ides of March, in the year 44 BC.

The Second Triumvirate, formed by Caesar's adopted son, Octavian (later to become the Emperor Augustus), Marcus Antonius (Mark Antony) and Lepidus, emerged victorious from the renewed powerstruggle against the aristocracy. Octavian also aspired to rule alone, but managed to avoid giving rise to suspicions that he wanted to become king. After his victories in 42 BC over Caesar's murderers, Brutus and Cassius, at Philippi, and over Antony and Cleopatra in 31 BC in the naval battle of Actium, Octavian was given the honorary title of *princeps* (first citizen), and in 27 BC he invited the Senate to confer on him the name Augustus, the "august" or "respected." He reigned over the Roman Empire under this name until 14 AD, and it is as Emperor Augustus that he has become known to history.

The Julian-Claudian dynasty and the Flavians

Although Augustus proclaimed the "restoration of the republic," he was *de* *facto* sole ruler. He commanded the army, all government officials were accountable to him, and the Senate was reduced to being an honorary assembly without any real power. Those nobles most loyal to the emperor were appointed urban prefects and made responsible for public order; while the emperor himself was under the protection of the Praetorian Guard. Popular attention was diverted from politics with "bread and games" *(panem et circenses)* which kept the masses happy, while a whole series of very necessary administrative reforms (reorganization of the army, improvement of the water and grain supply, creation of a civil service, and the revival of religion) led chroniclers of the period to speak of a "golden age", an "age of peace."

For these reasons Augustus, who had already become the object of a cult in Italy and the provinces during his lifetime, was elevated to the status of *divus* (a god of the state) after his death, as Julius Caesar had been before him.

Although the republic continued in name, it was a form of hereditary monarchy that was practiced after the reign of Augustus. His successor, Tiberius, had been adopted by him, while Caligula, Claudius and Nero were his blood relatives. Under Tiberius, Caligula and Nero, autocracy turned into vicious despotism; only the sober Claudius (41-54 AD), the successful conqueror and colonizer of Britain, tried to negotiate with the Senate. The half-mad Nero, who succeeded him, was declared a public enemy by the Senate and committed suicide.

In the year of the four emperors (68/69 AD), Galba, Otho, Vitellius and Vespasian were all simultaneously declared emperor by different factions of the army. It was Vespasian who emerged as victor from the ensuing struggle for power. Ruling from 69 to 79 AD, he was the founder of the Flavian dynasty, under which the era of peace and prosperity in

the Roman Empire continued. His son Domitian (81-96 AD) came to power after the death of his brother Titus, and ruled until 96 AD, when he was assassinated at the instigation of the Senate. He was the last of the Flavian emperors.

The cultural heritage of the Julian-Claudian dynasty can be seen in the important monuments erected during this period, such as the Theater of Marcellus. the Pantheon, the Mausoleum of Augustus and the Altar of Peace (*Ara Pacis*). The first century AD saw the redesigning of the Forum Romanum and the construction of large palaces on the Palatine Hill – the Domus Tiberiana, the Domus Flavia and the Domus Augustana. Under Nero, the first large-scale thermal baths were built on the Field of Mars, and after the great fire which reduced Rome to ashes in 64 AD the magnificent Domus Aurea ("Golden House")

Above: Bronze statue of the emperor Augustus. Right: Daily life in the Forum Romanum at the beginning of the 3rd century.

project was started, in which large parts of the city center were turned into a gigantic villa complex.

After Nero's death Vespasian handed a large part of the complex back to the public. He had the large artificial lake filled in, and on its site work was started on the Colosseum, which was completed under Titus. To the east of the Forum Romanum, the fora of Augustus and of Vespasian were created. Because the earlier civil wars had occupied people with problems other than enlarging and beautifying their city, building activity during the early years of empire had to make up for lost time; Augustus could say with justification that he had found a city of brick and left one of marble. Most of the ancient Rome that we admire today the emperors of the first century AD.

Trajan, the Antonine and Severian Emperors

Nerva (96-98AD) was the first in a series of "adopted emperors." Nerva, Trajan, Hadrian, Antoninus Pius, Marcus Aurelius, Lucius Verus and Commodus were all selected as the "best" candidates and deliberately trained to hold the "office" of emperor. The most memorable ruler of all of them was Trajan (98-117 AD). His domestic policies included promoting trade and transport, defending social justice, and seeing to the maintance of widows, orphans and the education of the young.

Abroad, the Roman Empire reached the height of its territorial expansion under Trajan and his successors. It stretched from Spain to Armenia, and from Britain to Egypt. Generations later, Mussolini set up three maps engraved in stone in the Via dei Fori, below the Basilica of Constantine, which show the Roman Empire's tremendous territorial expansion during its first seven centuries.

The prosperity of the empire was based on the ruthless exploitation of the con-

quered countries; but it was accompanied by certain political rights, which were extended to the people of the newly conquered, now Roman territories. This was a logical step, as Trajan himself came from a province, Hispania. The population of the city of Rome had already exceeded the one-million mark.

The second century also saw brisk building activity. One of the most important projects resulted in the largest and most splendid of all the imperial fora, the Forum of Trajan. Closely related to this project was the building of the Markets of Trajan, for which the ridge between the Capitoline Hill and the Quirinal had to be leveled. Construction boomed, both in the public and private sector. The large thermal baths on the Oppian Hill set the tone for the type of imperial baths later adopted by Caracalla and Diocletian, in which every minute detail was carefully planned.

Under Hadrian and Antoninus Pius, building activity reached its peak. Whole districts with multi-storey tenement houses were constructed, while the villa Hadrian had built at Tivoli, proved such a succesful synthesis of functional architecture and the philosophical consideration of every aspect of daily life that it became a kind of model for the architecture of the second century. The villa's designers quoted architectural styles from every part of the empire; combining them into a harmonious whole in the dwelling of the supreme ruler was a fine symbol of the Roman Empire's unity. Other important monuments to this period are the famous equestrian statue of Marcus Aurelius, and the columns of Trajan and Marcus Aurelius, on which the rulers' deeds are immortalized in bas-reliefs.

The death of Marcus Aurelius, the "philosopher emperor," which was probably caused by a plague spread by his own troops, and the murder of his successor, Commodus, meant the end of the Antonine epoch and its long period of peace. Increasing unrest along the frontiers heralded the beginning of the great westward migrations of tribes through

Europe. Fortifying walls, or limes, were supposed to make the Roman borders safe from enemy attack. Yet Germanic tribes penetrated into Italy, the Balkans and Asia Minor, bringing about the Empire's the first major crisis.

The soldier emperors and Diocletian

The founder of the Severian imperial dynasty, Septimius Severus, had to contend with four years of civil war (193-197). The third century, which saw a series of emperors follow one another in quick succession, is known as the century of the soldier emperors. Caracalla (211-217) granted Roman citizenship to everyone living within the confines of the empire. But as hostile tribes penetrated the north and east, while rulers in the capital squabbled over succesion, the empire gradually began to dissolve. In 270 emperor Aurelian built a new city wall to protect the capital, which was called, logically enough, the Aurelian Wall. Although Aurelian succeeded in re-establishing some measure of unity within the empire, the new wall remained a symbol of its military vulnerability, and heralded its long and irreversible decline.

In 284, Diocletian was proclaimed emperor by his troops. His rule established the absolutist state of late antiquity, the so-called "dominatus". Reorganizing the government to take the specific needs of the third century into account, he divided the empire into four parts, making it a tetrarchy governed by four regents.

The city of Rome experienced a new spurt of growth. After a disastrous fire in 283 destroyed a large part of the city center, existing monuments, such as the Curia, were restored, and new buildings, including the Baths of Diocletian, the Basilica of Maxentius and the Arch of Constantine, were erected. The early fourth century also saw the creation of monumental staues of the emperors, a new art form: one example ist the statue of Constantine in the Basilica of Maxentius. However the main thrust of the building activity was directed to the preservation of the old buildings, which were gradually ceasing to be used for their original functions and were falling into ruin.

The cult of the state god *Sol Invictus* (the unconquered god of sun) as well as the mystic religions that were coming into Rome from Asia Minor and Egypt (including the cults of Isis and Mithras) showed that the Roman mentality was turning away from the traditional Graeco-Roman pantheon towards a monotheism which prefigured Christianity. The new religion of the gospels had already taken root among the lower classes and slaves of Rome. As early as the first century Paul preached to crowds in cities of the Roman empire and in Rome itself. Small groups of Christians established themselves and were soon numerous enough for the emperor Nero to consider them a danger and to single them out for persecution. The early Christians had to remain literally hidden and meet in caverns and cellars. They were often made scapegoats for Rome's increasing economic and political problems. By the time of Diocletian Christianity had spread upward to wealthy and influential families. They were a dissident movement, protesting against the cruelty of the amphitheater, and demanding fair treatment for women and slaves. Their pacifist, egalitarian views were anathema to Diocletian, who clung to the old Roman customs and tried to destroy the new religion in a campaign of bloody suppression.

Christianity becomes the state religion

Over the years, Rome had lost its status as single capital of the empire: imperial

Right: The Donation of Constantine (fresco from the 13th century).

courts were held in Milan, Trier, in western Germany, and Sirmium and Nicomedeia in Asia Minor. The two Roman emperors, Diocletian in the east and Maximianus in the west, were each assisted by a deputy and heirapparent, known as a Caesar. However, when the two emperors stepped in 305 AD, this succession did not take place, and the empire's original capital became once again the center of events. The Roman legions in Britain nominated their commander, Constantine, then aged 32, to be the next emperor. Constantine defeated the two Caesars, Maxentius and Licinius, in a series of brilliant campaigns, with a final victory at Milvian Bridge in 312.

The new Emperor completed the military dictatorship which Diocletian had begun, and secured the power of the aristocracy.

In 313, in the Edict of Milan, he granted Christianity equal status with other religions, thus laying the cornerstone for Rome's becoming the capital of Christendom and the seat of the popes. At the same time he adopted the new faith himself and effectively assumed leadership of the church at the Council of Nicaea in 325. Christianity thus became identified with the Roman state, though it did not become the sole official state religion until 381.

The new ecclesiastical power manifested itself in the Christian churches, which started out in converted private houses, but later became separate, and important, buildings. Imperial constructions such as St Peter's in the Vatican and S.Paolo fuori le Mura were modeled on the great courthouse basilicas of antiquity; the beautiful churches of S. Agnese fuori le Mura, S. Lorenzo or S. Sabina on the Aventine Hill all date from this period.

The earliest Christian art was ornamental rather than illustrative, but the old Roman "love of the picture" soon made itself felt. Mosaic techniques which had been passed down from antiquity reached new heights in the depiction of the new Christian subjects.

27

As classical buildings served as models for the Christian churches or were even converted into them (the church of S. Costanza, for example, had been an imperial mausolem), a new city rose up alongside, and on top of, the old one: Christian Rome.

The division into a western and an eastern empire

In 324 Constantine declared the ancient and formerly Greek city of Byzantium to be the new imperial capital. It received its city charter in 330, when its name was officially changed to Constantinople. Rome and the western part of the empire increasingly lost their importance as Constantine's successors divided up the empire among themsleves or ruled as

Above: Rome under siege by the Ostrogoths (a colored wood engraving from the 19th cent.) Right: Charlemagne is crowned emperor in Rome in the year 800 AD.

despots. The last ruler of the empire as a whole, Theodosius I, forbade all heathen rites; a result of this was that the pagan temples of Rome – those that had not been converted into Christian churches – fell further and further into decay. The affluent Romans fled to the eastern part of the empire, to Constantinople and Asia Minor, where there was less danger of invasion by Germanic hordes. Their empty villas were left to fall into ruin.

After Theodosius' death in 395 there was nothing to prevent the permanent division of Rome into an Eastern and a Western empire from taking place. The city of Rome was finally captured and plundered in 410 by the Visigoths under Alaric; in 455 it suffered the same fate again, this time at the hands of Gaiseric, king of the Vandals. Although it is often asserted that the Germanic tribes (who were generally termed barbarians) set out to destroy Rome's historic monuments and art treasures, there is no concrete proof that these original acts of "Vandalism" ever actually occured. Rome certainly suffered damage in the fighting: many important buildings were destroyed, and many works of art were spirited away in the looting which inevitably followed. On the other hand, one must not forget that some 4,000 bronze statues had already been removed from Rome to adorn the new capital, Constantinople.

The last emperors of the Western Empire transferred the seat of government from Rome, first to Milan and then to Ravenna. Emperor Romulus Augustulus abdicated in 476, and the Gothic king Odovacer, and his successor Theodoric, ruled Italy from the new capital, Ravenna, for the next half century. Thus the Western Roman Empire came to an end. The Eastern Empire held on for almost a thousand years more, until the Turks captured Constantinople in 1453.

Rome at its nadir

With the sieges and sackings of the Gothic Wars (535-553), famine, and plague, the once-proud city of a million people became a ghost town of 25,000, parts of it deserted completely. In the struggle between the Germanic tribes and the Byzantines to secure the succession to the Western Roman Empire, the city temporarily returned to the Eastern Empire in 553.

Popes Leo the Great (440-461) and Gregory the Great (590-604) tried to protect it, but without much succes. Still, it was the papacy which was to form the foundation of the city's future significance. It took over the administrative function of the former, now-vanished, secular government.

Christian institutions, such as the diaconia or hospices for the poor, caused new life to blossom from the ruins. In place of the Forum and the Capitoline, the Lateran, the seat of the head of the church, became the new center of there awakening city.

THE MIDDLE AGES
The development of the Papal State

After 568 the Lombards, who had arrived in the last great wave of Teutonic migrations, controlled virtually the whole of Italy. Pope Gregory was able to negotiate a peace treaty, thus temporarily averting the threat to Rome's independence, but in 754 Pope Stephen II was forced to call upon Pippin, King of the Franks, for help. The Lombards were indeed vanquished by Pippin, and their territories handed over to the Pope in what came to be known as the Donation of Pippin. This provided the basis for the Papal State. When Pope Leo III crowned Charlemagne emperor in St Peter's on Christmas Day, 800, the close links between the German kings and the papacy within the "Holy Roman Empire" were officially recognized and confirmed.

Thus imperial sovereignty was recognized to exist alongside the sovereignty of the popes, although the Frankish king also had an obligation to protect the church of Rome. Trying to reconcile the powers of the Emperor and those of the Pope became a bone of contention which led to repeated power struggles throughout the Middle Ages, and was to play a decisive rule in the history of the city.

The German emperors in Rome

Charlemagne's coronation as emperor, meant a rebirth of the Western Roman Empire, and its old capital regained something of its former glory.

Pope Leo III had the Lateran Palace expanded in magnificent style so that it could stand up to comparison with the great imperial palace in Constantinople, and at the same time form a link to the city's power under the reign of Constantine and to the classic Rome of antiquity. The popes increased, stabilized power was also reflected in the building of churches. S. Prassede was built, SS. Quattro Coronati extended and elaborately decorated, and the precious inlay work of the Cosmati family in the floors, altars, chandeliers and thrones, developed into a typical element in the flourishing new art of Roman church decoration. It has survived to the present day in such churches as S. Lorenzo fuori le mura, S. Maria in Cosmedin and S. Clemente.

The outward show of splendor was encouraged not least by the frequent presence of the German emperors in Rome. Appearances notwithstanding, the economic and political situation remained unchanged. One threat was posed by the Saracens, who pillaged the churches of S. Pietro and S. Paolo fuori le mura, situated outside the city walls, in the middle of the 9th century. In reaction, Leo IV had the Leonine Wall built around the southern half of what is today Vatican City. It was intended to protect St Peter's tomb, which was becoming an

Right: The cloister in the courtyard of S. Paolo fuori le Mura.

increasingly popular destination for Christian pilgrims from all over Europe and Asia Minor. Even within the city, things were far from peaceful. Charlemagne's successors had what might be termed a complicated relationship with Rome, while the popes were less than happy about their dependence on the imperial dynasty. The more intense the disgreements between the emperors and the papacy, the greater became the influence of powerful patrician families such as the Frangipani, Colonna, Pierleoni, Crescenzi, Tuscolani, Annibaldi, Orsini and others, who engaged in bloody power-struggles amongst themselves. They also interfered in the political process, installing and removing popes as they saw fit and regarding themselves as the successors to the patrician families of antiquity, who had once held the destiny of Rome in their hands. Since many popes were themselves patricians, they were pulled into the quarrels between the great families. The ordinary people also took sides, sometimes with the Pope and sometimes against him. There were repeated violent disturbances and uprisings, and only Otto III, who ruled on the Aventine Hill in the years 1000 and 1001, hoping thus to make Rome a new center for the Holy Roman Empire, managed to bring a brief hiatus to the fighting. The papacy meanwhile, became more and more entangled in squabbles over secular power; the highest office of Christianity was corrupted and made to function as a purely political instrument. Under Benedict IX the papacy reached its nadir. This pontiff lived in the lap of luxury, surrounded by immense wealth and beautiful women. A conspiracy succeeded in deposing him, but his successor was hardly better. Not until Leo IX and Alexander II, who reigned in the 11th century, did Popes make any attempt to reform the morally depraved Church; they demanded the sole right of the Church to elect the Pope and vest bishops.

But when the Church made such claims to power, it led to bad feeling with the Emperors. Pope Grepory VII took the desire for ecclesiatical power to its limits by demanding the Pope's right to depose the Emperor; this gave rise to a bitter conflict with Emperor Henry IV, who was ultimately excommunicated. Since this meant his losing most of his followers, he felt he had no alternative but to make a penitential pilgrimage, the Walk to Canossa, to seek the Pope's pardon and to swear allegiance to him.

In the course of a second dispute, the Emperor marched against Rome and besieged the city. Gregory VII called upon the Norman Robert Guiscard, Duke of Apulia, for help. Guiscard did free the Pope, but then set about pillaging and burning the city with complete abandon. The people held Pope Gregory responsible for their suffering and hardship; he was driven out of the city and died in Salerno in 1085.

Again and again in the course of the following century Rome was the setting for the struggles between the popes and anti-popes, supporters of the papacy and followers of the Emperor.

The Concordat of Worms, Germany, concluded in 1126 between Pope Calixtus II and Henry V, proved a point of compromise in the long-running controversy, but it did not last.

The people of Rome, meanwhile, saw no reason to acknowledge either the Emperor or the Pope as overlord. Led by a monk, Arnold of Brescia, a resolute opponent of the secular power of the Pope, they wanted to create a republic modeled on that of ancient Rome. Pope Hadrian IV therefore imposed the so-called Interdict on the city, which prohibited church services and the administration of the sacraments. The people were thus forced to surrender Arnold, who was executed in 1155.

A renewed attempt in the 14th century to shake off the papal yoke also failed. This time it was the papal notary, Cola di Rienzo, who wanted to create a new Roman republic. His first attempt in 1347

failed because of opposition by the Roman aristocracy, while his second attempt in 1354 was no more successful, since he had himself developed into a vainglorious tyrant. He was so intensely hated by the Romans that they murdered him.

The "Babylonian Captivity"

Shortly before this there began an episode which again brought Rome to the brink of ruin: the so-called "Babylonian Captivity" of the Church. Pope Clement IV, who originally came from France, gave way to pressure from the French kings in 1309 and moved the papal residence to Avignon, where it remained until 1377. Thus Rome was no longer the capital of western Christendom. Streets and squares, palaces and churches fell into ruin, cows grazed on the Forum and

Above: The arrest of Cola di Rienzi in 1350. Right: Pope Julius II. (1443-1513), drawing by Raphael.

the Capitol changed its name to Monte Caprino (Goat Hill). The population dropped to 15,000. Even when, at the instigation of Catherine of Siena, the Popes finally did return to Rome, there was at first little change. The "Great Schism" (1378-1417), which led to two or more popes reigning at the same time had divided the Christian world in two. Not until the schism was resolved – which led to a renewed strengthening of Papal power – and the power of the German emperors begin to wane did Rome begin to recover something of its old flair.

THE MODERN ERA
The Renaissance

Rome again became the center of the Catholic world. On their return, the popes found the Lateran Palace in ruins: they therefore made the Vatican their main residence, systematically adding to and expanding the building from this time onwards. Pope Nicholas (1447-1455) was the first in a line of popes to commission buildings; the ensuing period of papal patronage was to last for over two centuries. The papacy became increasingly worldly, something which was reflected in many magnificently appointed churches. The "papal monarchs," Eugene IV (1431-1447), Sixtus IV (1471-1484), Alexander VI (1492-1503), Julius II (1503-1513) and Leo X (1520-1521) led Rome to its first period of prosperity after a long decline. The population began again to increase; under Leo X, it reached the figure of 100,000.

As many popes had contacts to the great artistic centers of Italy, notably Florence, non-Roman artists dominated the artistic production of the city. Outstanding artists and architects – Fra Angelico, Perugino, Botticelli, Ghirlandaio and many others – came to Rome and left a wealth of great works. Under Julius II and Leo X, Michelangelo, Bramante and Raphael were active, working to make their art effective, monumental, a display. St Peter's with its colonnades, the magnificently painted rooms of the Sistine Chapel and Raphael's Stanze in the Vatican, and the redesigned Piazza of the Capitol are just a few examples of the splendor by which their papal clients set such store. Paul III (1534-1549), in particular, was very keen to secure the services of a man as celebrated as Michelangelo. He insisted that the artist stop work on the tomb he was designing for Julius II, and concentrate solely on the Sistine Chapel. "I have cherished this desire for thirty years," he is supposed to have said, "and now that I am Pope I intend to fulfil it. I will tear up the contract for the tomb. I have made up my mind to have this work done, come what may." And thus it was that Michelangelo created the superb fresco of the Last Judgment, of which Vasari says: "...it is clear that Michelangelo not only surpassed the masters who had worked in the Chapel before him, but even succeeded in surpassing his own renowned frescoes."

Michelangelo at last realized his new concept of placing sculptures as free-standing entities at the center of a space, rather than incorporating them into buildings around them in the equestrian statue of Marcus Aurelius in the Piazza del Campidoglio on the Capitol. This concept was to have a lasting influence on late Renaissance urban planning. Sixtus V (1585-1590) used the idea to help guide pilgrims from one patriarchal church to another: free-standing obelisks, placed at prominent points on the broad avenues he had laid out, stood like great stone compass-needles to orient travelers.

The streams of pilgrims who were once again pouring in to Rome in ever greater numbers, led to the building of the great churches for different nationalities, with adjacent pilgrims' hostels. The Renaissance popes gave such priority to the visible signs of their power that they did not devote much attention to ecclesiastical matters. One consequence was that they did not take seriously enough the danger represented by Martin

33

Luther's reform movement north of the Alps. The bitter quarrel between Pope Clement VII and the Emperor Charles V finally led to the infamous "Sack of Rome" by the Emperor's mercenaries. They rampaged through the city, pillaging and murdering, destroying churches and palaces, and leaving famine and plague behind them. The suffering population was again reduced to about 20,000, but recovered relatively quickly from this blow. The optimistic view of Mankind, however, which had grown out of the humanistic ideals of the Italian Renaissance, was shattered.

The age of the Baroque popes

After the sobering shock of the Sack of Rome, Pope Paul III tried to keep the ecclesiastical state neutral and to revitalize the Church. At the Council of Trent

Above: The Sack of Rome – German Protestant soldiers mock the Pope. Right: Bernini put his mark on 17th century Rome.

(1545-63) the Roman Catholic Articles of Faith were clearly defined in relation to the reformist movements. At the same time the Counter-Reformation was introduced by Ignatius of Loyola (1491-1556), the Spanish priest who founded the Jesuit order.

The energetic building activity which had been interrupted by the Sack of Rome soon resumed. The popes of the Baroque period wanted above all to build churches of great splendor, but they also aimed to modernize the city with broad formal avenues and grand piazzas adorned with many magnificent fountains.

The Roman aristocracy built splendid town palaces, at the cost of many classical ruins which were torn down and used as building material. This practice wasn't stopped until the Age of Enlightenment in the 18th century, when men such as the German archaeologist Winckelmann (1717-1768) insisted that the precious monuments of antiquity should be preserved. At last people began to take care of the ruins of ancient Rome, and collect valuable art treasures in museums for the first time. Thus the Capitoline Museum was founded in 1742, and the Vatican Museum in 1760; in 1772, at the instigation of Winckelmann, Pope Clement XIV commissioned the Pio Clementino Museum in the Vatican.

As in the Renaissance, so did the Baroque period produce many buildings which today seem characteristic of Rome, a part of the image of the city. The churches of Il Gesù and S. Ignazio, the Spanish Steps, the Fountain of the Four Rivers in the Piazza Navona and the Trevi Fountain are but a few of the edifices dating from this time. Important artists and architects, in particular Maderna, Bernini, Borromini, Domenichino and many others, left their mark on the city's art and architecture. Typical of the style of the period are the animated, sculptural façades and high rounded domes of the major churches, or the juxtaposition of the earthly and the divine, the representation of ecstatic visions and dramatic martyrdoms, in the visual arts.

Rome began to develop a certain cultural flair. Artists working in the city were joined by visitors drawn by the prospect of studying the great works of Roman art. Among these were such famous artists as Rubens, Velasquez, Poussin and Claude Lorrain. Institutions such as the French Academy (in the Villa Medici) and the German Institute (in the Villa Massimo) were founded so that gifted foreign students on scholarships could continue their education and research on the spot. The literary movement known as the Arcadians was founded, as was the Accademia Nazionale dei Lincei; and the salon of Queen Christina of Sweden became a meeting point for the city's intellectual elite.

The Settecento

It was no accident that the Classical style, which developed in the second half

of the 18th century, had its origins, more than anywhere, in Rome. Anyone interested in art was virtually obliged to travel to Italy and stay in Rome to explore the omnipresent classical ruins. Seeing them for the first time upon his arrival in Rome, Goethe cried, "I have finally come to the capital of the world." People in other parts of enlightened Europe had less favorable things to say about the state of the city. The French *Encyclopédie* (1745-1752) says of Rome: "It can be calculated that the population of Rome is one sixth that of Paris and one seventh as large as London's. It has half the number of inhabitants of Amsterdam, and where wealth is concerned, the disparity is even greater. It has no navy, no manufacturing industry and no trade. Its much-touted palaces are not as beautiful as their reputation, many being poorly kept up; most of the private houses are in a miserable state. The paving is bad, and the streets are filthy and narrow. The city, which is crammed with churches and monasteries, is almost empty in its east-

ern and southern quarters." There seems to be a certain historic precedent for the Romans' cavalier treatment of their cultural treasures – which has persisted to the present day.

By this time Rome no longer had any political importance. The popes concentrated almost exclusively on church matters, and life was relatively peaceful and uneventful until Napoleon's troops occupied Vatican City and Rome in 1798.

Revolution and Restoration

The French revolutionary army marched into Rome, and Marshall Berthier proclaimed the new Roman Republic from the Castel S. Angelo. Pope Pius VI was taken off to France, and his successor Pius VII agreed to the *Concordat* with Napoleon in 1801. However, Bonaparte occupied the city again from 1803

Above: View of the city of Rome in the 18th century. Right: The freedom fighter Giuseppe Garibaldi (1807-1882).

to 1809, declared Rome the second capital of his empire and named his son a King of Rome in 1811. When Pius VII excommunicated the French revolutionaries who had been responsible for the invasion of the Vatican, he had to spend five years in exile in France. At the Congress of Vienna in 1814/15 the Vatican was finally restored to the Pope, and Pius VII returned to Rome to re-establish the old order.

Although at first the Romans were little affected by the tide of revolutions which swept through Europe after 1840, this turbulent decade eventually left its mark. The process of industrialization upset the even tenor of life, especially in the cities. Railway construction, which was being carried out with enthusiasm all over Europe, meant that more imports were coming in from abroad, driving down prices for domestic products and threatening the livelihoods of farmers and craftsmen alike.

At the same time, a rise in nationalist sentiment prompted the King of Piedmont, in northern Italy, to declare war on neighboring Austria.

Pius IX, who assumed the papacy in 1846, was at first thought to be a liberal pope, winning over the people with minor reforms and a decree of amnesty. But he was so shocked at the uproar of the masses who swept through Rome in the revolutions of 1848-49 that he suddenly turned against everything that seemed to be new. He embodied the very opposite of liberalism when he withdrew his support of the King of Piedmont in 1848, not daring to side against Austria, the most powerful Catholic country in Europe. The interests of the Church were more important to him than national unity. When a papal minister was murdered in the uprising of November 1848, the Pope took up an unequivocal position against the democratic movement and, as a result, was forced to flee to Gaeta early in 1849. Not until 1850 was he able to return to Rome under the protection of French troops. Meanwhile elections had been held in Rome, and the democrats of Giuseppe Mazzini, who in 1831 had founded a revolutionary party to fight for the unification of Italy had won a majority. On 9th February, 1849, a new Roman Republic was proclaimed; Mazzini assumed political leadership and Garibaldi took command of the Republican army.

On his return, the Pope ruled with an iron hand, strictly opposing all democratic tendencies and progress of any kind. In 1854 he established the doctrine of the Immaculate Conception of the Virgin Mary. In an index of false doctrines entitled the *Syllabus Errorum*, he rejected all scientific discoveries and modern social theories which were not acceptable to the Church.

In 1869-70, for the first time in three centuries, the Ecumencial Council convened and proclaimed the dogma of Papal Infallibility in all questions of morality and faith. The meeting's sole pur-

pose was to consolidate the power of the Church over all the world's Catholics.

The Vatican state itself, meanwhile, had become a well-organized machine, in marked contrast to the crumbling monarchies in the rest of Europe. The only kingdom left in Italy was that of Sardinia, ruled by Victor Emanuel II of Savoy. In a referendum held in several Italian provinces, a majority voted for union with Sardinia. Garibaldi and his redshirts, together with the king's armies, gradually succeeded in uniting all of Italy – with the exception of Rome and Venice – under Piedmontese rule. In 1861 Victor Emanuel II became King of Italy. However, in order to complete the *Risorgimento* or rebirth of Italy, Rome had to become the capital of the new state.

Garibaldi made several unsuccessful attempts to conquer the Vatican State. French troops had been stationed in Rome for twenty years to enforce and protect the secular power of the Pope, and it was not until they left the city in 1870, called away to fight in the Franco-

Prussian War, that the Italian soldiers under General Cadorna managed to breach the Aurelian Wall at the Porta Pia and enter the city.

On 1st July, 1871, Rome was officially declared the capital of the Kingdom of Italy. The Pope, however, was not prepared to surrender his secular power. Deeply offended, he withdrew into the Vatican, declaring himself a prisoner, and died there in 1878.

The successors of Pius IX also imposed on themselves a voluntary ordinance never to leave the Vatican. Relations between the Vatican and the state of Italy remained strained until Mussolini and Pope Pius XI negotiated the Lateran Pact in 1929, which led to the solution of the so-called "Roman question." The pact declared the Vatican to be an independent state with the Pope as its sole

head. While the secular power of the papacy thus came to an end, its moral authority remained undiminished. Every year thousands upon thousands of pilgrims continued to travel to Rome to experience something of the fascination that the papacy still exerts.

The "Third Rome"

When Rome was proclaimed capital of the Kingdom of Italy, it had the character of a large village: with over 200,000 inhabitants, it didn't even have an adequate, modern system of roads. Hardly any progress had been made towards industrialization: the only businesses which used machinery to any great extent were printers' shops and textile mills. Luxury articles were in greater demand than industrial goods; with the vast amount of money they had at their disposal, members of the papal court and the aristocracy were willing to pay the high prices for hand-crafted goods. Apart from the craftsmen, it was the peasants who were

Above: Sad state of the "Colonnacce" in the Forum of Nerva during the 19th century. Right: The Caffé Greco in 1856.

responsible for most of the trade in the city. They came in from the countryside of the Campagna to sell their produce in the markets of Rome. The rest of the population was decidedly poor. More than half of the city's inhabitants were unemployed, and beggars sat in the doorways of the great palaces hoping for charity from the rich. The diet of the lower classes was very meager. The need to make use of anything that was at all edible led to the creation of dishes made from vegetables and offal, which are still typical today of the rather coarse Roman cuisine (see the feature *Eating Out*). Undernourishment and inadequate sanitation led to numerous epidemics. Added to this was the constant threat of malaria, which was widespread as a result of the city's marshy, humid surroundings.

There was no public education system and 78% of the Roman population could neither read nor write. On the other hand, anyone given permission by the papal authorities could open a school – the only requirement being that the applicant be a good Catholic. As no other particular qualification was necessary, the standard of teaching was quite low. The subjects taught were mainly religious, and a mastery of the Catechism was the only specific objective. Anyone who wanted to continue his education could go to one of the many Jesuit schools; even the university came under church administration.

In spite of the economic and social deprivation in Rome under papal rule, it is not surprising that this most backward of all Italian cities was chosen to be the capital of the new Italy. Its unique past gave it considerable symbolic value. Having been the city of emperors and popes, it now became that of the kings of united Italy.

This "Third Rome" grew apace. The central administration was moved here, and buildings to house it sprang up throughout the city, buildings which combined the style of the 19th century with those of earlier epochs. Banks and great enterprises were founded, which attracted many people from all over Italy.

As the population increased rapidly, Rome eventually became the most populous city in the entire Mediterranean world. (This expansion has continued up to the present day and there is no end to it in sight). A trend set in toward unscrupulous building speculation; the Vatican itself was actively involved. Gradually, many open spaces disappeared and historic buildings and monuments were pulled down to make way for new streets, squares, official buildings and residential developments. A large part of the Capitoline Hill, for instance, together with its ancient buildings, was removed to make way for the construction of the Vittorio Emmanuele II Monument, which outshines everything around in its gleaming white ugliness.

But the city's new status also brought about some positive changes. Important reforms were implemented, such as the introduction of a public education system

Above: During a state occasion at the Vittorio Emmanuele II Memorial.

and the abolition of censorship, while the Jews were at last granted the same rights as other citizens.

The banks of the Tiber were reinforced as a measure against the all-too-frequent flooding, and the worst of the slum areas were cleared.

The great contrasts between old and new which are still so typical of Rome today began to emerge and define the city, which had been celebrated with so much romantic enthusiasm by the travellers and poets of the 18th and 19th centuries. The historian Ferdinand Gregorovius, who witnessed these radical changes and recorded them for posterity in his *Roman Diary*, wrote in 1871: "Rome has become a white washed sepulchre. The houses, even the venerable palaces, are being painted white; the patina of centuries is scraped away, and it becomes clear for the first time how ugly is the architecture of Rome... The conversion of the Holy City into a secular one is the exact reverse of that time when the heathen Rome was transformed with the same enthusiasm into its Christian counterpart... The old Rome is disappearing. In twenty years there will be a new world here. But I am glad that I have lived for so long in the old Rome. It was only there that I could write my history books."

But the character of Rome did not change as quickly as Gregorovius thought it would. The new capital continued to retain a rather rustic atmosphere. Cows, sheep and goats were driven through the streets every day, and as late as 1865 twelve cows were killed when their shed caught fire right in the center of the city. Pigs roamed freely in front of the Porta Flaminia, and fruit and wine were brought into the city in ox-carts from the Campagna.

Rome remained the "paradise for exiles" that Shelley, the English poet and lover of Rome, had called it. The Piazza di Spagna continued to be the meeting place for artists from abroad, while the Caffé Greco in the Via Condotti was still as popular as ever. Nor had Rome lost any of its fascination for the traveller, for whom the ancient ruins had a much greater attraction than anything that really important cities such as Naples, or even Florence, had to offer in the way of culture.

Only those who stayed in Rome for longer periods became aware of some of the problems with which the city was struggling. The feud between the Vatican and the government also split Roman society down the middle. The aristocratic families were torn between two camps. Some, known as the "Black Aristocracy," aligned themelves with the Pope and refused to recognize the King as their ruler, while others supported the King and the monarchy.

The King was also remarkably popular with the common people, who gave him a jubilant welcome when he arrived in Rome. The building program, which began with the arrival of the armies of

civil servants, meant work and an improvement in living standards. Poverty-stricken peasants poured into the city by the thousands; the population had risen to 460,000 by the turn of the century. However, the authorities were not at all prepared for this invasion. Forced to live with their families under bridges and in wretched shacks, the construction workers fomed a new under-class, and eventually built their own shanty-towns which were a blot on the city's landscape for decades. In stark contrast to all this were the living conditions of the civil servants and officers, who found pleasant homes in the newly developed residential areas, and enjoyed in full all the other amenities which the city continued to offer to everyone who could afford them.

The most important buildings from the late 19th and early 20th centuries were the Palace of Justice, the Ministries of War and Finance, the Policlinico Castro Praetorio (a group of hospitals), and of course the abovementioned national monument to King Vittorio Emmanuele II. Many visitors from abroad nevertheless found the new buildings crude and ugly, and felt they had ruined the overall look of Rome. The young writer James Joyce, who lived in Rome at the time, said that the city seemed to him like someone who earned a living by showing strangers the corpse of his grandmother. Even so, more and more foreigners came to Rome, and despite the speculative building and the relentless destruction of all the villas, parks and gardens, most of them still found Rome "an overwhelming experience," as Sigmund Freud put it.

Rome of the Fascists

In 1915, Italy entered the First World War against her old enemy Austria in order to regain territories on her northern borders. But Italy was heavily defeated at Caporetto; not until in the final weeks of the war did its soldiers manage to inflict a

mortal blow against the demoralized Austrians. However, the war cost the country dearly, both in money and lives, and left Italy very weak.

When, in 1918, Benito Mussolini boasted that he was the man to deal with Italy's numerous economic and social problems, his followers were still a rather motley assortment with a wide range of political affiliations.

At first the *fasci di combattimento* (militant Fascist groups), who came together under the sign of the *fasces*, the ancient Roman symbol of authority, had relatively little success. Gradually, however, their brutal and uncompromising way of attacking everything which had even the slightest taint of Bolshevism won them increasing support among the people, who thought that order could only be restored by such methods.

In 1922 the Fascists finally seized

Above: Mussolini's march on Rome on 28th. Oct. 1922. Right: Demonstration by Fascist Youth in the Piazza Venezia.

power in Ravenna, and since the king adopted a neutral position, Mussolini dared to undertake his notorious "March on Rome." On 28th October, 1922, 26,000 Fascists reached the city; Mussolini himself did not arrive until two days later. He presented himself to the citizens of Rome as the *Duce*, a leader who put the nation above all else. This sparked the people's imagination, and they gave him a triumphant welcome. The enthusiasm continued as Mussolini set to work with great energy and resolve to bring order into the city's affairs. He delivered rousing speeches from the balcony of the Palazzo Venezia, and was constantly dashing from one place to another to supervise the numerous building projects which he had commissioned.

Mussolini's aim was to transform Rome into a megalopolis with skyscapers and buildings unequalled anywhere in the world. In order to create the space needed for this, everything that was "filthy and picturesque" – in other words, anything medieval was to be cleared

away. He presented his plans to the Rome city council with the following words: "In five years Rome must be a place for the whole world to marvel at – immense, well-ordered and powerful, just as it was under the first empire of Augustus."

To create room for the monumental Fascist edifices, fifteen early Christian churches were, among other buildings, demolished what was put up in their place was intended to demonstrate of size and power rather than to satisfy any aesthetic citeria. Without the slightest concern for the heritage of antiquity, the new Via dei Fori Imperiali was laid out between the Piazza Venezia and the Colosseum, straight through the old imperial Fora. In the Borgo, on the other side of the Tiber, the broad Via della Conciliazione carved a path through this ancient quarter levelling many medieval houses, streets and squares.

The only really historic achievement of Fascism was the conclusion of the Lateran Pact, which led to the building of this avenue. When Mussolini ended the feud between the Vatican and the Italian state in 1929 with this *patti lateranensi*, which returned Vatican City and some lands outside it to the Pope, relations between the two seats of power were at last normalized after eighty years of unbroken conflict.

Another large-scale project was the new EUR (Esposizione Universale di Roma) complex built for the world exhibition that was planned to celebrate the 20th anniversary of the March on Rome.

There were a few projects which can be seen in a positive light, and which were not, as so many of Mussolini's plans, merely announced, but were actually carried out. The draining of a large part of the Pontine Marshes, for example, elimated the problem of malaria in the region, while the building of canals and new roads created jobs for people from all over Italy. The result was that the Italian people idolized their *Duce*, and even the many who were against Fascism were not necessarily opposed to Mussolini himself.

But the mood changed when, on 10th June 1940, Mussolini declared war on Britain. And by 1943, after the catastrophic consequences of World War II for Italy had become all too evident, people were openly discussing how they could get rid of the *Duce*. Up until this point, the King had maintained a position of neutrality where Mussolini was concerned. However, after a devastating Allied air raid on Rome killed hundreds of people and badly damaged the Basilica of S. Lorenzo fuori le Mura, he decided the moment had come to have Mussolini arrested.

The news was greeted with wild enthusiasm in Rome and throughout Italy. Suddenly, it seemed that the entire population had always been comprised of nothing but anti-fascists. Fascist institutions were stormed and there was dancing and celebration in the streets. The photograph of Pietro Badoglio, the new head of government, even appeared on the front page of Mussolin's own newspaper, *Popolo d'Italia*.

But the war continued. The Allies landed in Sicily and prepared for their invasion of the mainland. On September 13, 1943, Italy negotiated a surrender. Taken completely by surprise, Hitler ordered his troops into Italy to take over the country. Germany immediately occupied Rome.

Rome – open city

Under the Nazi occupation Rome was declared an open city, meaning that it was not to be defended if attacked. The administration of the city was in German hands, and the new Fascist government under Mussolini (who, freed from prison by the Germans, governed from Salò on Lake Garda) was also under German supervision. A curfew was imposed on

Right: April 1945, and everywhere the Allied troops are given an enthusiastic welcome.

Rome: anyone on the streets after 5pm was to be shot without warning. Men of enlistment age were drafted by the Fascist authorities, and anyone capable of working was forced to join a labor unit. As a result of these repressive measures hundreds of people disappeared from the city every day or went into hiding. Of the 1.5 million inhabitants of Rome at this time, about 200,000 had gone underground.

Until this point, the Roman Jews had been able to live in relative peace; but a dangerous period for them had now begun. On 26th September 1943, the head of the Gestapo in Rome, Colonel Kappler, suddenly demanded that the Jewish community give him 20 kilograms of gold. This demand could only be met with the help of selfless support from non-Jewish fellow citizens. The synagogue was attacked, and people living in the ghetto were threatened with the destruction of their houses and shops. Many Jews fled in blind panic, about 8,000 of them finding refuge in churches and monasteries. Still, some 2,000 were arrested and deported to German concentration-camps.

Many Romans risked their own lives and freedom to help those persecuted by the regime.The first Committee of National Liberation was founded; many similar groups followed. Organized underground resistance began: acts of sabotage and attacks on the German occupation forces were daily occurrences.

One famous event was a Communist group's bombing a German army unit in the Via Rasella: 32 German soldiers were killed.

As a reprisal Hitler ordered that 10 Italians should be shot for every German killed. The execution of randomly selected victims took place in the sand-pits on the ancient Via Ardeatina.

Meanwhile, conditions in Rome were becoming more intolerable every day. Food was rationed ever more strictly;

water, gas and electricity were available only sporadically; and the black market flourished.

The Vatican was sharply criticized for its failure explicitly to condemn the excesses of the German occupiers, although it did generously supply 100,000 meals a day to the poorest people for only 1 lira per head.

The city was repeatedly bombed by the Allies. Although the raids were directed at strategic targets, many civilians lost their lives.

At the end of May 1944, as the allies began their final advance on Rome, the Germans evacuated the city. The first Allied tanks were greeted with jubilation. But the Italians' hatred for *Il Duce* had to be exorcised in a final macabre act.

In April 1945, Mussolini and his mistress, Clara Petacci,who had been in hiding, were caught by partisans and taken to Milan. There they were both executed and their bodies hung ignominiously upside-down from lamposts before being buried in a paupers' cemetery.

The road to the Republic

The administration of the city was now in the hands of the Allies. Their first and most difficult task was to feed the population, swollen by the influx of refugees to almost 2.5 million, and restore electricity and water supplies. The Allies managed to solve these problems remarkably quickly, and also made efforts to return the administration to Italian hands as soon as possible.

Thus Rome gradually became once again the city of the Romans, who quickly recovered their habitual humor and optimistic attitude toward life. In a referendum held in June, 1946, the population decided in favor of re-establishing a republic. The monarchy was abolished and the king sent into exile.

From 1946 to the present

The collapse of Fascism and the beginning of the Republic did not mean any violent upheaval of Roman society and cul-

ture. After the end of the Mussolini era, the political climate indeed changed with the return to democracy, but basically the myth of the universal and eternal city continued to be used as a cover for the speculative interests of the new ruling classes. This can be seen even in the physical development of the post-war period. Important building projects which had been started under the Fascists were completed after the declaration of the Republic. Large areas of the Borgo were finally pulled down in the Holy Year of 1950. During the 1960 Olympic Games (when the population of Rome passed the 2 million mark), the city spread out to the west like an oil-slick, just as the Fascists had planned in 1931.

The legacy of twenty years of Fascism was also reflected in Rome's cultural life. On the one hand, the return to democracy was accompanied by the intellectuals'

Above: Many corners of Rome have preserved a charming village atmosphere. Right: The ubiquitous cats of Rome.

call for a renewal of society, chiefly expressed in leading newspapers such as *Nuovi Argomenti* and *Il Mondo*. Italian cinema, meanwhile, entered its golden age of neo-realism; while literature and art devoted themselves to reclaiming a cultural identity for the common people, which had been virtually quashed under Fascist repression.

On the other hand, some of the more sensitive artists – who had abandoned the Caffé Greco for the two Rosati cafés on the Piazza del Popolo and Via Veneto – recognized the contradictions inherent in the kind of developments being imposed on the city. They also denounced the provincialism of a civilization that was riddled with hedonism, and a love of scandal and gossip. In popular mythology, Rome's new function was tellingly expressed in Federico Fellini's movie *La Dolce Vita* (1960).

There is a stark contrast between Fellini's Via Veneto, the Eldorado of a cinematic fantasy world, and the chaotic reality of the outskirts of the city as do-

cumented by Rossellini and Pasolini, among others. The "eternal city," the center of the Catholic world, has two contradictory faces: one good-natured, ironic, and down-to-earth, who works off his frustrations over a glass of wine in the *osteria*; the other a tough, streetwise kid from the slums on the edge of the city, who, ambitious for the trophies of the consumer society, advances ever more threateningly into the territory of Rome's wealthiest citizens.

New political themes and movements paased across the city's stage: the student uprising in 1968, or the workers' protests in the "hot autumn" of 1969. The cultural scene tried to keep peace: the new poets of the period after 1968 made efforts to achieve a dialogue with the people by singing in clubs and dives and improvising "happenings;" actors abandoned public theaters and tried to come closer to the "people" by performing in tents and small studio theaters.

The murder of Pier-Paolo Pasolini in 1975 was a dramatic embodiment of so-cial, political and cultural tensions which were summed up in the term *mali di Roma* ("Roman sickness"). The young murderer came from one of the outlying districts which the Fascist regime created in the 1930s and '40s in order to isolate the poor sections of the population in the Campagna, far from the city; particularly affected were former inhabitants of the Centro Storico, who were moved out, so that their old houses could be renovated and occupied by the affluent.

Primavalle, Trullo, Quarticciolo, Tru-fello, San Basilio and Pietralata are examples of these *borgate*, which were made famous by the neo-realist cinema. Swallowed up by the city's rapidly spreading web, they had become centers of a violent subculture. Ironically, it was exactly these people whom Pasolini had been trying to help.

In the second half of the 1970s and early '80s the City Council tried out a new policy aimed at improving the quality of life and creating a sense of civic identity. Particularly because of the

47

efforts of Giulio Carlo Argan, an art critic and historian of international renown who served as mayor from 1976 to 1979, Rome seemed at last to be on its way to becoming a modern European city. For the first time, efforts were made to check and rationalize the perennial problem of *abusivismo* (illegal building), and a number of initiatives were planned with the aim of making life more human and tolerable in the big dormitory towns on the outskirts of the city.

Culture, seen as a basic need for many citizens, received particular attention. The city's Department of Cultural Affairs organized a variety of events (theater, cinema, dance, animation, poetry readings and so on), including the *Estate Romana* ("Roman Summer").

But these attempts to create a cultural impetus were short-lived. In the 1980s, when the political climate changed in

Above: The watchful eye of the law caught momentarily off guard. Right: The Romans' love of driving.

Rome and in the rest of Italy, the old market-driven system returned, and culture was pushed into the background. Institutions such as the *Teatro Stabile* and *Teatro dell'Opera* were in crisis, and subsidies for the *Estate Romana* were drastically reduced.

In spite of the efforts of many intellectuals both old and young, Rome can no longer be numbered among the great cities of Europe. Nowhere else are culturally-minded tourists so continually confronted with the problem that the major museums seem always to be closed, for any number of reasons. In many respects Rome is beginning to resemble a Third World city. There is a famous quote from a journalist about Fiumicino Airport: "If you're coming from Cairo, you think it's the gateway to Europe, but if you are coming from Paris, it seems more like the gateway to the Middle East."

The football World Cup in 1990, which organizers tried to make popular by presenting it as a great opportunity to make sweeping changes, was a bitter dis-

appointment from this point of view. Although a few important projects were carried out, chaotic traffic conditions and smog continued to dog the daily life of the citizens of Rome. The great enthusiasm that the "Three Tenors" concert with Pavarotti, Domingo and Carreras in the incomparable setting of the Baths of Caracalla aroused around the world could not hide the meager results achieved by "Italia 90" in the wider sphere of tourism and culture.

And yet there's reason to be optimistic at the prospect of Rome in the year 2000. In spite of economic and moral crises, Rome's citizens have not given up their desire to improve the cultural level of their city.

Recently the *Opera di Roma* has put on some first-class performances, while in the theaters one finds an increasingly knowledgeable audience. Thanks to the excellent new movies produced in Rome by young directors, many of the old studios in Cinecittà have been reopened, while in the world of popular music young performers with intelligent texts and a whole new musical vocabulary are drawing large audiences to the Studio Flaminio, Palazzo EUR or the Campo Boario.

Meanwhile the Romans seem to have grasped that they need to change their way of living and working and conform to the accepted standards of northern Europe. The recently passed law *per Roma Capitale* has the aim of making Rome into a modern city, in which past and present exist harmoniously side by side. Rome's future has roots in antiquity, and in order to become a genuinely modern city it must look to its multicultural past and see itself in the year 2000 as a bridge between the European Union and the Mediterranean world.

But the political structure that had prevailed since 1945 has broken up. The two major parties, Christian Democrats and Communists, have virtually disappeared and a new movement, the Liga Nord, has gained support for a separate state in the prosperous north, based in Milan.

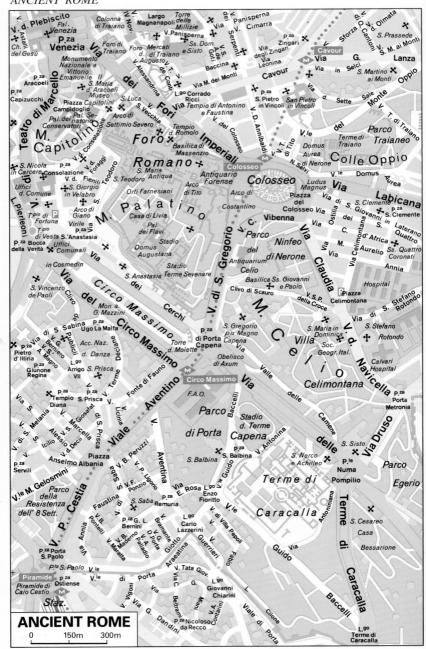

ANCIENT ROME

0   150m   300m

ANCIENT ROME

FORUM ROMANUM
PALATINE
COLOSSEUM
IMPERIAL FORA
CAPITOL
CIRCUS MAXIMUS
BATHS OF CARACALLA

FORUM ROMANUM

The Forum Romanum is the largest extant grouping of the buildings of ancient Rome. The area, originally a swampy region between the Capitoline, Palatine, Quirinal and Viminal hills, became a meeting-place for the inhabitants of the various hills as early as the first, pre-Republic, monarchies. A system of drainage helped dry out the ground, and gradually, public and private buildings were erected on it.

During the Republic the Senate was located here, as were the Temple of Vesta with its sacred flame, the Temple of Castor and Pollux, law courts, and shops. At the beginning of the imperial age, the Forum, with its large and splendid buildings, became a symbol for the wealth and power of the city. Time and again, it was laid waste by fire; each time, it was repaired and rebuilt.

With the decline of the city at the end of the 5th century AD, the Forum gradually fell into disrepair, until it was no more than a cow pasture (*Campo Vaccino*). It wasn't until the end of the 19th century that archaeologists began to undertake systematic excavations, exposing the ruins once again to the light of day.

From the observation terrace near the *Tabularium*, the archive of ancient Rome, which is situated below the Senatorial Palace on the slope of the Capitoline Hill, you have an excellent overview of the Forum Romanum.

Immediately in front of you, to the right, are the eight columns which are all that remain of the Temple of Saturn. Saturn was one of the most important gods in ancient Rome. In his honor, the *Saturnalia* were held on 17th December, a riotous celebration during which the differences between social classes were temporarily suspended, servants and masters gave each other gifts, and there were all kinds of wild goings-on. Near the Temple of Saturn stands a fragment of the *Miliarium Aureum*, the Golden Milestone, where all of the Empire's consular highways once converged.

Beyond the mighty triumphal Arch of Septimius Severus, you can make out the façade of the Curia. Behind this are the foundations and broken pillars of the Basilica Julia, the columns of Phocas and the remains of the Basilica Aemilia. Beyond the basilica stand the three columns of the Temple of the Dioscuri, the Temple of Antoninus and Faustina (today

Previous pages: View of the Forum Romanum. The Colosseum by night.

the Church of S. Lorenzo in Miranda), with the round temple to the deified Romulus just beyond it. Then come the mighty arches of the Basilica of Maxentius and, finally, the façade of the church of S. Francesca Romana, with the foundation of the Temple of Venus and Roma at its side. Beyond the Arch of Titus, the majestic bulk of the Colosseum completes the panorama.

The main entrance to the Forum Romanum is in the Via dei Fori Imperiali. A model right beside the ticket booth shows how the Forum must have looked in its heyday. From here, the path leads down past the former Temple of Antoninus and Faustina down to what was once the street level of the Forum. On the right rise the ruins of the **Basilica Aemilia**, built in 179 BC by the Censors Marcus Aemilius Lepidus and Marcus Fulvius Nobilitor. The building had to be rebuilt many times

after being destroyed by fire; the remains we see today date from the Augustan period. In the vaulted hall of the basilica legal cases were heard and debated, and business deals concluded.

Turning towards the Capitoline, you'll come to the **Curia**, the assembly hall of the Roman Senate. The simple brick building was converted into a church in the 7th century, and not restored to its original state until the early 1900s. Its ancient bronze doors now close over the main portal of the church of S. Giovanni in Laterano.

In front of the Curia the **Lapis Niger**, a stone of black marble, marks the spot where Romulus, the founder of the city, is supposedly buried. A staircase leads down to this shrine, which was worshipped from the earliest days of the city's history. A stele bearing an inscription is accounted the oldest written memorial in the Latin language.

Beyond it rises the **Arch of Septimius Severus**, 70 ft (21m) high and 75 ft (23m) wide. It was built in 203 to cel-

Above: Part of the Arch of Septimius Severus. Right: The House of the Vestal Virgins and the Basilica of Maxentius.

ebrate the victory of the emperor and his sons, Caracalla and Geta, over the Parthians in Asia Minor. Episodes from this war are depicted on the four marble reliefs. The inscriptions sing the praises of the emperor and his sons, but Geta's name was removed from them at some later date, perhaps when Caracalla became emperor.

To the left of the triumphal arch stretch the foundations of the **Rostra**, originally the dais for the orators. The name is derived from the *rostri*, or figureheads, of ships in Cleopatra's fleet captured at the Battle of Actium, which used to decorate the platforms. Left of this is the **Umbilicus Urbis**, or "Navel of the City," a cone-shaped brick structure which once marked the very center of Rome.

The group of columns erected in 608 AD in honor of the eastern Roman emperor, **Phokas**, were the last monument to be built in the Forum. Beside them grow the sacred fig tree, olive tree and vine, all of which have great symbolic importance.

The square in front of the Rostra, paved with travertine marble, is the actual Forum, where people gathered to listen to the impassioned speeches of the *oratores*. South of this stand seven brick pedestals, once covered with marble, which support ceremonial columns from the time of Diocletian. Leading past these is the **Via Sacra**, which runs across the whole Forum from east to west. Once the most important commercial street in Rome, it was also lined with the most important shrines, and marked the course for religious processions and triumphal marches.

The right side of the Via Sacra was once taken up by the **Basilica Iulia**, a building with three aisles begun under Julius Caesar and used as law courts. All that remains of it today are its foundations and the stumps of columns. Scratched on the steps you can recognize checkerboards and games of tic-tac-toe, with which spectators amused themselves when proceedings got slow.

Beyond the Basilica Iulia, on the other side of the *Vicus Tuscus*, is the temple dedicated to the Dioscuri, the holy twins

Castor and Pollux. A legend is associated with this temple: in the year 499 BC, in the course of a decisive battle between the Romans and the Latins, at a now forgotten place called Lagus Regillus, two young riders came charging in and helped the Romans to victory. When the two rescuers then took their horses to drink at the spring of Juturna, which bubbles up at the foot of the Palatine, the Romans recognized them as the heavenly twins and built the temple to them as a sign of thanks.

To the east of the Temple of the Dioscuri lies the **House of the Vestal Virgins**, abode of the keepers of the Eternal Flame in the neighboring **Temple of Vesta**, which could never be allowed to go out. The six Vestals were bound in service to the goddess Vesta in early childhood. For as long as they served her they had to maintain a vow of chastity; anyone who transgressed was buried alive. The pious virgins lived in a kind of convent and enjoyed certain honorary privileges. Their accommodation on the Forum consisted of a two-storeyed house around a beautiful courtyard or *atrium*. Over the centuries both the house and the temple were burnt down on numerous occasions.

North of the temple stands the **Regia**, which, legend has it, was the home of Numa Pompilius, the second king of Rome. Later it became the official seat of the *Pontifex Maximus* or high priest, whose authority extended even to the Vestal Virgins. Next to it are the scant remains of the **Temple of Julius Caesar**. Crossing the Via Sacra we come to the **temple which the emperor Antoninus** built in 141 AD in memory of his late wife, Faustina. Because it was later converted into the **Church of S. Lorenzo in Miranda**, the 56 ft (17m) high columns of its portico and podium survived; the

Right: Ancient statues in the House of the Vestal Virgins.

church received its present Baroque facade in 1602. To the right of this stands the **Temple of Romulus**, son of the emperor Maxentius. The circular building is remarkably well preserved: even its bronze door, whose lock still functions, dates back to imperial times.

The vast Basilica of Constantine or Maxentius, 330 ft (100m) long and 213 ft (65m) at its widest point, was started in 310 under Maxentius and completed under the reign of Constantine. What you see today is the northern aisle, where orchestra concerts are often given in the summer. Inside the Basilica there used to be a huge statue of the emperor Constantine; today, its head and foot are exhibited in the courtyard of the Palazzo dei Conservatori on the Capitoline Hill. Only one of the 48-ft-high (14.5m) columns which once supported the vaulted roof of the nave has survived; it now serves as a pedestal for the statue of the Virgin Mary at the center of the Piazza Santa Maria Maggiore.

Passing the Basilica of Constantine we come to the large double **Temple of Venus and Rome**, which was converted into the **Church of S. Francesca Romana.** The temple was built by Hadrian and dedicated in 135 AD. With an area of 360 ft by 174 ft (110 by 53m), it was the largest temple in Rome. The *cella* of the Temple of Rome, which faces the Forum, has survived almost intact. The pieces of the columns which formed the portico were reassembled in 1935. In the first floor of the church's monastery is the **Antiquarium Forense**, where archaeological finds from the Forum are on display.

The last important monument in the Forum is the **Arch of Titus**, built in honor of that emperor. The side walls of the arch are decorated with impressive reliefs glorifying the emperor's victory over the Jews in 70 AD. On one relief you can see the booty which was taken from Jerusalem and carried in the trium-

phal procession through Rome. This includes the first classical representation of the seven-armed menorah. For this reason, orthodox Jews even today refuse to pass through the Arch of Titus.

THE PALATINE

Leaving the Forum Romanum, we walk up the Clivus Palatinus to the most famous of the city's seven hills, the Palatine. This hill stands at the very core of Roman history. It is here that traces have been found of the huts where shepherds lived in pre-Roman times, the seed of today's sprawling city. In the days of the Roman Republic, the 165 ft (50m) high hill, which overlooks the island in the Tiber, was the preferred residence of the rich and the aristocracy. After the age of Augustus, who was born here, the hill was transformed into the living-quarters of the Emperors, who built magnificent palaces for themselves (the word "palace" is derived from the name *Palatium*) until the entire hill was a single vast complex of imperial buildings. Their vast lower walls extending down the slopes of the hill can still be seen from the Circus Maximus and Forum Romanum.

When Constantine transferred the imperial seat to Byzantium, all these ornate buildings began to go to seed, although some of them were still occupied by Germanic princes and Roman governors sent from the Eastern Empire. During the Christian Middle Ages, many of these "heathen" buildings were transformed into churches and monasteries, and in the 16th century wealthy noblemen such as Cardinal Alessandro Farnese laid out gardens and vineyards among the ruins. Not until the 18th century did people start taking an interest in the magnificent imperial buildings they had learned of from Latin authors.

In the course of systematic excavations, more and more remains are coming to light; the most important of these will be described in the following paragraphs.

If you climb out of the Forum Romanum by following the Clivus Pa-

59

latinus, which begins by the Arch of Titus, you'll come first to the **Farnese Gardens**, which could be described as the first botanical gardens in the world. From the *loggia* there is a superb view over the Fora. Next to the gardens is the **Temple of Cybele** (or *Magna Mater*), whose cult was introduced to Rome in the republican era. The temple was built in 204 BC and was intended to house the Black Stone of the Goddess, as required by the mystic Sibylline Books. In front of the temple are remains of walls dating from the Iron Age; tradition has it that they were a part of Romulus's house.

The **House of Livia**, named after the consort of the emperor Augustus, is typical of the homes of wealthy Romans. It was attached to the Palace of Augustus and consists of a series of rooms with beautiful, relatively well-preserved mu-

Above: Painstaking archaeological work on the Palatine. Right: Ruins of the Temple of Castor und Pollux.

rals in what is known as the Second Pompeian Style, depicting mythological scenes with ornamental and floral motifs. Inside, the house gives an impression of comfort and good taste, though the exterior looks quite modest – a sign of the shrewdness of the first emperor of Rome. More elaborate in appearance was the **Domus Tiberiana**, which was completely buried under the Farnese Gardens and yet to be fully excavated.

The most important palace complex, comprising the Domus Flavia, the Domus Augustana and the Stadium, was commissioned by the emperor Domitian from his architect, Rabirius. Even at the time the poet Martial extolled the splendid edifices, which took up the whole central part of the hill and stretched down to the Circus Maximus.

The **Domus Flavia** was intended as a showpiece. It consisted of a triple-aisled basilica, the Aula Regia, where the emperor held audiences; the peristyle with a garden in the center; and, most magnificent of all, the *triclinium*, or dining-hall, with a raised apse, decorated with mosaics and colored marble, on which the emperor sat enthroned. The spacious hall opened on to the Nymphaeum, which is in a good state of preservation. The emperor actually lived in the **Domus Augustana**, which continued to fulfil this function into the Byzantine era. The southern part, with its *exedra* looking out on to the Circus Maximus, is relatively well preserved. Today, no one is actually certain whether the **Stadium** of Domitian was really an arena for sporting events or was simply a garden laid out in the shape of a stadium.

All in all, Domitian's palace buildings and grounds are important testimony to the size and splendor of the absolute empire. It served political purposes as well as acting as a showcase and functioning as the arena for the actual, day-to-day exercise of imperial power.

In the **Palatine Antiquarium** you can see frescoes, parts of statues and other artifacts found among the Palatine ruins.

Next to the exedra of the Domus Augustana is a small building with several rooms known as the **Paedagogium**, which was used for the education of the imperial page-boys. The graffiti on the walls, not so very different from what you might find in universities even today, bear vivid historic testimony to the period. A wall in the second room, for example, bears the inscription: *labora, aselle, quomodo ego laboravi et proderit tibi* (Work, O donkey, just as I have worked, and it will profit you.)

THE COLOSSEUM

The **Colosseum** is *the* symbol of the city of Rome. What we can see today is, however, scarcely one third of the building constructed between 27 and 80 AD by the Flavian emperors, Vespasian and Titus. There is a saying in Rome that the Eternal City will finally disappear when the Colosseum falls down. Presumably to

prevent this, a Roman bank announced in 1992 that it was prepared to advance the money necessary for a comprehensive restoration of this gigantic monument. Visitors to Rome in the next few years will have the not very pleasing sight of the Colosseum covered in scaffolding, but the Romans are happy.

The building is elliptical in shape and some 160 ft (50m) high. Its greatest length is 617 ft (188m) and the width is 512 ft (156m). In ancient times it could comfortably hold as many as 73,000 spectators, who came to watch the grisly spectacles in the arena. Its inaugural festivities lasted without interruption for one hundred days, in the course of which more than 5000 wild animals were killed. No-one bothered to keep count of the number of gladiators who died during the same period.

Apart from the foundations, which extend far underground, and as well as marble and other materials, the building required no less than 120,000 sq. yds (100,000 sq. m.) of travertine. The iron

supports which held the stone blocks together, weighing more than 300 tons apiece, were removed in the Middle Ages, you can still see the holes where they used to be.

The lowest arcades, ornamented with Doric pilasters, formed the entrances to the arena. On the next level, the pilasters are Ionic, while Corinthian pilasters decorate the top. The fourth storey was not added until the reign of Titus. This level had 240 rectangular window openings and as many consoles; the latter were used to hold the masts supporting the vast awning, rigged by 100 specially-trained sailors, that shielded the spectators from the sun or rain. The seating was cleverly arranged so that the spectators could reach their places and leave them again in the shortest possible time. The seats were strictly segregated on three levels according to social class. On the lowest tiers sat the emperor, the senators and the *equites*

Above: Inside the Colosseum. Right: Hackney carriages by the Arch of Constantine.

(knights). Above them came the middle-class citizens, and right at the top were the commoners, including women and slaves.

Of the arena itself only the walls of the underground cages and corridors have survived. One of the latter led out to the **Ludus Magnus**, the training camp for gladiators, which lies between the Via Labicana and the Via S. Giovanni in Laterano.

Until 483 AD the goriest spectacles were presented; during the period when Christians were being persecuted, countless martyrs went here to their deaths. Animal-baiting continued until well into the 6th century. After that, the great building fell into disuse. Earthquakes and fires hastened its demise, and in 1348 the side facing the Celio collapsed. In the Middle Ages the powerful Frangipani family took over the Colosseum and rebuilt it as a fortress.

Later, especially during the Renaissance, it provided stones for new building projects, the Palazzo Venezia among

them. Though it was originally called the Flavian Amphitheater, it acquired the name Colosseum in the Middle Ages, probably because of the colossal statue of Nero that stood nearby, roughly where the Via dei Fori Imperiali meets the Piazza del Colosseo.

Standing not far from the Colosseum, the **Arch of Constantine** is the largest triumphal arch to have survived to the present day. It was erected by the Senate in the years 312-315 AD to celebrate Constantine's victory over Maxentius. Consisting of a large central arch and two side-arches, it was partly built from stone taken from the ruins of other buildings; even some of the decorative elements predate the arch itself, such as the figures of the eight captured barbarians which decorate the Attica, the medallions above the side arches or the reliefs of hunting and sacrificial scenes, which have little to do with Constantine's military achievements. Having been incorporated by the Frangipani into their fortifications, the triumphal arch was not fully exposed to

view until the 19th century, and restoration was only completed in 1990.

To the left of the Colosseum, on the far side of the Via Labicana, rises the **Colle Oppio**, one of the three heights which make up the Esquiline. Here, set in a beautiful park, are the ruins of the **Baths of Titus**, the **Baths of Trajan** and, most important of all, the remains of the **Domus Aurea**, the gigantic palace built for the emperor Nero, which stretched along the valley of the Colosseum as far as the Temple of Venus and Rome. After Nero died, the magnificent residence was given back to the people of Rome, and Vespasian ordered the Colosseum to be built on the site of its artificial lake.

In the rooms, now below ground level, which were probably used for private and state receptions, valuable ancient works of art, frescoes and marble statues were found, including the famous Laocoon group, which can be admired today in the Vatican Museum. Many of the rooms hidden beneath the park were common knowledge as early as the 15th century.

Admittedly, in those days they were thought to be caves or grottoes, which is why the murals discovered in them were called *grottesche*, a term which in the Renaissance came to be applied to a certain style of ornamental motif. Unfortunately, because they're under restoration, the rooms of Nero's *Domus Aurea* are not open to the public at the moment.

THE IMPERIAL FORA

Today, the **imperial Fora** are for the most part buried under the broad street which bears their name: Via dei Fori Imperiali. In the days of the emperors, they were built to glorify the current ruler and to represent his power and authority. Little by little, the residential and commercial district which originally occupied the area was pulled down demolished to make way for these fora,

which were squares of various sizes, large or small, surrounded by such public buildings as temples, basilicas, colonnades and the like.

The first of the great imperial Fora was the **Forum of Caesar**. It lies to the north of the Forum Romanum, partly buried beneath parking lots and grassy park areas. It was built between 54 and 46 BC by Julius Caesar; the Roman Forum had become too small for Rome's many citizens, and he wanted to present them with another arena for daily public life.

Today, nothing remains of the colonnades which once surrounded the 558 ft by 246 ft (170 m by 70 m) square on three sides. The three lovely Corinthian columns which are still standing were part of the temple dedicated to Venus Genetrix which stood on the square's fourth side; the Julian emperors claimed to descend from this goddess. The Basilica Argentaria, which Trajan later built next to the Temple of Venus, housed the money-changing booths and trading exchange of imperial Rome.

Above: In the Forum of Caesar.
Right: The spiral-shaped reliefs on the Column of Trajan.

The second Forum is the **Forum of Augustus**. Its focus was the **Temple of Mars Ultor** (Mars the Avenger) of which the foundations and four columns can still be seen. Augustus dedicated the temple to the war god Mars after he had killed Brutus and Cassius, the assassins of Julius Caesar, at the Battle of Philippi in 42 BC. Caesar's sword was kept in the *cella* of the temple. Colonnades with two exedrae each lined the long sides of the square; beyond the right-hand colonnade you can still see the remains of the so-called *Aula del Colosseo*, where there's a pedestal for a huge 40-ft-high (12 m) statue of the emperor.

Next to the Forum of Augustus is the **Forum of Nerva** (96-98 AD) also called the **Forum Transitorium** (Transit Forum), because it was crossed by the *Argiletum*, a road linking the Forum Romanum with the densely populated and rather notorious district of *Subura*. In the middle of Nerva's Forum stood the Temple of Minerva; two of its elegant Corinthian columns with attractive friezes on their entablature, known as the *Colonacce*, are still standing.

To the right of the Forum of Nerva lies the **Forum of Vespasian** (69-79 AD), also called the **Forum Pacis** because the Temple of Peace once stood in the middle of it. All that remains of the temple are a niche below the medieval Torre de Conti and the lower part of the *cella*. Most of the Forum lies under the Via dei Fori Imperiali; on the other side of the street stands the **Church of SS. Cosma e Damiano**, which was converted from a Roman library in the Forum.

The largest and most important of the imperial Fora, however, was the **Forum of Trajan** (98-117 AD). To make way for this the architect Apollodorus of Damascus had the entire Velia Hill, which linked the Capitoline with the Quirinal, removed. The Forum was 330 yds (300 m) long and 200 yds (185 m) wide, and was inaugurated in 113 AD to celebrate

Trajan's victory over the Dacians (who occupied what is now Romania). It was laid out on the lines of a military camp. One passed through a triumphal arch, which has not survived, to gain access to the broad square, an equestrian statue of the emperor at its center. At the far side of the square was the five-aisled **Basilica Ulpia.** Measuring 185 yds (170 m) long and 65 yds (60 m) wide, it was the largest ever to be built in Rome. It had a gilded roof and was completely encircled by a superbly worked frieze, parts of which were later used to ornament the Arch of Constantine. All that remain of the great Basilica today are parts of the foundations and stumps of columns.

The basilica had two libraries attached to it, one for Greek literature and one for Latin. Between them stands **Trajan's Column.** Nearly 130 ft (40 m) tall including its plinth, it is the same height as the hill which was removed so that the Forum could be built. In 1587, a **Statue of St Peter** replaced a statue of Trajan which had been lost in the Middle Ages;

the ashes of the emperor himself, however, were interred in a golden urn in the plinth. The column consists of 18 marble cylinders; winding around them, a continuous spiral relief 3 ft (1 m) high and 660 ft (200 m) long depicts Trajan's campaign against the Dacians. The reliefs are at once an important historical document and one of the great masterpieces of ancient sculpture. (A copy of it can be seen in the **Museo della Civiltà Romana** in the EUR). Unfortunately, the 2500 figures on the original have been badly damaged by air pollution--like all major Roman monuments.

Next to the Forum of Trajan are the **Markets of Trajan**, a group of brick buildings three storeys high built into the side of the hill above the Forum. These contained shops where inexpensive goods were sold, as well as rooms where private business deals could be negotiated and where grain was distributed to the public. Through the Markets of Trajan ran the *Via Biberatica*, or Street of the Drinking-houses. Strolling through these almost perfectly preserved shopping streets, it's easy to imagine yourself back in the days of ancient Rome. The entrance to the markets is in the Via IV Novembre; this street also leads to the **Torre delle Milizie**, which is the largest medieval tower to have survived to the present day. It was built in the 13th century by the aristocratic Roman family of Annibaldi and later passed into the possession of the Caetani. You need special permission to climb the tower, but it is worth the effort, because from the top you get a marvellous view over ancient and medieval Rome.

THE CAPITOLINE HILL

Above: View of the Forum of Trajan. Right: Michelangelo's beautiful Campidoglio seen from above.

The *mons capitolinus* may have been the smallest of the classic seven hills of Rome, but from the very beginning it was

the political and religious center of the city. On its northern summit, the ancient *arx*, where today the **Church of S. Maria in Aracoeli** stands, the Temple of Juno Moneta was built; this goddess's sacred geese warned the Romans of an attack by the Gauls in 390 BC. Later the city's mint was built here, whence the word *moneta,* meaning "money" is derived. On the southern summit, the Capitol itself, stood the **Temple of Jupiter Optimus Maximus**; in the hollow between the two peaks, where the Capitoline Square lies today, was the *asylum*, a shrine in which the persecuted could take refuge.

In ancient times the Capitoline Hill was very inaccessible. Steep cliffs of tufa dropped away on three sides; from the most southerly of these, the Tarpeian Rock, that condemned men were hurled to their death. The whole hill was covered with shrines, although today, you can see only a few scattered remains. Nevertheless, the hill has managed to retain its aura of power and dignity throughout the centuries. Here culminated the triumphal processions of victorious Roman generals; here, in the Middle Ages, poets were crowned and crowds cheered the demagogue Cola di Rienzo; here, the mayor of Rome officiates today.

In Classical times, the buildings on the Capitoline faced toward the Forum. However, in the Middle Ages, new buildings began to be oriented to the northwest, towards the Vatican. At the beginning of the 16th century Michelangelo was commissioned to redesign the whole hill. He drew up the trapezoid **Piazza del Campidoglio**, bordered on its shortest side by the Senatorial Palace, and to the right and left by the Palazzo dei Conservatori and the "New Palace of the Capitoline Museum." A ceremonial staircase made the hill easily accessible for the first time. It leads past the memorial to Cola di Rienzo and on past the Dioscuri to the elegant square, whose center is occupied by the plinth of the famous equestrian statue of the emperor Marcus Aurelius (161-180 AD). The only reason that

67

the monument escaped being melted down in the Middle Ages was that people thought it represented Constantine the Great, the first Christian emperor. In 1990 it was painstakingly restored, and now stands in the Capitoline Museum. The statue was originally gilded and there is a popular belief that when the horse and rider are once again covered in gold, it will herald the advent of the Last Judgment.

Especially in the evening, the Piazza del Campidoglio affords a wonderful view over the roofs of Rome. And if you go to the left of the Senatorial Palace, past the raised **statue of the Lupa**, the She-Wolf, to one of the two observation terraces near the Tabularium, you'll have an impressive view of the ruins of what used to be the center of the world. Below the terrace stands the **Church of S. Giuseppe dei Falegnami** with its *Carcer Mamertinus.* It was here that the apostles

Above: A quiet stroll through the Baths of Caracalla.

Peter and Paul were imprisoned, and enemies of the Roman state, such as Jugurtha, King of Numidia, or the Gaulish leader Vercingetorix, were cruelly put to death.

CIRCUS MAXIMUS

South of the Palatine stretches the long oval of the Circus Maximus, which is the oldest stadium in Rome and is mentioned as far back as 329 BC. It was one of the largest sports arenas in the ancient world, with two 500-meter racetracks and a capacity of as many as 300,000 spectators. The chariot races, which took place chiefly during the *festival Ludi Romani*, were just as popular with the Roman people as football matches are today. The charioteers belonged to one of four teams and were idolized as heroes by their supporters, who placed bets on the outcome of the races. You can get some idea of how exciting these races must have been from the classic Hollywood film *Ben Hur*.

THE BATHS OF CARACALLA

Another leisure activity available to the ancient Romans was having a bath in one of the city's many thermal establishments. In the imperial period, the largest of these were the Baths of Diocletian, but the best preserved today are the Baths of Caracalla, which are almost as large. They were opened in 217 AD and continued to be used until the 6th century, when the Goths destroyed important aqueducts supplying them with water.

In their heyday, however, the buildings and gardens covered an area of 27 acres (10.9 ha.). The bath house itself measures 720 ft by 374 ft (220 by 114 m) and could accommodate about 1500 people at once. In addition to the hot baths and an open-air swimming pool, there were sports and entertainment facilities, restaurants, libraries and meeting rooms. The impressive remaining walls that we see today give only a rough idea of the former dimensions of the complex: vast halls with high domes and barrel- and cross-vaulted ceilings supported by massive columns, all decorated with marble, mosaics and frescoes; beneath these, a subterranean labyrinth of passageways built to house the complicated heating system.

These baths played a major role in public life in ancient Rome. It was an accepted part of the normal daily routine for a Roman citizen that he devote several hours a day to toning up his body while at the same time fulfilling social obligations, or even simply avail himself of the many services offered – a luxury which can hardly be matched by our modern "leisure centers." For the past few years opera productions have been put on among these mighty ruins and a concert with Domingo, Carreras and Pavarotti took place at the beginning of the Soccer World Championship in 1990. With a backdrop such as this they cannot fail to be an unforgettable experience.

ANCIENT ROME
Forum Romanum

Via dei Fori Imperiali; *Metro:* Line B to Colosseo. *Bus:* 11, 27, 81, 85, 87, 88. Open Mon, Wed, Sat, 9am until 1 hour before sunset; Sun until 2pm. Entrance: 10 000 Lire.

Palatine

Via di San Gregorio; *Metro:* Line B to Colosseo; *Bus:* 11, 15, 27, 85, 87, 88, 90, 90b, 118, 673. *Streetcar (tram):* 13, 30, 30b. Open Mon, Wed-Sat 9am-6pm, (in winter 9am-3pm), Sun 9am-1pm. Entrance: 10 000 Lire.

Colosseum / Imperial Fora
Markets of Trajan

Colosseum: Piazza del Colosseo; *Metro*: Line B to Colosseo. *Bus:* 11, 15, 27, 81, 85, 87, 88, 118, 673. *Streetcar:* 13, 30, 30b. Open Tue-Sat 9am-3pm, in summer until 7pm; Sun, Mon, 9am-1pm. Access to the underground rooms: Tue-Fri 9am-12 noon. Entrance free.

The Imperial Fora can be reached from the Via dei Fori Imperiali. *Metro:* Line B to Colosseo, *Bus:* 85, 87, 88. For permission to visit the Imperial Fora, you should apply to the **Soprintendenza Comunale ai Musei, Monumenti e Antichità,** Piazza Caffarelli 3.

Access to the **Markets of Trajan**: Via IV Novembre 94. Open Tue-Sat 9am-1pm; Sun until 12.30pm. Entrance: 3750 Lire, students 2500 Lire; free for children and senior citizens.

Capitol

Metro: Line B to Colosseo; *Bus:* 57, 85, 87, 88, 90, 90b, 92, 94, 95, 716, 718, 719.

The Capitoline Museums

Piazza del Campidoglio. Open Tue-Sat 9am-1.30pm, Tue again from 5pm to 8pm. In summer: 8pm-10pm; Sun 9am-1pm. Entrance: 10,000 Lire.

Churches on the Capitol
Other sights

Santa Maria in Aracoeli: Important frescoes by Pinturicchio and the miracle-working Christchild (*Bambino Santissimo*). Highly revered by the Romans, it is carved from the wood of an olive tree from the Garden of Gethsemane.

S. Giuseppe dei Falegnami with the **Mamertine Prison** on the eastern slope of the Capitoline, facing the Forum Romanum. Open daily 9am-12.30pm and 2pm-6pm.

Circus Maximus: Via del Circo Massimo. *Metro:* Line B to Circo Massimo.

Baths of Caracalla: Via delle Terme di Caracalla; *Metro:* Line B to Circo Massimo. *Bus:* 11, 27, 90k, 90b, 94, 118, 673. Open Tue-Sat 9am to 1hour before sunset; Mon, Sun 9am-2pm.

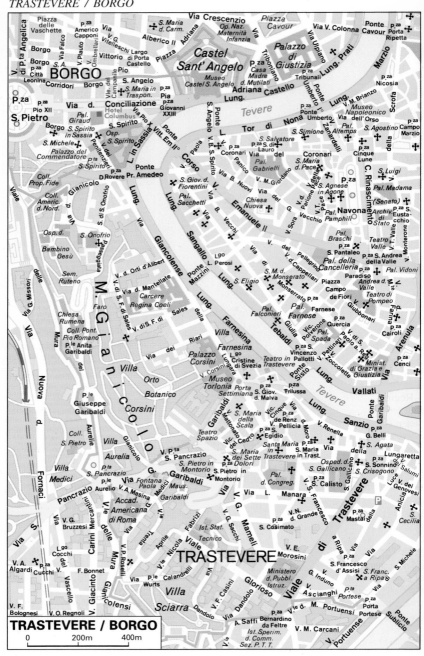

TRASTEVERE / BORGO

0   200m   400m

THE ROME OF THE PEOPLE

TRASTEVERE
GIANICOLO
BORGO

TRASTEVERE

Dentro Regina Coeli c' è 'no scalino. Chi nun salisce quello nun è romano. Nun è romano e manco tresteverino. ("In the Regina Coeli there's a stairway. Anyone who does not use it is no Roman, much less from Trastevere.") The words of this old Roman folk-song demonstrate the citizens' pride in being Roman, and especially in coming from Trastevere, seen as the most Roman of all Roman neighborhoods.

Regina Coeli is one of Rome's two penitentiaries. Its name, which ironically means "Queen of Heaven," derives from the convent of the same name which occupied the building until 1881. It is no coincidence that the government of the first all-Italian state of 1861 wanted to locate the capital's prison in the quarter – or *rione* in Italian – which a hundred years before had had the worst reputation in the whole of Rome. It is safe to assume that the first inmates of these cells were people from the immediate neighborhood, inhabitants of the dense labyrinth of streets and alleys where in those days the *bullo,* an odd mixture of dandy and small-time crook, plied his nefarious trade. Every Trasteverino who had run

Previous pages: Beware of the dog!

afoul of the law took the walk up the infamous staircase into the prison with a kind of dignified pride: everyone who passed this way proved his allegiance to a certain neighborhood, the most Roman in all of Rome.

No one would question Trastevere's distinctly "Roman" quality; but this actually developed relatively late in the day. Under the reign of Augustus the area, which was mostly farmland inhabited by poor artisans, Syrians, and Jews, was designated Trans Tyberim, the XVIth *regio* of the city. Later, under Aurelian, it was partially surrounded by a city wall.

All too often, the peasants who had settled there had to leave their fields for years at a time in order to take up arms and defend Rome against the Etruscans, whose attacks did not cease until 396 BC, when the Romans destroyed the neighboring Etruscan city of Veii. Even after this, the memory of the Etruscans remained vivid in the minds of the people; this, together with the fact that their *rione* was the only city neighborhood on the right bank of the Tiber until 1586 (the Borgo was at that time part of Trastevere), convinced the inhabitants that they were something unique and special.

Something of Trastevere's "special" quality has survived to this day. You can

often still see washing hanging out to dry on a clothesline stretched across the street. And just as often the Trasteverini sit out in the street on summer evenings for a chat with the neighbors in the cooler night air or a hand of cards at a table outside a bar.

As well as this traditional, folksy face, Trastevere can also display fancy restaurants and the so-called alternative boutiques. In the late 1960s and early 1970s it was still possible to buy an apartment here very cheaply, though it would have no heating and the toilet would be on the balcony. The attempt to turn the area into something like New York's Greenwich Village, at the expense of the old residents, has only partially succeeded: the few members of the smart set who have moved in have hardly altered the character of the place. It has kept its traditional, local color, and even today its residents are proud to be "Romans from Trast-

Above: In the Villa Farnesina. Right: Strictly male conversation in Trastevere.

evere" – even if they haven't climbed up the notorious staircase.

A good starting point for a walk through Trastevere is actually quite near the staircase: the beautiful Renaissance **Villa Farnesina**. Located at Nr 230 Via della Lungara, it was built between 1508 and 1511 by Baldassare Peruzzi for the Siennese banker Agostino Chigi. Frescoes in the villa's Galleria depict scenes from the myth of Amor and Psyche; in the next room you can see the marvellous fresco of *Galatea* by Raphael. On the ceiling is a representation of the horoscope of Agostino Chigi's birth on December 1, 1466 (the date has been deduced from the position of the planets). Located on the upper floor, the *Salone delle Prospettive*, or "Hall of Panoramas," contains *trompe l'oeil* views of Rome and mythological scenes painted by Peruzzi. On the walls you can still see the scribbles left behind by the *Landsknechte*, the German mercenaries of the emperor Charles V, who invaded the city in May 1527 and ransacked it for nearly seven months. The next room is the bedroom, where you can see Sodoma's fresco *The Wedding of Alexander and Roxane*.

Opposite the Villa Farnesina rises the elegant façade of the 18th-century **Palazzo Corsini**, designed by Ferdinando Fuga. A staircase flooded with light leads up to the first-floor rooms, which house a collection of 17th and 18th century paintings from Italy and other European countries.

A part of the former palace gardens is occupied by the **Botanical Garden**, which, with its hot-houses and centuries-old trees, stretches to the foot of the Janiculum Hill (Gianicolo). The entrance is at the end of the Via Corsini on the **Largo Cristina di Svezia**, a palace named after the Swedish queen who lived here from 1659 until her death in 1689.

Continuing along the Via della Lungara, you'll come to the **Porta Settimiana**, a triumphal arch which formed the entrance to the Baths of Septimius Severus in imperial times, and was later integrated into the wall that surrounded the *rione*. The arch leads you into the very heart of Trastevere, a labyrinthine network of narrow alleyways and enchanting hidden corners. Just to the right of the gateway, the **Church of Santa Maria della Scala** was built to house a picture of the Madonna which was said to have miraculous powers. It was painted on the outside staircase of a house in Trastevere, which is why the church is named "St Mary of the Stairs." The picture now hangs over the altar in the left transept and is surrounded by numerous tokens of profound piety. The Trasteverini's special reverence for the Virgin culminates every year in the third week of July, when the image of the so-called *Madonna de Noantri* is borne through the streets in a festive procession; the rest of the year, the image is housed in the **Church of S. Agata**, not far from the Viale Trastevere. Also dedicated to the

Mother of God is the basilica of this district, **Santa Maria in Trastevere**. Built by Pope Julius I (337-352), it is probably the earliest church in Rome dedicated to the Virgin. It stands on the spot where a miraculous jet of oil shot out of the earth in 38 BC; later, Christians interpreted this unusual event as a portent of the coming of the Savior.

The façade had a portico added to it in the early 18th century, and its upper part is decorated with mosaics. The richly appointed interior is comprised of three aisles separated by 22 ancient columns, which may well have come originally from the Baths of Caracalla. Note, too, the magnificent wooden roof and the mosaic in the apse; in the upper part, Christ is portrayed enthroned, with his right arm around his mother.

The **Piazza Santa Maria**, with its elegant late 17th century fountain, is today a center of Rome's nightlife. During the day, however, it's a meeting-place for local residents, filled with children playing around the square.

The Via delle Lungaretta ultimately leads you to the **Viale Trastevere**. This great traffic artery, built after the unification of Italy, cuts through the tangle of little streets and lanes and brings the noise and bustle of the big city into this peaceful quarter. Even if you have a full schedule, you should at least take a quick look at the **Basilica of S. Crisogono**, with its underground church from the 5th century (entrance through the sacristy with permission from the priest), which was built on the remains of various buildings from the days of the Roman empire.

On the other side of the Viale Trastevere lies the **Piazza in Piscinula**, on the left side of which stands the simple medieval **edifice of Casa dei Mattei**. This building was the setting for a tragic, and fatal, story of revenge in the year 1555, in the course of which three of the four siblings of the noble family of Mattei killed

Above: Children playing football in the Piazza S. Maria in Trastevere.

each other. In the corner between this house and the next stands a stone bearing an inscription stating that, under an edict of 1763, dumping garbage on this spot was forbidden, punishable by a fine and a flogging. The little notice, one of many which were put up all over papal Rome, is evidence of a bad habit among the Romans, which even today they have not quite been cured of.

If you turn right into the Via in Piscinula, follow it to the Via dei Salumni, and turn from there into the Vicolo dell'Atleta, you'll come to a beautiful medieval house, Number 14, which was probably a synagogue in the 12th century. Carrying on past this alley you come to the Via dei Genovesi; a little ways along this street to the left, the **Via Santa Cecilia** leads to the wonderful basilica of the same name. Behind the monumental 18th-century entrance, passing through a garden with a magnificent fountain made from a Roman ceremonial marble basin, you come to the church itself, dedicated to the aristocratic Roman

Cecilia, who is said to have invented the organ and is the patron saint of music. Over the main altar you can see the medieval ciborium; beneath the altar, the marble statue by the sculptor Stefano Maderna depicts the saint's body in exactly the same position in which her corpse was found when it was exhumed in 1599. The house in which she lived and where she died a martyr's death during the period of Christian persecution, in 230 AD, is probably one of those whose ruins have been found beneath the church; a nun can guide you to these and other Roman ruins on an organized tour. In the choir of the convent is a marvellous, though partly damaged, fresco of the *Last Judgment*. This work was painted by Pietro Cavallini in 1293, but covered up when the nuns' gallery was added to the church in the 16th century, not to be rediscovered until 1900. It was restored in the 1980s.

Going straight ahead from the church, you come to the **Piazza dei Mercanti**, once a favorite meeting place for sailors who came from the nearby harbor, which no longer exists today. Instead, the customers of the famous restaurants which lie around the square are entertained by Roman folk singers.

GIANICOLO

Trastevere has always been distinguished by a certain rusticity, which the other *rioni* don't generally possess at all, and certainly not to the same extent. Some of the green parklands with which the patriotic Italians, at the end of the last century, wanted to beautify their city, are still extant on the Gianicolo. This quiet hill, once dedicated to the god Janus (hence its name, the Janiculum) has had an eventful history: its pines and oaks have sheltered the meetings of the group of intellectuals known as the Academy of Arcadia for three centuries; but they also witnessed Garibaldi's volunteers, the Redshirts, fighting the French army in one of the bitterest battles of the Risorgimento in 1849.

To see one of the most interesting sides of the hill, return to the Porta Settimiana and walk up the **Via Garibaldi**. After a few hundred yards there's a beautiful garden gate on the right, which unfortunately is nearly always locked. It leads to the **Bosco Parasio**, where the academicians of the Arcadia still meet, as they have done since 1690.

On the left is the **Church of S. Maria dei Sette Dolori**, a creation of Borromini's, which, unfortunately, was never finished. A little further up, you'll come to another fine church, its terrace affording a marvellous view over much of Rome. **S. Pietro in Montorio** stands on the spot where, according to legend, St Peter, the apostle and first Pope, was martyred. Behind the simple Renaissance façade is a richly decorated interior, where the first chapel on the right contains the dramatic painting *of The Scourging of Christ* by Sebastiano del Piombo (1518). The mortal remains of **Beatrice Cenci** were supposedly kept beneath the high altar until the end of the 18th century; Beatrice was beheaded on 11th September 1599 as punishment for killing her father. She was so beloved for her great beauty among the people of Rome that Masses for her soul are still said today on the anniversary of her death. In the courtyard of the church stands the wonderful **Tempietto del Bramante**, which was built in 1502 on the spot where, according to tradition, St Peter was crucified. Bramante was one of the greatest Renaissance architects: the perfect balance of forms in this building, and the purity of its lines, make this small circular temple with its 16 columns one of his masterpieces, a true jewel of Renaissance architecture.

Somewhat above the church you come to the **Fontana dell'Acqua Paola**, named after Pope Paul V, who had the

ancient Aqueduct of Trajan restored to use in 1612. The fountain, built, by a strange coincidence, by an architect named Giovanni Fontana, in locally known as *Il Fontanone,* the big fountain. It's virtually an obligatory background for the souvenir photos of the many weddings held in S. Pietro in Montorio, especially in September.

To the right, the **Passegiata del Gianicolo** is a beautiful path, ideal for strolling, which leads along the side of the hill to the **Salita S. Onofrio**. The first sight that awaits you here is the **equestrian statue of Garibaldi**. It shows the national hero with his gaze directed toward the Vatican, though since 1932 he has appeared to be looking across at his wife Anita, a few yards down the hill, who is represented, also on horseback, in a very warlike pose. From the terrace on clear days there is a superb view of the city.

Above: The Garibaldi Memorial on the Gianicolo at sunset. Right: In the Botanical Garden (Gianicolo).

If you follow the Passegiata downhill, you'll come to a large curve in the road after which a flight of steps on the right leads up to the remains of the old oak tree where the poet Torquato Tasso is said to have spent many hours during the last days of his life, before he died in the nearby **monastery of S. Onofrio**. In any case, this monastery is certainly worth a look, not only because of the marvellous paintings, attributed to Baldassare Peruzzi, in the apse, but also for its attractive cloister, where frescoes that are perhaps not quite as valuable as Peruzzi's, but are nonetheless impressive, depict scenes from the lives of the saints. When you can tear yourself away from this oasis of peace, continue down the Salita S. Onofrio to the **Porta Santo Spirito**.

THE BORGO

Through this Porto, begun in 1538 based on designs by Antonio de Sangallo, but never completed, you pass into the last of the 14 *rioni* of old Rome. Of all the city districts, the Borgo is undoubtedly the one which has suffered the most throughout its history. Founded by pilgrims from Saxony – the name *Borgo* derives from the German word *Burg, or "castle"* – it was destroyed by two fires in the 9th century and then plundered by the Saracens. After flourishing anew over the next few centuries, it went into another decline during the exile of the papacy in Avignon, but managed to recover yet again when the popes returned to Rome and settled down in the Vatican. Then, in 1527, it was ransacked by the troops of Charles V. By this time, construction had already started on the new Basilica of St Peter. This building work dragged on for two centuries and, in a way, had a decisive effect on the future of the Borgo: Bernini's colonnades made it necessary to build a new, wide street. This project wasn't actually tackled until 1936. Not only was part of the Borgo destroyed in the process, but the aesthetic value of the result is open to debate.

On the corner, to the right, stands the **Church of S. Spirito in Sassia** with its fine Renaissance façade and elegant, single-aisled interior. Next to the church is the entrance to the **Palazzo del Commendatore**. In the beautiful courtyard of this building is an unusual clock dating from 1827: there are only six figures on its face, according to the *ora Romana*, the ancient Roman time reckoning which divided the day into six parts.

Opposite the palace runs the wall of the ancient *Corsia Sistina* of the **Ospedale di S. Spirito**, in the middle of which a Baroque door opens on to the so-called *Ottagono*, a beautiful Renaissance chapel with an elegant *ciborium* dating from the same period. The Hospital of the Holy Ghost was founded by Pope Innocent III in 1198; the story goes that he was moved to found it after he had seen a couple of fishermen pulling in the dead body of a new-born baby from the Tiber with their net. The story may well be apocryphal,

but it is true that one of this hospital's major goals was to take in unwanted children. Beside the gateway you can see the "The Foundlings' Wheel," where mothers could "unburden" themselves of the fruits of unwanted pregnancies. Beside the wheel is a block of travertine with a slit in the center, through which alms for the foundlings could be dropped.

Turn left from the Via Pio X into the **Via della Conciliazione,** named for the "Reconciliation" between the Catholic Church and the Italian state, which was concluded in 1929 with the signature of the Lateran Treaties. Prior to this, the Church had refused any form of union with the Italian state, which had removed the church's authority over Rome by taking it for itself on 20th September 1970. In place of the impersonal boulevard you see today, which, in spite of a few lovely Renaissance palaces, remains rather sterile, the area was originally occupied by two streets, Borgo Vecchio and Borgo Nuovo, as well as the beautiful Piazza

Scossacavalli. The demolition of the old buildings in 1936 has deprived us of an experience which famous visitors to Rome in past centuries used to rave about: originally, when you emerged from the Borgo's narrow alleyways you found yourself confronted with St Peter's square and the colonnades. Trying to rescue at least a few of the beautiful buildings which used to stand on the sites today marked by an uninterrupted stream of car traffic, officials had them dismantled and rebuilt rather haphazardly in other parts of the city.

The **Church of S. Maria in Traspontina** (1566-87), which stands on the grandiose modern thoroughfare running up to St Peter's Square, is worth a visit. The reason for its oddly small dome, which seems out of proportion to the rest of the building, is that the church once stood beneath the Castel Sant'Angelo, and it got

Above: One of the many "Madonnine" on the walls of Roman houses. Right: A neighborly chat at the newspaper kiosk.

in the way of the cannon fire directed against the troops of Charles V. When the church was moved and rebuilt on the Borgo Nuovo, pains were taken to provide it with a dome too small for the enemy to take refuge behind against the papal artillery's attacks.

From here the **Vicolo del Campanile** branches off to the right. It was in this narrow street that Rome's last hangman, Giambattista Bugatti, known as Mastro Titta, lived. Between 1796 and 1864 he carried out 514 death sentences, conscientiously entering the name of each condemned man in a notebook, together with details of the crime which had brought him to the scaffold. The alley leads to the so-called **Passetto di Borgo**, the wall which connects the Vatican with Castel Sant'Angelo and formed the city limits until 1527. On May 6, 1527 Pope Clement VII only just managed to escape to safety over this wall ahead of the hordes of *Landsknechte,* who had already forced their way into St Peter's.

To encourage the people of Rome to make their home beyond the new city wall, the Pope promised a reward to anyone who built a house there. This even applied to prostitutes (referred to in the Papal Bull as *impudicae et inhonestae mulieres*) – provided they invested at least 500 *scudi* in the undertaking, which they were doubtless able to earn easily from their trade. Perhaps it's because of these plebeian origins that this neighborhood, just like Trastevere, has preserved the traditional character of its narrow, winding streets. They have odd names like: Vicolo delle Palline (Lane of the Little Balls), Via dei Tre Pupazzi (Street of the Three Jumping-jacks), Vicolo del Farino (Flour Lane), Via del Falco (Falcon Street), Via dei Ombrellari (Street of the Parasol-makers). Only one bears the name of a historical figure, the ancient Roman poet and writer of comedies, Plautus; but this was once called Vicolo delle Fogne (Sewer Lane), probably be-

cause a dark and dirty gutter ran through it. The name was changed at the request of the residents; it is not difficult to imagine why.

At the corner of the Vicolo del Campanile and Borgo Pio you will see one of the many images of the Virgin Mary which one comes across everywhere in Rome. Cemented into the wall below it is a round, dark-colored stone, whose purpose was to show the minimum size permissible for a loaf of bread. Shoppers could come here to check whether or not the baker had tried to put one over on them. Incidentally, throughout the period of papal rule, the price of bread was kept extremely low for political reasons; on certain holidays it was even given away free.

Strolling through these quiet lanes, only a few steps away from the busy embankment beside the Tiber, you will come across many curious sights, such as the bell foundry at Nr 34 Vicolo delle Palline, which, according to a sign in the window, has been in existence for over 400 years. The **Piazza delle Vaschette** was named for its three small fountains, only one of which remains. It stands a little below the level of the street and can be reached by two attractive, curving flights of steps. The water that bubbles from the fountain as called *Acqua Angelica*, not, as you might think, because it tastes heavenly, but in honor of Angelo de Medici who became Pope in 1559 under the name Pius IV.

The square, which is surrounded by rather shabby buildings, nevertheless exudes a discreet charm: the graffiti on the walls, the children playing, mothers chatting to each other, old folk sitting on benches, and the gentle splashing of the water from the fountain all combine into a harmonious ensemble. It is rare to find such an atmosphere of quiet and tranquility in the Rome of today; it's as if a little piece has survived here of the old city, the rest of which was rudely awakened from its centuries of slumber on 20th September 1870 by the guns of Garibaldi's liberation army.

TRASTEVERE / GIANICOLO / BORGO

Transport connections

Rome on the far side of the Tiber can easily be explored in one day on foot. Begin your walk from Trastevere through Gianicolo and into the Borgo or vice versa. Don't forget that most of the galleries in the palaces are only open until 2pm, and that the churches close for a while at midday. The best way to visit Trastevere is on foot, from the Ghetto and across the island in the Tiber, or you can take one of the many buses which cross the bridges and then run along the Lungotevere e.g routes 23, 41 and/or 280. The streetcar (tram) route 13 also takes you to Trastevere.

Sightseeing / Churches

Santa Cecilia in Trastevere, Piazza di Santa Cecilia; *Bus:* 23, 26, 28, 44, 75, 97, 170, 710, 718, 719, 774. Viewing the *Last Judgement* in the monastery Tue and Thur 10am-11.30am. **San Crisogono**, Viale di Trastevere, Piazza Sonnino; *Bus:* 26, 44, 56, 60, 65, 75, 170, 710, 718, 719. **Santa Maria in Trastevere**, Piazza di Santa Maria in Trastevere; *Bus:* 23, 28, 28b, 56, 60, 65. **San Pietro in Montorio**, Via Garibaldi, *Bus:* 41, 44, 75, 710.

Palaces / Museums / Galleries

Museo del Folklore e dei Poeti Romaneschi, Piazza S. Egidio 1/6, Tel: 5816563, daily 9am-1.30pm; Tue, Thur also 4.30-8pm. **Villa Farnesina,** Via della Lungara 230; Tel: 6540565; *Bus:* 23, 41, 65, 280; daily except Sun and holidays 9am-1pm; closed in August; entrance free. **Palazzo Corsini**, Via della Lungara 10 (opp. the Villa Farnesina); *Bus:* 23, 28, 28b, 65; Tue-Fri 9am-7pm, Mon, Sat 9am-2pm, Sun 9am-1pm.

It is worth visiting the **Fontanone** above the church of San Pietro in Montorio. One of the finest lookout points, with a view over the city, is on the Piazza Garibaldi. Best to go just before sunset. On Sundays don't forget: the Porta Portese flea market on the Viale Trastevere!

Relaxation

If you take the bus 170 coming from S. Paolo Fuori le Mura, get out in Trastevere one stop after Piazza Ippolito Nievo, and walk up the Viale Aurelio Saffi, along the Aurelian Wall, until you reach a gap in the wall which leads into the **Villa Sciarra**, a charming little 18th century park.

Not far from here the city's largest stretch of parkland, the **Villa Doria Pamphili**, is beside the Via Aurelia Antica (*Bus:* 31, 42, 144). Near the Villa Corsini, at the end of the Largo Cristina di Svezia, the **Botanical Garden** is open Mon-Fri 10am-6pm, in summer until 7pm. (Entrance 2000 Lire).

Restaurants

Alberto Ciarla, Piazza San Cosimato 40, Tel: 5818668, absolutely first-class fish dishes, considered the best place to eat in Rome, also open for lunch from October to May. Closed Suns and 1–13 January and 12–28 August; book ahead. **Carlo Menta**, Via della Lungaretta 101, Tel: 5884450, seafood specialities, book ahead. Closed for lunch, closed Mons and 16 Juli–10 August. **Corsetti-il Galeone**, Piazza S. Cosimato 27, Tel: 5816311, closed Weds and 17– 25 July. **Cul de Sac 2**, Vicolo dell'Atleta 21, Tel: 5813324, book ahead, closed for lunch, closed Suns and August. **Da Fieramosca**, Piazza dei Mercanti 3a, Tel: 5890289, excellent Roman cuisine. **Gino in Trastevere**, Via della Lungaretta 85, Tel: 5803403 and 5806226. **Ivo in Trastevere**, Via S. Francesco a Ripa 158, Tel: 5817082. **La Tana de Noiantri**, Via della Paglia 1-3, Tel: 5806404, hidden behind the church of S. Maria in Trastevere, typical Roman cuisine, big helpings, low prices. **Meo Patacca**, Piazza dei Mercanti 30, Tel: 5892193, folkloric songs and dancing.

Romolo, Via Porta Settimiana 8, Tel: 5818284/5813873, one of Trastevere's favorite restaurants, Roman cuisine, pretty garden.

Sabatini, Piazza di Santa Maria in Trastevere 13, Tel: 5812026, and Vicolo Santa Maria in Trastevere 18, Tel: 5818307, superb fish restaurants. In summer it's nice to sit out on the piazza. **Taverna Trilussa**, Via del Politeama 23, Tel: 58118918, closed Sun evenings, Mon and 30 Juli–28 August. Bohemian haunt. **Tentativo**, Via della Luce 5, Tel: 5895324, book ahead, closed for lunch, closed Suns and in August.

Evening in Trastevere / Theater

Teatro Spazio Uno, Vicolo dei Panieri 3. **Teatro in Trastevere**, Vicolo Moroni 3. **Belli**, Piazza S. Apollonia 21 a, Tel: 5894875. **Folk Studio**, Via Gaetano Scacchi 3, Tel: 5892374. **Il Tarchio**,Via Morosini 16, Tel: 582049. **Metateatro**, Via Mameli 5, Tel: 5895807.

Nightlife

Action Club, Via Benedetta 23, Tel: 5894016. **Belle Epoque,** Vicolo del Leopardo 31, Tel: 5895540, piano bar. **Calisè**, Piazza Mastai 7, Tel: 5809404, bar with music. **Invidia**, Via della Scala 34/B, Tel: 5806408, piano bar. **L'Angelo Azzurro**, Via Cardinal Merry del Val 13, Tel: 5800472, Disco. **L'Asino Cotto**, Via dei Vascellari 48, Latin-American. Live music, Tel: 5898985. **New Scarabocchio**, Piazza dei Ponziani 8/C, Tel: 5800495, Disco.**Yes Brazil**, Via S. Francesco a Ripa 103, Tel: 5816267, bar with music.

EARLY CHRISTIAN ROME

THE PATRIARCHAL BASILICAS
THE TITULAR CHURCHES

Rome has more churches than any other city in the world. It would take an age to visit them all. Beside all the old churches there are countless new ones, for the city has spread out like an oil slick in recent decades, and each of the new districts, or *borgate*, has its own church, modern and not always very attractive. So visitors to Rome will doubtless want to restrict themselves to the old and famous churches. Foremost among these are the seven patriarchal basilicas, or senior churches, which are under the direct supervision of the Pope. Practicing Catholics still visit these pilgrimage churches to receive indulgences, exactly in the way prescribed by Filippo Neri in the 16th century. Most important of all is St Peter's, followed by the former papal church of S. Giovanni in Laterano (St John Lateran); the others are S. Paolo fuori le Mura (St Paul outside the Walls), S. Sebastian on the Via Appia, S. Croce in Gerusalemme (the Holy Cross of Jerusalem), S. Lorenzo and S. Maria Maggiore. Each of these churches has an altar where only the Pope is allowed to say Mass, and each of them is at least 1,500 years old.

Previous pages: Village life in the metropolis – a street in Trastevere. Left: In the Piazza S. Giovanni in Laterano.

THE PATRIARCHAL BASILICAS

S. Giovanni in Laterano, also called the Lateran Basilica, is the first and oldest Catholic church in the world, "mother and chief of all the churches in the city, and upon the globe." The popes dwelt in the Lateran from the days of the emperor Constantine in the 4th century until 1309, when the Popes went into exile in Avignon. The great Councils of the Middle Ages took place here, and it was here, too, that the first Holy Year was proclaimed in 1300 AD.

The land on which the church was built once belonged to the Laterani family and formed part of the dowry of Fausta when she married the Emperor Constantine. This first Christian basilica became the architectural model for all early Christian churches. Its location was in line with the wishes of the emperor, who wanted to keep the new Christian places of worship away from the city center, so that the great "heathen" tradition of Rome might be preserved. The ground-plan follows the form of the Roman basilica: a longitudinal central nave, with two lateral transepts and an apse at the east end. This sacred building was clearly meant as a counterpart to the emperor's secular basilicas, courtrooms and palaces of assembly. In the apse stood the *cathedra*, the official throne for the bishop of Rome, and later for the Pope. It is from this that the word "cathedral" is derived.

In the course of its eventful history the magnificently appointed church was plundered by Vandals and Normans, damaged by earthquakes, and finally burnt down in a major fire in 1308. Once rebuilt, the church received its present shape under Pope Innocent X, who had it completely remodelled in 1650 by the Baroque architect Francesco Borromini. The grandeur of its imposing interior, with two aisles on either side of the nave and the Gothic main or papal altar rising up in the transept, is emphasized by the huge figures of the apostles carved into the pillars by a sculptor of the School of Bernini. The mosaic floor in the style of the Cosmati and the Baroque cofferwork ceiling are typical elements of Roman decorations of the period. The mosaic in the apse dates from 1288-94 and shows Christ holding a cross set with precious stones. There is an old legend that the heads of the apostles Peter and Paul are kept here, and Pope Martin V is buried in the *confessio* below the altar. The cloister at the side of the church, which dates from around 1222-30, is a consummate example of the work of the Cosmati, but the many fragments displayed around the walls come from the original church.

The Lateran Palace is built on to the church, and near it is the **Baptisterium**, the Baptistry of St John. Every Easter Saturday, people come in a ceremonial procession to be baptized at the font in the center of this ancient, octagonal building. In the reign of Constantine, it was built for the Laterani family over a *nymphaeum*, or pump room. Although it has been renovated many times in the course of its history, it has retained its original appearance and served as a model for many later baptistries.

Opposite the present-day Lateran palace are some remains of the former papal residence. The private chapel of the

Popes, the "sancta sanctorum," is there, and leading up to it is the deeply venerated Holy Staircase. These are the stairs Christ is supposed to have walked down after being condemned to death; Helena, the mother of Constantine, brought them from Jerusalem to Rome.

In 432 AD, when work on the most beautiful early Christian church on the Aventine Hill, S. Sabina, was nearing completion, construction began on the first and largest of Rome's churches to the Virgin, **S. Maria Maggiore**. Legend has it that the Virgin Mary appeared to the patriarch John and the Pope Liberius on the night of 5th August, 352 AD, and told them they were to build a church and that she would give them a special sign

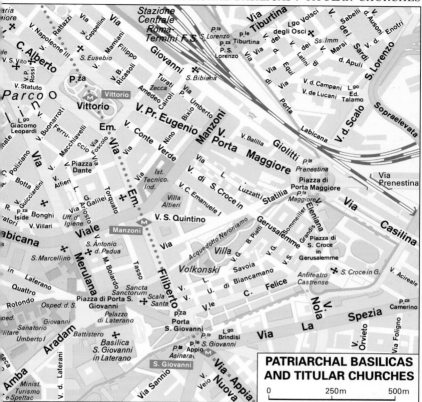

PATRIARCHAL BASILICAS AND TITULAR CHURCHES

0   250m   500m

showing where it was to be sited. Sure enough, they woke the next morning to find snow upon the Esquiline Hill, and a church in honor of the Virgin was duly built there. This day is still celebrated by the congregation of S. Maria Maggiore with a special service; during it, white petals flutter down from the gilded coffers of the ceiling. The gold on the ceiling was the first to arrive from the New World, a gift from King Ferdinand and Queen Isabella of Spain.

S. Maria Maggiore is also famous for its mosaics, which are some of the most beautiful to survive from the 5th century. There are 36 mosaic pictures along the walls of the nave. Those on the left wall depict the lives of the Old Testament pa-

triarchs Abraham, Isaac, Jacob and Esau; those on the right, the lives of Moses and Joshua. Above the high altar, the biblical scenes on the golden triumphal arch have an almost mystical glow: the Annunciation, the Adoration of the Three Kings, the Massacre of the Innocents and, on the right, the apostle Peter and the Presentation of Jesus in the Temple, the ordering of the flight into Egypt, the encounter of the Holy Family with the King of Egypt, and that of the Three Wise Men from the East with King Herod. In the apse the mosaic pictures glorifying Mary, on their gold background, are the work of Jacopo Torriti. The floor is in the Cosmati style, the principle nave is supported on ancient columns, and in the steps up to the high

87

altar is an inconspicuous tombstone whose inscription tells us that here "the noble Bernini family await their resurrection." On November 28, 1680, "at the second hour of the night" the great Gian Lorenzo Bernini was quietly laid to rest here. In 1743 the architect F. Fuga covered the old façade with a second one, considered modern at the time, which serves to protect the 13th century mosaics. The restored mosaics depicting the legend of the church's founding can be seen in the loggia.

Between S. Giovanni in Laterano and the ancient Roman gate of Porta Maggiore stands the third pilgrimage church, **S. Croce in Gerusalemme**. This late Baroque building dates back to the papacy of Benedict XIV (1740-58), who had the existing church remodelled from the ground up. So, unfortunately, almost nothing remains of the original Basilica

Above: The impressive structure of S. Maria Maggiore. Right: The Porta Maggiore, the gateway to the Campagna.

of the Holy Cross in Jerusalem, which was built in the grounds of an ancient Roman palace, the *Sessorium*. The church was probably built at the behest of Saint Helena, the mother of Constantine the Great. She wanted a building to house and venerate the precious relics she had brought home from her journey to the Holy Land, including, so legend has it, fragments of the True Cross.

The underground **Chapel of St Helena**, built upon sacred soil from the hill of Calvary, remains a memorial to this pious royal lady. In the Chapel of the Relics in the left-hand aisle is a shrine containing three fragments of wood and a nail from the cross of Jesus, found in Jerusalem, as well as two thorns from the Crown of Thorns and a remnant of the sign bearing the inscription I.N.R.I. (standing for the Latin words for "Jesus of Nazareth, King of the Jews").

Not far from the church is the ancient **Porta Maggiore,** the gateway to the two Roman roads, the Via Labicana and the Via Prenestina, which led into the south-

ern region of the Campagna. This was also the junction of the aqueducts which brought water from the mountains in the southeast. You can still see the five water channels that converged here: two streams flowed between the Attic columns of the monumental gate, while at the sides you can still make out the dry beds, of three more ducts, one above the other, which are covered with a veneer of chalk and today, in part, with concrete. The water used to flow into a tank below the Baths of Diocletian, near where the Stazione Termini train station now stands; from there it was distributed further throughout the city.

In front of the gate stands a curious stone cube, through which holes have been bored; this is the grave of the baker Eurysaces. It is probably 70 years older than the Porta itself, which was built in 52 AD, during the reign of Claudius. When the Aurelian city wall was hastily erected in the third century as a defense against barbarian invaders, the whole structure of the gate, along with the grave, was incorporated in the defensive works. The whole thing didn't come to light again until the 19th cen., thanks to the work of architect Giuseppe Valadier.

In 1917, workers building the railway unearthed a subterranean basilica from the 1st century AD. It is near the Porta Maggiore, and the details of its past are still shrouded in mystery. But it has been established that it was a place of worship for the cult of the Neo-Pythagorians. This, like the cult of Mithras, was a religion of salvation which was especially widespread among the patrician families. The cult probably had to practice in secret, which would explain the underground site. However, archaeologists are still rather baffled. The room where the worshippers met has reliefs on the ceiling depicting scenes from Greek mythology, which were intended to help believers overcome their fear of death; today, however, you need a special permit to enter it.

The last of the pilgrimage churches, S. Lorenzo fuori le Mura, is described in connection with the district of the same

89

name in the section on 19th-century Rome (p. 159).

THE TITULAR CHURCHES

Apart from the legacy of Constantine the Great, many of the earliest Roman churches owe their existence to the often considerable private fortunes of affluent Christians. During the difficult period when Christians were persecuted, they did not, as is often claimed, hide in the catacombs – this hiding place was very well known to the imperial authorities. Instead, patrician converts often made available their homes, offices, or warehouses – or individual rooms therein – for the religious services of congregations or Christian leaders. The house generally retained the name of its owner even if he had given part or all of it to the church. After freedom of religion was

Above: Worried about the Vatican's financial crisis? Right: The glowing golden mosaics in the apse of S. Clemente.

granted by the Edict of Milan in 313, these sites were converted into proper churches or used to build new ones. They are still called "titular churches," even though, in general, nothing is left of the original building and only underground remains of walls testify to their former existence. Twenty-five such titular churches are known, the most famous being S. Clemente, SS. Quattro Coronati, SS. Giovanni e Paolo and S. Martino ai Monti.

A little way behind the Colosseum stand the three superimposed strata of building that make up **S. Clemente**, probably the most impressive example of post-Imperial Roman architecture. Past the Ludus Magnus, the barracks where the gladiators of the emperor Domitian trained for combat in an amphitheater which has partially survived, in the dip between the Colle Oppio to the north and the Celio to the south, there was an *insula*, or ancient Roman tenement building. It probably belonged to the family of the man who became St Clement, and was one of the first places where Christians could assemble. The church, therefore, dates from before the age of Constantine; it was probably used by a cult of some kind even before Christianity had reached Rome. Written evidence dating from the 3rd and 4th centuries attests to the fact that a Christian church existed on this site; it remains, today, one of the most interesting early churches in Rome.

A small, modest side entrance leads into the **upper church**, which, begun under Pope Paschal II in 1108 and consecrated in 1128, is the most recent part of S. Clemente. The main entrance lies in an atrium at the end of the nave, which is supported by 16 classical columns. As in many churches in Rome the floor was paved by craftsmen of the Cosmati workshops. Work of this kind is found principally in and around Rome, because only here was the supply of marble from the ruins of the ancient city plentiful enough

that it could be sawn up into tiny pieces and laid out in imaginative patterns. The decoration of the church dates almost entirely from the Middle Ages. This is true of the Easter candelabrum, two ambones (an early variant on the pulpit) and the reading desk in the *schola cantorum* in the nave; although the marble for the cantorum itself date from the 6th century, having been appropriated from the lower church for the purpose. Also well preserved are the high altar, the choir screen, the stalls for the clergy and the bishop's throne.

The mosaics in the apse date from around 1120 and are among the finest in Rome. They depict the glorification of the cross. Portraits of the early church fathers Ambrose, Hieronymous, Augustine and Gregory the Great; characters from the legend of St Clement; stags drinking from the rivers of Paradise flowing from the cross, snakes, and lambs (symbolizing Christ and the Twelve Apostles) coming out of the holy cities Jerusalem and Bethlehem, are the figures

decorating the arch of the apse. Over these, at the top of the arch, floats the figure of Christ, surrounded by the four beasts of the Apocalypse which are at the same time symbols of the evangelists.

For the price of a small contribution to the Irish Dominican monks who have looked after the churches since 1789, you can climb 16 ft (5 m) down into the 4th-century basilica, which was plundered and largely destroyed by the Normans in 1084. The fact that the apse is located at the west end – a feature retained in the medieval church – shows that the church is very old. The steps take you past some ancient archaeological finds, including a statue of Mithras, into the narthex, the vaulted anteroom of the early church in which the faithful used to meet.

On the walls, frescoes dating from the 11th century depict legends from the life of St Clement. One shows St Cyril, missionary to the Slavs and father of the Cyrillic alphabet, who brought St Clement's relics back from the Crimean peninsula to Rome and buried them in

this church. In 869 he, in turn, was laid to rest here; which is why both St Cyril and his brother Methodius, the missionaries to the Slavs, are worshipped here. In the church, which has two side-aisles and a nave, there are further frescoes, including one of the legend of St Alexis. He returned from Syria as a beggar and lived in poverty below the steps of his father's house on the Aventine Hill until the Pope had a vision which revealed his true identity.

If you descend even further, an ancient staircase will bring you into the Rome of the 2nd century, in a house with a **shrine to Mithras**. There may even have been something like a school devoted to Mithras here, for opposite the domed, cavern-like shrine a larger room was found, which may have been used to explain the cult to would-be initiates. Mithras, supposedly born of a rock, was worshipped only by men, frequently by soldiers. Said

Above: Inside S. Maria in Cosmedin. Right: The nave of SS. Giovanni e Paolo.

to be the son of Apollo, the God of Light, he was to lead his followers to redemption after he had killed the primordial bull. The Mithras cult originated in Persia and spread through the Roman empire at about the same time as Christianity, first to Italy and later to the provinces north of the Alps, especially Germany and Britain. (A Mithraic temple was unearthed in the City of London in the 1950s.) Because this mystery cult conflicted with the official religion of the Roman gods, it could, like Christianity, only be practiced in secret. In many respects the cult, with its doctrine of redemption, resembled the teachings of Christianity; this may have been one reason why it was banned by imperial decree, and not, one may surmise, without the influence of the by-then officially recognized Christian community, in the 4th century.

Not far from S. Clemente in the Lateran district, the wealthy patrician quarter of the ancient Romans, is **SS. Quattro Coronati**, the Church of the Four Coronati (figures with haloes). This church goes back to the Titulus Aemilianae, a building owned by the family of that name which, like other classical remains, can be found below the church. Tradition has it that the bones of four or five martyrs lie here. They were stonemasons from Pannonia (a province in what is now Hungary) who, for refusing to make a statue of Aesculapius, the Roman god of medicine, were summarily thrown into the river Save. Another version of the church's origins has it that the eponymous four figures were four Christian legionaries under the reign of Diocletian, who refused to worship a statue of Aesculapius, and were martyred.

The original church on this site was built in the 4th century, only to fall victim to the Norman invasion. The present church was built in the 12th century on the ruins of its predecessor. This explains its rather higgledy-piggledy structure. The former atrium was in the first courtyard and in the second was part of the earlier basilica, which you can see from the pillars on the right. Today's church is much smaller than its 4th-century predecessor: the central nave of the old building was divided into the nave and two side aisles of the new one. Steps below the altar lead down to the circular 9th-century crypt, where four sarcophagi hold the bones of the martyrs. A side cloister, dating from 1220, contains fragments from the interior of the earlier building, including a basin with lions' heads which used to stand in the atrium. With its charming garden and fountain, this cloister is one of the hidden delights of Rome.

Outside the church on the right is the **Chapel of St Sylvester**, dedicated to the first Pope of that name. The story of his life, already know in the 5th century and since widespread, forms the basis for the legend of the Donation of Constantine. This story is depicted in wonderfully impressive 13th-century frescoes on the chapel walls; in the anteroom, a rare fre-

sco of the calendar of Christian festivals has survived.

On the western slope of the Celio, one of the seven hills of Rome, is the **Church of SS. Giovanni e Paolo**, dedicated to two high-ranking Roman officials who were martyred for their Christian faith. The church dates back to the period around 400 AD; it was built on the remains of a house which belonged to one Byzantius and so bore his *"titulus."* The church's external appearance has remained for the most part the same, but its interior was so thoroughly "Baroqueized" in 1718 that barely a trace of its former beauty remains. A stone in the nave is all that's left to indicate that the church's patron saints were murdered in the house that lies beneath it.

In 1887 a two-storied building was uncovered beneath the church, which can be visited if no restoration work is in progress. Its rooms, dating from the imperial Roman period, still contain rare frescoes with early Christian motifs from between the 2nd and 4th centuries. They indicate

that Christians used to meet here for worship and, little by little, the church was built on top of it. At present there is a large sign at the end of the right-hand aisle forbidding people from entering this unique monument, because it is in danger of collapsing. A few years ago, a commercial TV channel belonging to the media mogul Berlusconi – after the 1994 elections, Italy's new right-wing political leader – moved into premises nearby and the vibration from their heavy trucks is endangering the excavations. They squeeze through the Clivo di Scauro, a narrow, ancient alleyway, and are damaging the seven medieval arches which span this romantic little street. Under the name of Via di S. Paolo della Croce, the street continues on to the Via della Navicella, at the top of which lies the little Piazza della Navicella with the church of S. Maria in Domnica and the Navicella

Above: A Roman marriage in S. Maria in Domnica. Right: The magnificent frescoes in S. Stefano Rotondo.

Fountain. For this fountain, Pope Leo X donated a little ship ("navicella") carved in marble, probably copied from an ancient Roman vessel.

The **Church of S. Maria in Domnica**, also called S. Maria della Navicella after the fountain, can probably be traced back to a 5th century oratory which was part of a patrician Roman house. Built in the reign of Pope Paschal I (817-824), it was completely renovated in the 16th century, and given its Renaissance façade, designed by Andrea Sansovino in 1514. The interior is divided by 18 classical columns; on the walls of the nave is a frieze executed by Perino del Vaga. One of the church's artistic highlights are the early medieval mosaics on the triumphal arch and in the apse.

To the left of the church, a gateway guarded by two buxom marble figures leads to the **Villa Celimontana**, one of the loveliest and most peaceful parks in Rome. Nestling amongst the dense subtropical vegetation stands the Italian Geographical Institute.

Opposite the church the old Via di S. Stefano Rotondo leads to an important circular church, the **Church of S. Stefano Rotondo**. This building is another incomparable source of information about Roman history and the city's development. In its early centuries young Mithras in his swirling red cloak and gilded helmet struggled with the mythical bull in its vaults; this, at least, is how he appears in a colored marble statue in a shrine of Mithras underneath the present-day church. Excavators stumbled upon the ruins of a barracks for soldiers who were passing through Rome, and the shrine to the Persian god was integrated into these.

Early Christianity was superimposed on this cult, according to a rule that held good even in those days: "once holy, always holy." The church, consecrated by Pope Simplicius (468-483), originally consisted of a round central room, surrounded by two concentric corridors and narrowing above into a massive cupola which was suffused with light. The circular elements were intersected by the four arms of a Greek cross, one of which remains to form the vestibule. The ancient Roman throne which you can still see is said to have been used by Pope Gregory the Great.

Time and again, this unusual building, which is based on an eastern design, was vandalized or partly destroyed. It had evidently fallen into a sorry state of disrepair by the time Innocent II, shortly after his coronation as Pope in 1130, dictated this descriptive entry for the *Liber Pontificalis,* the official papal chronicle: "...the roof stripped, the stucco shattered and the marble facing removed!"

Since the late 16th century this unique church has been in the care of the German-Hungarian theological college and is the titular church of the Archbishopric of Munich and Freising. In recent years, considerable financial help from the Germans has made a thorough restoration possible.

Built around the shrine of the relics of the Chains of St Peter, not far from the

Colosseum on the piazza of the same name, is **S. Pietro in Vincoli.** Around 400 AD it was built on the site of a magnificent house on the slopes of the Esquiline Hill. This church, too, has undergone frequent restorations, and has retained hardly anything of its original appearance. The relics are contained in a bronze Renaissance tabernacle underneath the altar; while there's no proof of their authenticity, they have, like many other relics in Rome, proved extremely effective in historic terms.

At the end of the right-hand aisle stands the monument to Pope Julius II, adorned with the famous sculpture of Moses; this is all that was completed of the huge tomb which Michelangelo planned for St Peter's. The paintings over the second and third altars in the same aisle are works by Guercino.

Hidden away in an alley near S. Maria Maggiore you will stumble across the

Above: Michelangelo's famous statue of Moses in S. Pietro in Vincoli.

modest side entrance of a small church which contains mosaics that are among the best examples of early medieval Roman mosaic art: **S. Prassede**. The building dates back to the 5th century but was so thoroughly restored four centuries later that it has become the most important church building of what is known as the Paschalian Renaissance, which can be compared with the flowering of art and architecture under Charlemagne in northern Europe. The paintings in the apse and on the triumphal arch demonstrate the ninth century's advances in artistic technique. Deservedly well-known is the **Chapel of S. Zeno**, which Pope Paschal I (817-824) built as a funeral chapel for his mother Theodora. The mosaics adorning the chapel walls are so beautiful that the chapel has been nicknamed the "Little Garden of Paradise." The Easter service in this church is particularly impressive. Together, all of these early Christian churches are a symbol of the strong influence that Christianity has had upon the Eternal City.

ROMAN CHURCHES

The seven Patriarchal Basilicas

S. Pietro, Città del Vaticano, Tel: 6983712; *Metro:* Line A, Ottaviano; *Bus:* 23, 32, 34, 46, 49, 51, 62, 64, 65, 81, 98, 280, 490, 492, 881, 907, 982, 991, 994, 999. *Streetcar (tram):* 19, 30. Open daily 7am-6pm, in summer till 7pm. Dome: daily 8am-4.15pm, in summer till 6.15pm.

S. Giovanni in Laterano, Via Vittorio Emanuele Filiberto (Main entrance), Piazza S. Giovanni in Laterano 4 (Side entrance). *Metro:* Line A, S. Giovanni. *Bus:* 16, 85, 87, 88, 93, 218, 650, 673. 8am-5.30pm, in summer till 6.30pm.

S. Paolo fuori le Mura, Via Ostiense 184, Tel. 5410178; *Metro:* Line B, S. Paolo. *Bus:* 23, 123, 170, 223, 673, 707, 766. Open 8am-5.45pm; in summer till 6pm.

S. Croce in Gerusalemme, Piazza S. Croce in Gerusalemme 112; *Metro:* Line A, S. Giovanni. *Bus:* 11, 27, 81, 87, 88. Open 8am-6pm, in summer till 6.30pm.

S. Maria Maggiore, Piazza di Santa Maria Maggiore, *Metro:* Lines A and B, Termini. *Bus:* 3, 4, 16, 27, 70, 71, 93, 93b 93c. *Streetcar:* 14, 516, 517. Open 7am-12 noon; 4pm-6pm; in summer till 7pm.

S. Lorenzo fuori le Mura, Piazza San Lorenzo; *Bus:* 11, 71, 109, 111, 309, 311, 411, 415, 492. *Streetcar:* 19, 19b, 30, 30b. Open 8am-6pm, in summer till 7pm.

S. Sebastiano, Via Appia Antica 136; *Bus:* 118. Open 8am-6pm, in summer till 7pm. Catacombs: Mon-Wed; Fri-Sun 8.30am-12 noon, 2.30-5pm, in summer till 5.30pm.

Other important churches

Most churches in Rome, apart from the great Basilicas, are closed from 12 noon till around 4pm.
S. Clemente, Via S. Giovanni in Laterano; *Bus:* 85, 88. **San Luigi dei Francesi**, Piazza di San Luigi dei Francesi; *Bus:* 26, 70, 81, 87, 88, 90, 94. **S. Pietro in Vincoli**, Piazza di San Pietro in Vincoli; *Metro:* Line B, Cavour; *Bus:* 11, 27, 81. **Santa Maria in Aracoeli**, Via di Teatro di Marcello; *Bus:* 57, 90, 90b, 92, 94, 95, 716, 718, 719. **Santa Maria della Concezione**, Via Veneto 27; *Bus:* 52, 53, 56, 58, 90b, 95, 490, 492, 495. Unusual feature of the church: the cemetery of the Capucines. In five chapels macabre decorations have been created from the skulls and bones of 4000 Capucine monks. Daily 9am-12 noon, 3pm-6pm. **Santa Maria in Cosmedin**, Piazza Bocca della Verità; *Bus:* 15, 23, 57, 90, 90b, 92, 94, 716. **Santa Maria di Monserrato**, Via Giulia/Via di Monserrato; *Bus:* 23, 38, 28b, 65.

Santa Maria del Popolo, Piazza del Popolo; *Metro:* Line A, Flaminio. *Bus:* 1, 2, 2b, 90, 90b, 95, 115, 202, 203, 205, 490, 492, 495. **Santa Prassede**, Via Santa Prassede; *Bus:* 16, 93, 93b, 93c. **Santa Sabina**, Piazza Pietro d'Illiria; *Bus:* 23, 57, 92, 94, 95, 716. **Santi Cosma e Damiano**, Via dei Fori Imperiali; *Metro:* Line B, Colosseo. *Bus:* 11, 27, 81, 85, 87, 88. **Santi Giovanni e Paolo**, Piazza dei Santi Giovanni e Paolo; *Bus:* 11, 15, 27, 118, 673. *Streetcar:* 13, 30, 30b. **Santi Quattro Coronati**, Via dei Santi Quattro Coronati; *Bus:* 15, 81, 85, 87, 88, 118, 673. *Streetcar:* 13, 30, 30b. **Santo Stefano Rotondo**, Via di Santo Stefano Rotondo; *Bus:* 85, 88, 673.

Relaxation

Assimilating so much culture can be exhausting, and since most of the churches are closed at lunchtime, one can use this period to enjoy a long, unhurried meal at one of the many *trattorie* to be found in the vicinity of the old churches. There is also an opportunity to relax in shady parks and public gardens, where you can eat a picnic and then sleep it off for a while.

Restaurants

Agata e Romeo, Via Carlo Alberto 45, Tel: 4466115, 4465842. **Antica Hostaria "Da Franco"**, Via S. Giovanni in Laterano 48, Tel: 7096339. **Bassetti di Bassetti**, Via Marsala 68, Tel: 490694. **Da Michele**, Via Merulana 236, Tel: 4872672 and 4873111. **G. Catena**, Via Appia Nuova 9, Tel: 7591664. **Guido alla Scala Sancta**, Via D. Fontana 26/28, Tel: 7002557 and 7000618. **Hostaria Isidoro**, Via Ostilia 23, Tel: 7008266. **Il Cartoccio**, Via E. Filiberto 48, Tel: 4467057. **La Diligenza Rossa**, Via Merulana 271, Tel: 4881216. **La Pentola**, Via Gallia 190/192, Tel: 776244, serves fish and giant pizzas. **La Tana dei Rei**, Piazza dei Rei di Roma 49, Tel: 7577762.
Le Tavernelle Da Antonello e Nicola, Via Panisperna 48, 4740724 and 4744008. **Mino**, Via Magenta 48, Tel: 4959202. **Nazzareno**, Via Magenta 35 / corner of Via Marghera, Tel: 4957782 and 4959211. **Nerone al Colle Oppio**, Via delle Terme di Tito 96, Tel: 4745207. **Pommidoro**, Piazza dei Sanniti 44, Tel: 4452692. **Ricardo**, Via Tuscolana 384, Tel: 7824240. **Ristorante La Matriciana**, Via Viminale 44, Tel: 4881775. **Ristorante Roma Roma**, Via delle Cave 42 abc, Tel: 7880286. **Scoglio di Frisio**, Via Merulana 256, Tel: 4872765 and 4873115. **Trattoria Vecchia Roma**, Via Ferrucćio 12c, Tel: 4467143. **Vecchia Puglia**, Via Principe Amedeo 325, Tel: 4464906.

THE CENTRO STORICO

PIAZZA VENEZIA
THE JEWISH GHETTO
THE TIBER ISLAND
CAMPO DEI FIORI

AROUND THE PIAZZA VENEZIA

The area we know today as the *Centro Storico*, the city's historical center, was called the *Campus Martius* in Roman times and lay, for the most part, outside the *Pomerium* or sacred district of the city. This area was dedicated to Mars, the god of war, and it was in fact here that the legions trained for their campaigns. The land remained unsettled and swampy, probably because of the Tiber's frequent floodings; and its somber atmosphere was augmented by a subterranean shrine dedicated to the gods of the underworld, Dis and Proserpina. But this region, once so deserted and eerie, today roars with big city traffic; while its buildings reflect characteristics of all the intervening ages, from the late empire up to the monarchy of united Italy.

Providing a sharp contrast to the bombastic national monument on the Piazza Venezia is the elegant Palazzo Venezia, a masterpiece of Renaissance architecture which stands on the right-hand side of the **piazza** (looking from the Via del Corso). It was commissioned in the mid-15th century by Paul II, a very liberal pope

Previous pages: Market on the Campo dei Fiori. Left: The poet Goethe is said to have enjoyed dining here in the 18th century.

who loved the good life and was extremely popular with the Romans. It was he, for example, who arranged for Carnival to be celebrated in the Via Lata, now the **Via del Corso**, so that he could watch the festivities from the windows of his new residence.

The palace was built to a design by L.B. Alberti. After the popes vacated it, it housed the Venetian Embassy--whence its present name--followed by the emissaries of Austria and, finally, the leader of the Fascist government, Benito Mussolini. The dictator used the so-called **Sala del Mappamondo** as his private office, and used the famous balcony at the front of the palace for his addresses to the people. Today, people frequently arrange to meet "under the Duce's balcony,", since it's one place in Rome that everybody knows. The palace now houses a museum (entrance in the Via del Plebiscito) displaying ancient terra-cotta figures, sculptures from the Middle Ages and the Renaissance, and numerous objets d'art which served to decorate the magnificent residence in the days of the mighty Venetian republic. It is also used for a variety of temporary exhibitions.

Next to the Palazzo Venezia stands the **Basilica di San Marco**, whose origins date back to early Christian times. Its Renaissance façade is adorned with an im-

posing portico, attributed to Giuliano da Mariano. In the right-hand section of the portico is the gravestone of Vannozza Catanei, mistress of Pope Alexander VI and mother of his three children: the Duke of Gandia and the two Borgias, Lucrezia, the famous poisoner, and Cesare, who inspired Nicolò Machiavelli to write his cynical manual, *Il Principe*.

THE JEWISH GHETTO

Between the boundary of the Corso Vittorio Emanuele to the north and that of the Tiber in the south lies the area known as the Ghetto. Paul IV, who assumed the papal crown in 1555, forced the Jews of Rome to settle here. The people of Rome hated this terrible pope so deeply that they knocked the head off his statue on the Capitoline hill after his death.

Before they were moved, the Jews had lived on the other side of the Tiber in Trastevere. Mainly active in the areas of

Right: A typical corner of old Rome.

trade and medical science, the community gradually became very affluent. But the tolerance which had enabled the Jewish population to do so well since the early 13th century began to diminish. Pope Innocent III ordered the Jews to wear a yellow circle as a distinguishing mark. Once they were moved to the Ghetto, they were forbidden to leave it, and also prohibited from pursuing any career other than the trade in second-hand goods. Until 1870 they were denied the rights to take part in public life or to own land. Yet this quarter, once seen as disreputable and dangerous, is now a flourishing commercial area, filled with shops selling textiles and clothes as well as excellent restaurants serving Roman-Jewish specialities.

The Via del Teatro di Marcello leads to the **Theater of Marcellus**, which was begun under Julius Caesar and completed in 13 AD, during the reign of Augustus. The emperor dedicated the building to Marcellus, the son of his sister Octavia, who died at the early age of twenty-five.

The building, which is currently being restored, was of considerable size, with a seating capacity of 15,000 to 20,000. It served as a military stronghold throughout the Middle Ages. In the 16th century, Baldassare Peruzzi transformed it into a palace for the Savelli family, and it later became the property of the Orsini family. After the 13th century, the little shops under the two-storeyed arcade were rented out to butchers and craftsmen; the area was a hive of activity well into the 1930s. Today, the shops have all disappeared.

At the top of the Piazza Venezia, where the Via del Plebiscito becomes the Corso Vittorio Emanuele II, is the principal Jesuit church in Rome: **Il Gesù**. Its grandiose architecture, the model for countless churches during the Counter-Reformation, and its gloriously colorful interior reflect the Jesuits' idea that the church should draw believers into its circle by offering them a vision of elaborate splendor. Vignola, who was entrusted with the church's design and construction

in 1568, created a building which completely accorded with this goal. He built a single enormous nave, in order to hold as large a congregation as possible. In the interior is the tomb of St Ignatius Loyola, the founder of the Jesuit order, bedecked with layer upon layer of gold and precious stones. In the 17th century, Baciccia painted the fresco *Triumph of the Name of Jesus* in the barrel vault of the nave, as well as the frescoes in the dome.

According to an old legend, the square in front of the church is the windiest in Rome. The story has it that the wind was taking a walk with the Devil through the neighborhood, when the Devil popped into the church, assuring the wind he would "only be a moment." The wind, of course, has been wandering around waiting ever since.

Leading down from the Piazza del Gesù is the Via del Gesù, where the once-mighty Italian Christian Democratic Party has its headquarters. Of greater interest is the **Palazzo Altieri,** which Pope Clement X had built as a residence for his

family. The Pope didn't want to evict the old woman who lived in a shanty on the site where his building was to go up, so the little house was incorporated into the palace. You can still see one of its windows on the ground floor.

In the midst of the warren of streets that make up the Ghetto lies the elegant Piazza Mattei, where you can see the oldest of the palaces commissioned by the powerful Mattei family. It was built in about 1600 by Carlo Maderno for the rich Asdrubale Mattei. Beneath the windows of the palace is the **Fontana delle Tartarughe**, the Turtle Fountain, sculpted by Taddeo Landini in 1585. The figures of four youths each hold a dolphin with one hand, and streams of water from the dolphins' mouths plash into marble seashells; in their other hand, the boys support little turtles which are drinking out of the basin on top of the fountain. More

Above: The Turtle Fountain in the Piazza Mattei. Right: The Ponte Cestio connects the Tiber Island with Trastevere.

than once, the turtles have been abducted from their places in this idyllic scene; today, what we see are only copies.

Amid all the bustle of the Ghetto, between the Lungotevere Cenci and the Via Arenula, is the **Palazzo Cenci**, once home to the ill-starred aristocrat Beatrice, daughter of Count Francesco Cenci. Together with her brother Giacomo and her stepmother, she murdered her tyrannical father, and was subsequently sentenced to death by Pope Clement VIII.

On the northern edge of the Jewish quarter lies the **Largo di Torre Argentina**. Until the 1930s, this was a tangle of narrow streets; today, it's a major traffic intersection, heavily traveled by cars and buses, and thus one of the most exhaust-polluted places in Rome. The name Argentina has nothing to do with the country in South America, but is derived from the diocese of *Argentoratum,* once governed by Burckard, the Bishop of Strasbourg, who built the eponymous tower (*torre*) there that has since been integrated into a later building.

In the middle of the Piazza Argentina, far below street-level, well away from the hectic traffic and thus relatively well protected, some important ancient ruins have recently come to light. They are the remains of four temples which date back to the time of the Roman republic, but which no one has yet been able definitely to identify. Among the ancient ruins live countless cats, who know full well that they receive the very best of care here, fed as they are regularly and generously by the locals. Probably the best known *gattara* (cat-lady) was the actress Anna Magnani: up until the day of her death, they say, she came here every day to look after *her* cats.

On the southern edge of the Ghetto the Tiber describes a sharp curve. On the street along the river, named Lungotevere Cenci after the famous aristocratic family, is the huge domed cube of the **Synagogue**. For security reasons it is under constant guard and is not open to visitors.

THE TIBER ISLAND

Across from the synagogue, in the middle of the river, is the **Tiber Island** (Isola Tiberina). According to the Roman historian Livy, it grew from the grain of the Tarquins, which the people dumped into the river after the last Tarquin king was expelled. A different tale of its creation involves the hospital of the **Fatebenefratelli** ("Do-Good Brothers"): there is an ancient tradition that Aesculapius, the god of healing, settled down on this patch of land. The story goes like this: during a terrible outbreak of plague in 291 BC, the Sybilline Books were consulted for advice. On their recommendation, a delegation was sent to Epidaurus, in Greece, to bring the statue of Aesculapius to Rome. But when they got there, the emissaries were only given a snake, the symbol of the god, which was supposed to have mythical powers of healing. Upon their return to Rome, when

their ship had tied up at the *Navalia*, the military harbor beside the Campus Martius, the sacred snake slid into the water, swam to the bank of the Tiber Island, slithered ashore and disappeared. On the spot where the snake had disappeared, a temple was built dedicated to the healing god. The powers of healing associated with the island had not been forgotten in the Middle Ages, when a hospice for pilgrims was built here which then, in 1548, was converted into the hospital that we see today.

In memory of the god from Epidaurus a prow was built from travertine stone at the upstream tip of the boat-shaped island. On it you can see the snake of Aesculapius coiled around the stick which the god once held in his hand (only the arm remains).

On the downriver part of the island stands the **Church of San Bartolomeo**, which was erected on the site of an earlier church built by the German emperor Otto III in honor of St Adalbert. It stands on the spot where the temple of Aesculapius

once stood, and the well in front of the church is supposed to be exactly where, in ancient times, a spring flowed with the curative waters of the Roman shrine.

Dating back to the Middle Ages, the tower The **Torre della Contessa** was erected in memory of Mathilde of Canossa, who stayed here in 1078. Her name has gone down in history because Pope Gregory VII was a guest in her castle when the German emperor Henry IV knelt in the snow and entreated the Pope to forgive him for having challenged his authority.

Two bridges link the Tiber Island to both banks of the river. The Ponte Fabrizio, built in the year 62 BC, is the oldest bridge in Rome; it crosses over to the Ghetto. It is also known as the *Ponte dei Quattro Capi* (Bridge of the Four Heads) because of the four double stone heads on the parapet. The **Ponte Cestio**, which connects the island with Trastevere, also

dates back to the 1st century BC, but was destroyed towards the end of the 9th century and later rebuilt. At the southern end of the island you can see the remains of the **Ponte Rotto** (Broken Bridge) which was built on the piers of an old Roman bridge towards the end of the 6th century AD. Beneath the nearby **Ponte Palatino** the main sewer of ancient Rome, the **Cloaca Maxima**, still opens into the heavily polluted waters of the Tiber. In Roman times it was the heart of an extensive drainage system serving the whole city. Originally a tributary of the Tiber, it was covered over as early as 200 BC and is still in use today.

Over the last few years efforts have been made to give the river Tiber a more important role in the life of the city. To this end a river-bus service has been introduced, which runs from the Ponte Duca d'Aosta in the north of the city (near the Foro Italico) downstream to the docks at Fiumicino.

No description of the Tiber Island would be complete without a mention of

Above: The Ponte Fabrizio. Right: The statue of Giordano Bruno on the Campo.

106

the restaurant **da Sora Lella**. It belongs to the sister of a Roman actor, now deceased, who was known for playing mainly comic roles in the post-war years.

AROUND THE CAMPO DEI FIORI

The Via dei Giubbonari (Street of the Jacket-makers), which links the Ghetto to the Campo dei Fiori, is one of the many streets in the *Centro Storico* which are named after trades; other examples include the Via dei Baullari (the street of the chest-makers) and the Via dei Chiavari (the street of the key-cutters). The population of the area around the *Campo* (as Romans refer to the Campo dei Fiori) increased enormously after Pope Nicholas V moved his headquarters to the Vatican in the 15th century. From then on, the square became the hub of traffic running between the Capitoline Hill and the papal residence. To ease this congestion, the Via Papalis and the Via Peregrinorum were widened and paved. In 1474 Pope Sixtus IV had the bridge which bears his name built to link the district with Trastevere. From that time onward noblemen built palaces in the area and the streets began to fill with foreign envoys and countless pilgrims.

Activity in the spacious Campo dei Fiori begins early in the morning. Every day one of the largest, if not exactly the cheapest, markets in Rome is held here. The colorful market stalls throng around the statue of Giordano Bruno, whose stubborn and defiant face looks toward the Vatican, precisely reflecting the anticlerical mood of united Italy at the time when the statue was ceremonially unveiled in 1900. For it was on this spot in 1600 that the Dominican monk Giordano Bruno (born near Naples in 1548) was publicly burned by order of Pope Clement VIII. Even at the stake he remained true to himself and to his – admittedly heretical – teachings, as he had done for the previous eight years in the torture

chambers of the Inquisition. He had fearlessly defended Copernicus's hypothesis that the sun is at the center of the planetary system; furthermore, he took the idea one step further to postulate the "modern" idea of an infinite universe, with no center, that is continually in motion. Bruno saw the universe as a vast living organism, eternal, and animated by one principle alone: God. But it wasn't all of this that made Bruno a heretic in the eyes of the Inquisition; rather, it was his pantheistic concept of God, which went against the personal, anthropomorphisized deity of Christian dogma. To Bruno, God was not a "Creator," standing outside and above the world he had brought into existence: God existed only *in* the world, *in* the universe, operating as the inner, guiding force in their greatest and smallest elements. God *is* the cosmos and the cosmos *is* God. This doctrine was incompatible with orthodox Christian teaching.

The Vicolo del Gallo leads from the Campo dei Fiori to the Piazza Farnese.

Here you will find the **Palazzo Farnese**, where the French Embassy has been established since 1871. At that time the French government pledged to pay the Italian state a token rent of one lira every 99 years. The palace was built by Alessandro Farnese, later to become Pope Paul III, but the costs were so high that in 1514 construction work had to stop. It took many years to complete the building: originally designed by Antonio da Sangallo, it was later entrusted to Michelangelo, and it was ultimately Giacomo della Porta who completed it in 1589. Michelangelo had planned to link the Palazzo Farnese with the Villa Farnesina, another Farnese property in the Trastevere, with a bridge over the Tiber, but the bridge was never completed. Today, an arch leading over the Via Giulia to the river bank is all that's left to attest to his concept.

Above: Trompe l'oeil columns in the Palazzo Spada. Right: The courtyard of the Palazzo della Cancelleria.

Inside the palace is an **atrium** with cloisters and stucco decorations, the work of Sangallo, and a broad staircase leading up to the Hercules Hall with its giant statue of the god, copied from a Greek statue which was found in the ruins of the Baths of Caracalla (the original is in the National Museum in Naples). In 1655 Queen Christina of Sweden lived here and turned the place into a focus of Roman intellectual life. Her unconventional ways gave rise to not a few scandals within Roman society; among her provocative actions was that of removing the fig leaves from the private parts of her statues. Another deservedly famous hall, used by the French Embassy on ceremonial occasions, is the **Galleria Caracci**; its magnificent ceiling frescoes by the brothers Annibale and Agostino Caracci include the *renowned Triumph of Bacchus and Arianna.*

Near the Piazza Farnese is the Piazza della Quercia with the **Palazzo Spada**, named after Cardinal Bernadino Spada who bought the building in 1632. It was built, however, not for him but for another cardinal in 1540, probably by Mazzoni. Since 1889 it has been the seat of the Italian Council of State. In four of its rooms is the **Galleria Spada**, featuring the original 17th-century furnishing and decoration and containing a collection of valuable objects that belonged to Cardinal Spada and his family. Among these are some 2nd and 3rd century Roman sculpture, as well as paintings by such famous artists as Guido Reni, Il Guercino, Brueghel and Rubens. Another interesting feature is Borromini's optical illusion: a long colonnade leading to an inner courtyard with what appears to be a huge statue in it. In reality the gallery is only 33 ft (10 m) long and the statue is fairly small. The illusion works because the floor slopes slightly upwards and the pillars become progressively smaller.

Beyond the Largo Argentina and the theater of the same name lies the *Teatro*

dei Satiri in an inner courtyard of the **Palazzo Righetti**, which was built on the ancient theater of Pompey. The latter was built in 55 BC in honor of the consul who had defeated the Persian king Mithridates. In the shadow of the theater was the temple of *Venus Victrix*, the goddess of fortune in war, who was said to have protected Pompey and led him to victory. The temple was consecrated with *ludi circenses*, at which wild animals were made to fight each other. It was here, in the portico of the theater, close to the statue of Pompey, that, on the Ides of March in 44 BC, Brutus and the other conspirators killed Julius Caesar by stabbing him twenty-five times.

Beyond the Corso Vittorio Emanuele II lies the Piazza della Cancellaria with the majestic **Palazzo della Cancellaria**, built at the end of the 15th century by Raffaele Riario, the nephew of Pope Sixtus IV. It is said that he won the sum of sixty-thousand *scudi* necessary for the building's construction by gambling with Franceschetto Cybo. Both men belonged

to branches of the famous Roman patrician family of Cybo, another of whose members, just about that time, ascended the papal throne as Innocent VIII. The building served various functions: at first, it housed the official chambers of the papal chancellery, and later became the seat of the parliament of the short-lived 19th-century Roman Republic. On 16th November 1848, the prime minister of the republic, Pellegrino Rossi, was murdered as he entered the palace. The people of Rome immediately rose up and forced Pope Pius IX to flee to Gaeta. According to the story, the papal residence was being watched by the *Guardia Civica* and the Pope only managed to escape by means of a trick. The French ambassador requested an audience with Pius IX and pretended to be talking to him while the pontiff himself slipped quietly out of a back door.

On the far side of the Corso Vittorio Emanuele three more or less parallel streets lead to the river bank opposite the Borgo Pio and St Peter's: the Via dei Pel-

legrini, named after the pilgrims who used to walk along it to the basilica, the Via di Monserrato and the Via Giulia.

Today the **Via dei Pellegrini** is one of the last refuges of traditional Roman craftsmanship, along with the Via dei Capellari (Street of the Milliners), which runs parallel to it for a little way and then merges with it. The predominate trades are those of the restorers and antique dealers; its practitioners can still be seen working in the street, and their prices are quite moderate in comparison to the elegant antique shops in and around the Via dei Coronari. Many of the shops are supposedly situated over what was once a notorious dungeon, of which scarcely a trace remains. Beatrice Cenci and her brother Giacomo were imprisoned in it after they had killed their father.

The **Via di Monserrato** takes its name from the Spanish church of **Santa Maria di Monserrato**. The street continues

under the name Via dei Banchi Vecchi; here you will find the **Church of Santa Lucia del Gonfalone**, which belongs to the Honorable Brotherhood of Gonfaloniers (banner-carriers). Its members had the task of giving assistance in God's name to the poor and the sick. They were elevated to the status of brotherhood by Pope Gregory XIII in 1562. No one knows exactly why the square in front of the church was chosen as the starting point for the carnival procession of the Jews of Rome, which ended in St Peter's Square. But it is a fact that during the Carnival the Jews were forced to endure the mockery of the people. On the other hand they were allowed to do things at this time which were forbidden to them during the rest of the year.

The **Via Giulia** is one of the most exclusive and elegant streets in Rome, and apartment rents along it are astronomical. The few old tenants who have managed to hang on here, however, are still paying rents that are ridiculously low in comparison. The Via Giulia owes its name to

Above: In the Via Giulia life is very quiet and civilized these days.

Pope Julius II. He was a man of highly political, not to say belligerent, instincts, who wanted to expand the secular power of the Catholic Church. He first allied himself with France and Spain in order to break the power of Venice; he then switched sides and joined up with the Repubblicca di S. Marco, the Venetian republic, in order to launch a joint attack against his former ally, France. Julius II died in 1513, after returning to Rome in triumph from his military campaign. The street, whose construction began during his reign, was to have formed a splendid approach to St Peter's Cathedral, but the plan was abandoned after the Pope's death, never to be realized.

On the Via Giulia stands the church of **Santa Maria dell'Orazione e Morte**, a somewhat gloomy building which was intended to serve as a reminder to the faithful of the constant presence of death. Stone skulls adorn the entrance, while the crypt is lined with skeletons. Hanging from the ceiling is a macabre chandelier made from vertebrae.

The **Palazzo Falconieri**, which was built in the 17th century by the family of that name, is remarkable for the strangely carved female torsos with falcons' heads which lean out from each corner. Parts of the palace were designed by Borromini, including the loggia overlooking the Tiber at the rear of the building.

After passing the churches of Santa Caterina da Siena and Sant'Egidio agli Orefici, which was designed by Raphael, you'll come to the **Carceri Nuove**. This dungeon was built by Innocent X and remained in use until the end of the 19th cen. Today it houses a Museum of Crime.

In the church of **San Biagio alla Pagnotta** a charming old Roman tradition is kept alive every year on 3rd February, the birthday of St Blasius. When Mass is over, little loaves of bread (*pagnotte*) are distributed to the congregation; they are believed to be a protection against sore throats.

The Via Giulia finally brings you into the **Piazza dell'Oro**, which in Renaissance times was mainly inhabited by Florentines practicing the goldsmith's trade. The square is dominated by the church of **San Giovanni dei Fiorentini**. The man who commissioned it, Pope Leo X, was a Florentine by birth; his father was none other than Lorenzo de' Medici, the Magnificent himself. The Pope held a competition for the design of the church, for which both Raphael and Peruzzi submitted entries; ultimately, he decided on Sansovino's design. The building you see today, however, has little to do with the elegance of the Renaissance, since it was two centuries before the church was finally completed. Even Borromini, who is buried here, was involved in the project. He took his own life, but was nevertheless granted a Christian burial because he took a long time to die, and had enough time to repent his act and pass away in "the grace of God."

The simple structure of the building's exterior stands in sharp contrast to the Baroque richness of the main chapel. Three 17th-century artists collaborated here: Pietro da Cortona built the altar, Borromini designed the family tomb of the Falconieri, and Reggi was responsible for the sculpture depicting the Baptism of Christ.

The Lungotevere dei Tebaldi, which runs parallel to the Via Giulia, connects the **Ponte Sisto** with the Ponte Mazzini. The story goes that Pope Sixtus IV, who ascended the papal throne in 1471, lived in a monastery in the Via dei Pettinari before his election and often went from there to the Vatican. Walking along the river, he used to look at the remains of the ancient Ponte Agrippae, and resolved to have the bridge rebuilt if he was elected Pope. He was true to his vow: the Ponte Sisto was completed in 1475 by Baccio Ponticelli.

The wide traffic artery of **Corso Vittorio Emanuele II** forms the northern

boundary of this district on which the Renaissance popes left their imperishable mark. The Corso starts from the Via del Plebiscito and ends at the Ponte Vittorio Emanuele II. Following it in this direction, you come to the **Piazza Vidoni** with the Palazzo Caffarelli Vidoni, parts of which were designed by Raphael. Another street leading into the square is the Via del Monte della Farina, where you can find early 20th-cen. English furniture at reasonable prices in a cluttered antique shop called "Anticalia e Petrella."

Further on you come to the **Piazza della Chiesa Nuova**, named after the "New Church," as the church of Santa Maria in Vallicella is commonly known. It was built by San Filippo Neri and typifies the spirit of the Counter-Reformation, the movement aimed at clearing away abuses and corruption and returning to pure Catholic dogma. The church was completed in 1599, but the façade by Fausto Rughesi was added a little later, in

1605. The interior, which was originally pure white, was decorated with frescoes by Pietro da Cortona during the 17th century. At the side of the high altar are three paintings by Rubens, and the chapel on the left of the apse contains Filippo Neri's tomb.

Next to the church is the **Oratorio dei Filippini** with its broad, concave façade. The building was designed by Borromini, who worked on it from 1637 to 1662. Its elegant interior houses the Biblioteca Vallicelliana, which contains a wealth of early codices, and the Oratorium Hall, where, today as in the past, concerts of church music are still given.

The rectangular **Piazza Sforza Cesarini**, with its little park, is an oasis of peace, away from the roaring traffic of the busy thoroughfares. There are two pretty restaurants in the square, with outdoor tables. You can also see the house where Vanozza Cattanei, the mistress of Pope Alexander VI, lived for a time, and where Alexander's children, Lucrezia and Cesare Borgia, were born.

Above: Early morning on the Ponte Sisto.

THE CENTRO STORICO

In its strictest sense, the term Historic Center denotes that part of the city which has always been inhabited, even in the Middle Ages, when the population of Rome had dwindled to its lowest level. It takes in the ancient Campus Martius within the bend of the Tiber, in which the great Baroque churches and palaces were later built. In the following section attention is given principally to the monuments which form part of the medieval heart of the city.

Sightseeing

Between the Piazza Venezia and the Tiber island: the **Piazza Venezia**, one of Rome's busiest squares, can be reached by *Metro:* Line B (Colosseo station) or by *buses* on routes 46, 57, 85, 87, 88, 90, 90b, 92, 94, 95, 716, 718, 719. The square is dominated by the elegant **Palazzo Venezia**. It houses a museum and frequently changing art exhibitions, Tue-Sat 9am-2pm and Sun 9am-1pm. Continuing along the Via del Teatro di Marcello towards the **Theater of Marcellus**, beyond the Palazzo Venezia you come to the **Basilica di San Marco**. To the right of the Theater of Marcellus, narrow streets lead into the Ghetto. The **Synagogue** beside the Tiber is not open to visitors and is guarded round the clock. In the Ghetto one can sample the excellent Roman-Jewish cuisine, especially around the Portico d'Ottavia. In the Piazza del Gesù, where the Via del Plebiscito becomes the Corso Vittorio Emanuele II, stands the principal church of the Jesuits, **Il Gesù**. To get there from the Piazza Venezia take any of the numerous buses which run along the Corso Vittorio (routes 56, 60, 62, 64, 65, 70, 75, 81, 88, 90, 170). In the Via del Gesù you can see the **Palazzo Altieri**. The **Piazza Mattei** and the palace of the same name, in the heart of the Ghetto, forms the backdrop for the **Turtle Fountain** (Fontana delle Tartarughe), and not far from there, on the Lungotevere Cenci, is the **Palazzo Cenci**, in which the tragedy of poor Beatrice reached its grim climax. In the **Largo di Torre Argentina**, another hub of traffic in the old part of the city, you can escape the thundering vehicles, by visiting the **temple ruins** below street level.

The Tiber Island

The hospital of the **Fatebenefratelli** stands on ground that is steeped in medical tradition. Opposite is the church of **San Bartolomeo** and the **fountain,** from which healing waters once bubbled. The Tiber Island is linked to the river banks by the **Ponte Fabrizio** or **Ponte dei Quattro Capi** on the Ghetto side, and the **Ponte Cestio**

across to Trastevere. Looking downstream from the **Ponte Palatino**, you can see the huge mouth of the ancient sewer, the **Cloaca Maxima**.

Campo dei Fiori

Walking through the medieval streets of the Centro Storico you come to the **Campo dei Fiori** where a picturesque market is held every morning. Round about the Campo there are many restaurants and trattorias, and the pretty little boutiques are the perfect place to shop. The narrow Vicolo del Gallo brings you to the **Palazzo Farnese**, and nearby, at Nr 3 Piazza Capo di Ferro, stands the **Palazzo Spada** with its **Galleria Spada** (Tue-Sat 9am-2pm, Sun 9am-1pm) and Borromini's famous optical illusion. The **Palazzo della Cancelleria**, in the Piazza della Cancelleria, can be reached by buses 46, 62 or 64. In the **Via dei Pellegrini**, and in the **Via Monserrato** and **Via Giulia,** running parallel to it, there are many **antique-shops**. In the exclusive Via Giulia stands the church of **Santa Maria dell'Orazione e Morte** with its macaber decor of skeletons, the **Palazzo Falconieri** with its falcon-headed busts and the **arched gateway**, which was once intended to link the Palazzo Farnese with the Farnesina on the other side of the Tiber. The Via Giulia runs into the Piazza dell'Oro with its church of **S. Giovanni dei Fiorentini**.

Restaurants

Al Pompiere, Via Santa Maria dei Calderari 38, Tel: 6868377. **Al Salanova**, Via Florida 23, Tel: 6864298, closed Mondays and 4th–20th January. **Campana**, Vicolo della Campana 18, Tel: 6875273, closed Mondays and all of August. **Da Giggetto**, Via del Portico d'Ottavia 21/a, Tel: 6861105, Roman specialities. **Da Pancrazio**, Piazza del Biscione 92, Tel: 6861246, a taverna built on the remains of the Theater of Pompey, closed Wednesdays, 9th–16th January and 10th–20th August. **Da Sora Lella**, Ponte Fabrizio, Isola Tiberina, Tel: 6861601. **Evangelista**, Via delle Zoccolette 11/a, Tel: 6875810, book ahead; closed for lunch, closed Suns and all of August. **Il Convivio**, Via dell'Orso 44, Tel: 6869432, book ahead, closed Sun. **Le Streghe**, Vicolo del Curato 13, Tel: 6861381, open for the evening, closed Sun and August. **Quinzi Gabrieli**, Via delle Coppelle 6, Tel: 6879389, fish dishes, book ahead; closed Wed, Sun and all of August. **Rosetta**, Via della Rosetta 9, Tel: 6861002, seafood, book ahead, closed Sun and all of August. **Taverna Giulia**, Vicolo dell'Oro 23, Tel: 6869768, Ligurian specialities, book ahead for the evening, closed Sun and August. **Vecchia Roma**, Piazza Campitelli 18, Tel: 6864604, fish, closed Wed and 10th–25th August.

THE VATICAN AND CASTEL SANT' ANGELO

ST PETER'S
SISTINE CHAPEL
VATICAN MUSEUMS
CASTEL SANT' ANGELO
INSIDE THE VATICAN

ST PETER'S

The Basilica of St Peter is without any doubt the most famous church in Christendom, and until 1989 it was also the largest (the church in Yamoussoukro, the new capital of the Ivory Coast, itself built on the model of St Peter's, is even larger). The history of the church begins with the execution of the apostle Peter in the gardens or possibly the circus of Nero in the year 64 or 67 AD. His grave became a place of pilgrimage for early Christians, and the emperor Constantine the Great consequently had a basilica built on the site at the request of Pope Sylvester I. It was consecrated in 326.

After the return of the popes from exile in Avignon the old church was found to be in a somewhat ruinous state, so Pope Nicholas V decided in 1452 to commission a new building (it was no coincidence that this happened at the same time that Constantinople was conquered by the Turks). Several famous architects were entrusted with its construction over the centuries; first there was Bramante, who drew up the ground plan in the form of a Greek cross; then Raphael and

Previous pages: View over St Peter's Square. Left: Impervious to Rome's teeming nightlife – St Peter's.

Giuliano da Sangallo, who together designed a spacious nave; and finally Michelangelo, whose legacy included the whole west end of the church and the design of the dome. His successors, Vignola, Domenico Fontana and Maderno, completed the mighty task. Maderno lengthened the nave and added the façade, which is 376 ft (114.70 m) wide and 146 ft (45.50 m) high. He tried to make up for the façade's rather awkward proportions by incorporating pillars, balconies, windows and entrances into the design. The figures of Christ and the apostles on the parapet are 19 ft (5.70 m) high.

The portico has five entrances with bronze grilles. The double doors of the central portals are survivors from the days of Old St Peter's. "The Door of Death" on the left is the work of the modern sculptor Giacomo Manzù, while the Holy Door on the right is kept locked and only opened during Holy Year. Above the doors there is a row of balconied windows. It is from the central balcony that the Pope gives his annual blessing *urbi et orbi* (to the city and the world). This custom was abandoned in 1870, when the popes went into self-imposed isolation, but was revived by Pius XI in the 1930s.

The internal dimensions of St Peter's are massive. It is 610 ft (186 m) long; the

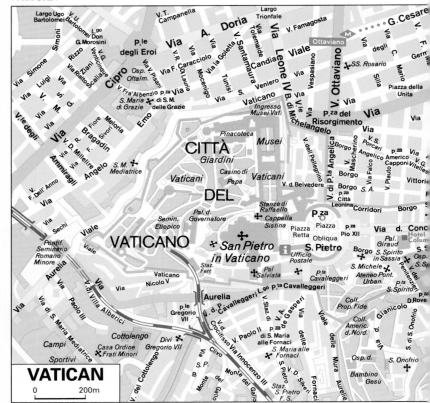

main nave is 150 ft (46 m) high; from the floor to the top of the dome is a distance of 390 ft (190 m); while the floor area of 160,000 sq. ft (15,000 sq. m) can accommodate some 60,000 worshippers.

Close to the main entrance is a circular red porphyry slab in the floor, which indicates the spot where on Christmas Day 800 AD Charlemagne was crowned emperor by Leo III. In the northern aisle on the right, protected by bullet-proof glass, is one of Michelangelo's early masterpieces, the *Pietà,* which he completed at the age of twenty-four.

Countless other works of art decorate the pillars, niches and chapels. Beneath the dome is the papal altar which Bernini crowned with a 95-ft-high (29 m) balda-

chin (the bronze he used for this came from the Pantheon). Under the altar is the *confessio* in front of St Peter's tomb, lit by 95 gilded oil lamps. In front of the back wall of the apse the famous bronze throne, the *Cathedra Petri,* is also by Bernini, as is the papal altar under the baldachin which is supported by richly decorated pillars. This is where the Pope celebrates Mass, while at his side stands his chief of protocol, a high-ranking prelate who never lets him out of his sight, whether in Rome or on his many travels. Helmeted Swiss Guards trained as bodyguards, standing impassively around the *confessio* with their halberds at the ready, protect His Holiness. They are proudly dedicated to their tradition. Ever since

drop for the gatherings of the faithful from all over the world. St Peter's Square is made up of the **Piazza Obliqua**, an ellipse 768 ft (240 m) wide, and the **Piazza Retta**, a trapezoid area which widens as it leads directly up to the steps of the basilica. Bernini surrounded the oval part of the piazza with 284 columns and 88 pillars of travertine stone, ranged in groups of four, which embrace the piazza like welcoming arms. The balustrades above the colonnades are adorned with no fewer than 144 statues of saints.

If viewed from either of two circular stones let into the ground, which indicate the focal points of the ellipse, the groups of four columns, one behind the other, appear to merge into one. The two fountains on the piazza are the work of Maderno and Bernini, while the 82 ft (25 m) high granite **Obelisk** formerly stood in Nero's circus. Pope Sixtus V had it moved to St Peter's Square, where it was erected by 900 workers under the direction of Domenico Fontana. The following story is told of this daunting operation: while raising the obelisk with the aid of windlasses and ropes, the workers were forbidden to speak on pain of death, so that all could hear Fontana's orders. In spite of this a sailor had the presence of mind to call out: "Throw some water on the ropes!" – a suggestion which prevented them from overheating and breaking. As a reward for his bravery he was granted the right to supply the Pope with palms every year on Palm Sunday, which is still exercised by his descendants to this day.

Charles V's mercenaries sacked and plundered the city of Rome in 1527, new recruits have sworn an oath every year on May 6th to protect the life of the pontiff to the last drop of their blood.

Beneath the floor of St Peter's are the tombs of numerous popes, among them that of Pius XII, at whose instigation extensive excavations were made between 1940 and 1957, which brought to light a large necropolis from ancient Roman times.

In the long line of those responsible for the overall development of St Peter's, Maderno's successor was Bernini. Between 1656 and 1667 he created the piazza in front of the church, with its colonnades, which form a magnificent back

THE SISTINE CHAPEL

The Sistine Chapel, built in 1477-88 at the behest of Pope Sixtus on the walls of an earlier court chapel, was not only used for solemn papal ceremonies and the Conclave, but also for the defense of the papal palace. Hence its fortress-like external appearance. However, it was not

Sixtus but Julius II who in 1508 commissioned Michelangelo to repaint the ceiling. Over a period of four years the prodigiously gifted sculptor, who now displayed his genius as a painter for the first time, created a series of frescoes which have remained without parallel to this day. In 1535 he set to work again. Clement VII had given him the commission to paint a *Last Judgment* on the altar wall. The whole of Rome must have gasped at the solemn inauguration in 1541, for frescoes of such luminosity had never been seen before. But even then their conservation soon began to pose a problem. The soot from the candles and from burning charcoal darkened the colors, and the frescoes were also damaged by rainwater leaking through the roof, so that a first restoration became necessary as early as 1564. But all efforts with tinctures and other agents were of little help. After a

Above: Mass being held in St Peter's. Right: A detail from Michelangelo's frescoes in the Sistine Chapel.

short while the colors were just as dark and dull as before. Any further attempts at restoration were abandoned, although from time to time down the centuries there were those of Michelangelo's admirers who regretted the loss of the original vividness of the colors.

It was not until 1980 that the decision was made in the Vatican, in the course of the complete restoration of the Sistine Chapel, to give the ceiling frescoes a thorough cleaning – to the horror of many experts. The team of restorers under Gianluigi Colalucci devoted ten years of painstaking work to washing the dirt off the frescoes with a special cleaning fluid. After Pope John Paul II personally closed a sponsorship deal with the Japanese Nippon company, every operation was recorded in greatest detail and a computer was used to store the data as work progressed. It is surely no exaggeration to say that this is the best documented restoration ever undertaken in the history of art. The result is so convincing that it is difficult to imagine what

the Sistine Chapel used to be like with its famous patina. In 1991 a start was made on the restoration of the *Last Judgment*, which was completed in April, 1994. It is to be hoped that this will shed new light on the work of Michelangelo and help us to gain a fresh understanding of this great artist.

THE VATICAN MUSEUMS

When Julius II had several masterpieces of classical statuary, which had just come to light in some of the first excavations in Rome, set up in the courtyard of the Palazzetto Belvedere in 1503, he probably didn't have the faintest idea that he had just sowed the seeds for what was to become the future Vatican Museum. The *Apollo Belvedere*, *Venus Felix*, the *Laocoon* group, *Nile* and *Tiber,* as well as the *Sleeping Ariadne,* were to formed the basis for a series of museums which, with their wealth of art treasures from every epoch, are a veritable papal cornucopia of artistic marvels. From Ancient Egypt and the Etruscans to Greek and Roman Classicism, from priceless tapestries to the earliest examples of cartography, from the artifacts of primitive tribes to the state coaches of His Holiness, from ancient frescoes to the superb paintings of Raphael and Michelangelo – you can see all of this in these museums. Since the reign of Paul VI (1963-1978), modern paintings have also been represented. Fifty rooms are dedicated to a varied collection of modern religious art, which, in the eyes of art experts, demonstrates a true spirit of adventure. It was put together by the Pope and his private secretary Don Pasquale Macchi, though apparently without any guiding principle. The works on display were for the most part donated by artists or their families, as well as by dioceses all over the world. Consequently they form a selection as idiosyncratic as the many gifts presented to the popes by visitors, which you can see lining the long corridors – and some of those are very curious indeed.

The museums, which are financially independent thanks to the admission fees paid by millions of visitors every year, are administered by a board of governors. Scientists and an army of restorers, specialists in stone, metal, mosaic and tapestries, see to the upkeep and conservation of the collections, while restoration work continues unceasingly in the Vatican's own workshops, which are an offshoot of the department responsible for the fabric of St Peter's.

The magnificent view from the dome of St Peter's is there for everyone to see. Visitors who are not deterred by the prospect of the climb into Michelangelo's architectural masterpiece will be rewarded with a completely new perspective of both the ecclesiastical and the secular Rome.

Below you spread the 109 acres (44 hectares) of the self-governing Vatican State, with its audience chamber and pontifical palace, its extensive and intricately laid out gardens, its own railroad station and heliport, its law courts and military barracks, mint, post office and telephone exchange, newspaper and radio station (the *Osservatore Romano* and Vatican Radio), and pharmacy and outpatients clinic. It also has a not inconsiderable portion of German-Roman history and tradition. In the shadow of the dome of St Peter's, where in Charlemagne's time the Germans lived gathered around the *Schola Francorum*, lies the **Campo Santo Teutonico**, the idyllic cemetery of many pilgrims to Rome. The inscription over the entrance speaks of the "Teutones in Pace," the German artists and clerics who found their last resting place here. Once, the Campo Santo (which now also includes a priests' seminary) stretched as far as St Peter's Square, and German members of the arch-confraternity still have a right to be buried here.

Right: The Castel Sant' Angelo – a symbol of papal power for 1500 years.

CASTEL SANT' ANGELO

The Castel Sant' Angelo is one of the most impressive buildings of antiquity. Three years before his death, the emperor Hadrian had this daunting edifice constructed as a tomb for himself and his successors. Originally this mausoleum consisted of a drum-shaped structure 65 feet (20 m) high and 209 ft (64 m) in diameter, covered with earth and planted with trees, and raised on a square plinth. Until the death of Septimius Severus in 211 AD, all members of the imperial family were buried here. Emperor Aurelian later made this funerary monument part of his city walls, and because of its useful strategic position Hadrian's mausoleum soon became Rome's most impregnable fortress, which even resisted the onslaught of the Goths in 537. It owes its present name to an incident in the 6th century. The Pope was taking part in a procession to intercede for the end of an outbreak of plague, when the Archangel Michael is said to have appeared to him above the fortress, placing his sword in its sheath and thereby bringing the epidemic to an end. A chapel was built on the grave mound to commemorate this vision. The bronze statue of an angel on the top of the Castel Sant' Angelo is the work of Piet van Verschaffelt and dates from 1753.

In the 13th century Pope Nicholas III connected the Castel Sant' Angelo with the palaces of the Vatican by means of the *passetto*, a wall containing a covered passage. The Castel Sant' Angelo thus became a haven for the popes whenever danger threatened: Pope Gregory VII, for instance, took refuge there from Henry IV in 1084; and Clement VII was able to escape to the fortress at the last moment during the Sack of Rome in 1527, when he was pursued by Charles V's mercenaries.

Over a period of 1500 years the Castel Sant' Angelo has repeatedly been altered,

extended and embellished. Having served as papal refuge, barracks, or prison, it has finally been converted into a museum where one can see models showing the architectural history of the castle, a collection of weapons, and a treasure chamber.

INSIDE THE VATICAN

"Habemus Papam" (we have a pope) is the traditional statement used to announce to the world that the cardinals gathered in conclave have chosen a successor to the throne of St Peter, who will chart the course to be followed by the Catholic Church. Before the *fumata bianca*, the column of white smoke, can mark the end of a successful election, a complicated and exhaustive procedure has to be followed, namely that of the Conclave, the election which takes place behind closed doors. Since the 16th century the Sistine Chapel has been the scene of this process, which can often last several days. In the same chapel whence mil-

lions of visitors come every year to admire Michelangelo's frescoes, the 120-strong electoral College of Cardinals assemble after the death of a pope to fill the vacant Holy See. Above each of the dignitaries is a canopy which is folded away after their vote has been made. The only one that remains in place is that above the head of the new pope.

Meanwhile, outside on St Peter's Square, the crowd of the faithful, with a fair sprinkling of journalists, has continued to swell. They wait with growing anticipation for the moment when His Holiness will appear on the central balcony of St Peter's and give his first blessing. The papal tailor from the house of Gamarelli Brothers, which has served generations of pontiffs, is fully prepared for this. For a long time he has been making made papal robes in three different sizes; for the Gamarelli craftsmen can draw on a wealth of experience. Only the short and stocky figure of Pope John XXIII, who was as popular as he was paunchy, caught them out. But they had

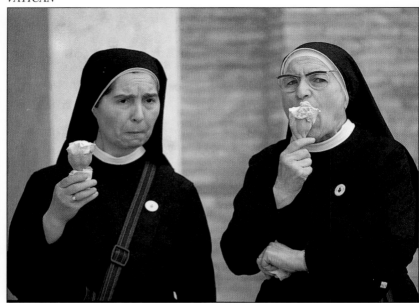

an inspiration which saved the day. The robes were simply slit down the back and held in place with pins, which made the Pope from Venice (who had a great sense of humor) laugh more than anyone. There were no such problems with the current Pope, John Paul II.

Pastor to the world – this is how Karol Wojtyla (his original Polish name) sees himself. He has succeeded in reaching millions of Catholics throughout the world by dint of his ceaseless travels. Nearly all his decisions on ecclesiastical matters are, however, characterized by rigid adherence to the authoritarian tradition of the papacy, and have consequently met with widespread criticism. But his unequivocal opposition to the Gulf War, and also his repeated admonitions on the conflict in the former Yugoslavia, have made it clear that the *Pontifex*

Above: Even nuns are sometimes allowed a treat. Right: Swiss Guards taking a break from duty.

Maximus is actively concerned with contemporary problems and is determined to make his voice heard in the arena of world politics.

His predecessor Paul VI, by contrast, gave priority to reforming the cumbersome administrative system of the Vatican, that tiny independent state whose worldwide influence can scarcely be overestimated even today. With his restructuring of the Curia, Paul VI succeeded in creating an administration which is universally acknowledged as being supremely efficient. In addition to the State Secretariat, which is concerned with the Church's relations with the outside world, there are nine Congregations which deal with a great variety of matters. Of these the Congregation for Dogma, the former Holy Office, has a particularly important role. Originally its task was to defend the true faith by whatever means necessary, even when that meant the Inquisition. Down the centuries anything that seemed to pose a threat to the dogmas of the Catholic

Church was placed on the Index, that infamous catalogue of forbidden publications, which has now been abolished.

For centuries, people speculated about the true extent of the Vatican's legendary wealth. There were repeated rumors of a vast fortune and majority stockholdings in dubious banks and large corporations. It is true that Paul VI ordered that steps be taken to disentangle and restructure the Vatican's finances; unfortunately these were in the hands of the Milanese banker Michele Sindona, who died mysteriously in prison in 1986, while an associate of his was found hanging under Blackfriars Bridge in London. Since June 1992 the fact has been inescapable: the Vatican is in the red. Presumably it was their financial straits which prompted the Vatican's "finance minister," Cardinal Castillo Lara, to take the unprecedented step of publishing the papal accounts. From the bare figures it became clear that the reputed wealth was nearly all tied up in priceless art treasures, and what is regarded as the cultural heritage of all mankind cannot be sold off so easily.

The Lateran Pact, signed by the Italian State and the Vatican on 11th February 1929, fixed, among other things, the compensation which the Holy See was to receive for the loss of the Papal States: 1,535 billion lire, in cash and state bonds. This settlement initially formed the Vatican's working capital. However, the "Peters Pence" taken in collections all over the world for St Peter and St Paul, remain a particularly lucrative source of income for the Pope. Today's Catholics would not be impressed by a picture of His Holiness lying on a meagre bed of straw, such as used to be distributed in large numbers, and which was still bringing in massive sums of money at the end of the 19th century. More reliance is now placed on persuading the faithful of their Church's manifold tasks, and obtaining larger contributions from local churches to help fill the deficit. However, there is

no desire in the hallowed halls of the Vatican to follow the example of Italy's own Catholic Church, which in 1990 hired a British advertising agency to organize a campaign aimed at extracting more money from churchgoers.

A particularly large dent in the Holy See's budget is made by the salaries of its employees (3,400 altogether: 2,360 lay people and 1,040 clerics). A job on the staff of Vatican Radio, the newspaper, post office, printing works, or the museums, was at one time considered a haven of peace and security. The salaries were admittedly not all that high, but tax-free gasoline and the specially low prices at the "Annona," the Vatican's department store, were useful perks. Recently, however, the complaints have been growing, and in 1991 (the year of John Paul II's social encyclical *Centesimus Annus*), the Vatican employees voiced their dissatisfaction in a public protest, caused by new performance targets which had been introduced without consulting those affected by them.

THE VATICAN

Metro: Line A, Ottaviano; *Bus:* 23, 34, 41, 42, 46, 49, 62, 64, 65, 98, 492, 881, 907, 991. *Streetcar:* 19, 30. Only a small part of the Vatican is open to visitors: St Peter's, the collections of art and antiquities, and a section of the Vatican Library. Remember to dress in a manner appropriate to the sanctity of the place (no shorts and no off-the-shoulder dresses or tops). The postal service of the Vatican (blue mailboxes), unlike that in the rest of Italy, is swift and reliable; postage-stamps from the Vatican are a present that will please any keen stamp-collector.

Papal audiences

Tickets for the public audiences, held on Wednesdays at 11am in St Peter's Square or in the Hall of Nervi in the Vatican, can be obtained the day before at the Prefettura della Casa Pontifica. Private audiences must be requested in writing, also from the **Prefettura della Casa Pontifica**, Città del Vaticano, Tel: 6982, Tuesdays, from 9am to 1pm.

The Vatican Museums

A shuttle-bus (leaving from the south side of St Peter's Square, in front of the Vatican Post Office) takes you through the Vatican Gardens to the entrance to the museums; there is another entrance in the Via del Vaticano. Opening times: Mon-Sat 9am-2pm, last admission 1pm (July-Sept. and Easter 9am-5pm, last admission 4pm); on the last Sunday of the month, open 9am-1pm; admission is free on that day only. You need to allow a lot of time for your visit to the Vatican Museums. But color-coded tours, which are graded according to their scope and time required, enable you to choose how intensively you want to immerse yourself in the treasures.

The following museums are the ones definitely not to be missed: **Pinacoteca**: valuable paintings from the Middle Ages to the present are displayed in 16 rooms. **Museo Pio Clementino**: The most important collection of sculpture in the world. **Museo Chiaramonti**: A very long gallery, furnished with Greek and Roman sculpture chosen by Antonio Canova. **Museo Gregoriano Etrusco** (Etruscan Museum): This museum contains – beside Greek and Roman works – everyday articles and works of art from the Etruscans, which give an insight into the life of this mysterious race. You can also see jewelry of Etruscan, Greek, Roman and Assyrian origin; and there is an extensive collection of vases. **Museo Gregoriano Profano**: This is where non-religious works of antiquity are displayed, for example, Roman sculpture of the imperial period, and Roman copies of Greek works of art. **Biblioteca Apostolica Vaticana:** The extensive collection in the Vatican Library – medieval manuscripts, incunabula, valuable printed books and priceless parchments – was begun in 1450 by Pope Nicholas V and built up systematically.

Appartamento Borgia: These private rooms, which Pope Alexander VI had built for himself and his family, were decorated with frescoes on the walls and ceiling by Pinturicchio. **Stanze di Raffaello**: The *Stanze*, or chambers of Raphael comprise four large rooms, in which the painter created his masterpiece: Two of them, the Pope's private office (*Sala della Segnatura*) and the "Burning of the Borgo" room (*Sala dell'Incendio di Borgo)* are decorated with murals by Raphael himself; the Hall of Heliodorus (*Sala d'Eliodoro*) and the Hall of Constantine (*Sala di Costantino)* were painted after Raphael's death by his pupils Giulio Romano und Gian Francesco Penni. **Cappella Niccolina**: The chapel of Nicholas V shows two cycles of frescoes, painted by Fra Angelico to celebrate the life and martyrdom of St Stephen and St Lawrence.

Galleria delle Carte Geografiche: Here you can see maps of all the regions of Italy, dating from the 16th century. **Galleria dei Candelabri e degli Arazzi**: This gallery displays valuable tapestries from the 5th to the 17th century, and Roman marble candelabras. **Cappella Sistina**: The Sistine Chapel has been almost completely restored since 1980. Only the altar wall with Michelangelo's fresco *The Last Judgement* is still in the process of restoration. The side walls and ceiling reveal in new and amazingly vivid colors the wonderful frescoes of the most celebrated painters of the 15th century: Michelangelo, Perugino, Botticelli, Rosselli, Pinturicchio, Signorelli und Ghirlandaio. **Collezione d'Arte religiosa moderna**: This collection shows plainly how little of note has been produced in the modern era, when compared with the famous works of art of previous centuries. **Museo delle Carrozze**: The Vatican Coach Museum in an underground room contains the state coaches used by ecclesiastical dignitaries, as well as uniforms of the papal troops and guards.

The Castel Sant' Angelo

Lungotevere Vaticano / Lungotevere Castello. *Bus:* 23, 28, 34, 64. Open Tue-Sat 9am-2pm, in summer till 6.30pm; Sun 9am-12 noon.

The Castel Sant' Angelo is now a museum. 58 rooms display a collection of weapons, models showing the history of the castle, several chapels and a treasure-chamber. Various temporary exhibitions are also put on here.

ROME OF THE BAROQUE POPES

PIAZZA NAVONA

PANTHEON

PIAZZA DI SPAGNA

PIAZZA BARBERINI

FONTANA DI TREVI

AROUND THE PIAZZA NAVONA

After the Classical Rome of antiquity, and despite the city's many stunning buildings from the Middle Ages and the Renaissance, Rome's Baroque period produced the greatest wealth of architectural treasures.

The best place to start a walk through the city's Baroque past is the **Piazza Navona**. As beautiful as the Piazza di Spagna (but not as fashionable), as lively as the Piazza S. Maria in Trastevere (but not such an integral part of its *rione*), the Piazza Navona is still the Romans' favorite square. Largely responsible for its erection on the ruins of the Stadium of Domitian, and for its present appearance, was Pope Innocent X Pamphili. The Pope's family owned several houses around the piazza; by building magnificent monuments, the Pope wanted to create an environment for them that was worthy of their own aristocratic splendor.

The piazza's main attraction is of course the superb **Fontana dei Fiumi** (Fountain of the Four Rivers) of 1651, one of Bernini's masterpieces and an im-

Previous pages: Under the colonnades of St Peter's Square. Left: The Triton Fountain in the Piazza Barberini.

pressive example of Roman Baroque. Grouped around a rugged chunk of travertine rock which supports an obelisk that originally came from the Circus of Maxientius are four allegorical figures repesenting the Nile, the Ganges, the Danube and the Rio de la Plata, in South America.

Popular tradition has it that their postes reflect Bernini's distaste for the façade and dome of the church of **S. Agnese**, which stands across from the fountain and was the work of his rival, Borromini. The figure of the Rio de la Plata, whom Bernini supposedly modelled on a cardinal who was ill-disposed towards him, reaches out an arm as if to protect himself from the dome's imminent collapse, while the figure of the Nile covers its face in order not to have to look at the church. In fact, S. Agnese (which was not the work of Borromini alone) was not built until two years *after* the fountain, and its curving, concave façade was even intended to harmonize with Bernini's work.

The interior of the church, which was built on the spot where St Agnes was presented naked to the crowd, was based on designs by Girolamo and Carlo Rainaldi, with a few touches from Borromini. Over the doorway Innocent X, who commissioned the church constuc-

129

tion, blesses the faithful from his vantage point atop the tomb Giovanbattista Maini made for him in 1730.

To the left of the church is the façade of the **Palazzo Pamphili**, built by Girolamo Rainaldi in 1650, which today houses the Brazilian Embassy. The palace was a gift from Innocent X to his sister-in-law Olimpia Maidalchini, who was apparently responsible for his being elected pope. Her arrogance, however, made her the object of the people's hatred. Although she was continually complaining that she was a poor widow after the death of her papal patron, she herself proved to be fabulously wealthy at the time of her death.

In front of the palace, the **Fountain of the Moor** (built in 1654) features the figure of an Ethiopian wrestling with a dolphin; the **Neptune Fountain**, at the opposite end of the piazza, was not completed until 1878.

Above: Sitting for a portrait in the Piazza Navona.

A favorite pastime of the Romans is strolling through the Piazza Navona, especially on summer evenings when the so-called *Ponentino*, a light breeze, comes inland from the sea and wafts through the city. The bars (which have increased in number), the street vendors selling costume jewelery, the portrait artists, card-layers and palm readers scattered throughout the square all contribute to the piazza's special flair for carefree liveliness.More than 150 years ago, the great Roman dialect poet G. G. Belli was already saying *Cuesta nun è una piazza, è una campagna, è un teatro, una fiera, un allegria* (This isn't a piazza; it's a holiday resort, a theater, a fair, a celebration).

The **Via di Pasquino**, which leads off the Piazza Navona on the south side of the Palazzo Pamphili, was named for the fragment of a classical Roman statuary group which was set up at the end of the street in 1501. The people dubbed it *Pasquino*, allegedly in memory of a tailor (some say a bar owner) who had his shop here and who was known for his sarcastic remarks. Over the centuries the statue has often been a forum for public protests. Vitriolic attacks in verse form directed at popes, princes and cardinals, known as *pasquinades*, were affixed to its surface.

The first street on the right brings you to the **Via S. Maria dell'Anima** which leads to the church of that name. But first, go to the left through the **Via di Tor Millina**, named for the medieval tower on the corner of the two streets.

Turning to the right again, you'll see the portico of **S. Maria della Pace** (1656) at the end of the street. As you approach it, your perspective gradually widens until you can see the façade, the wings, the entire backdrop of the **Piazza della Pace**, designed like a theatrical stage setting by Pietro da Cortona. This is a true masterpiece of Roman Baroque. Here, the whole concept of space leaves classical rules behind: no more the emphasis on a static scenario, it's the viewer's subjective ex-

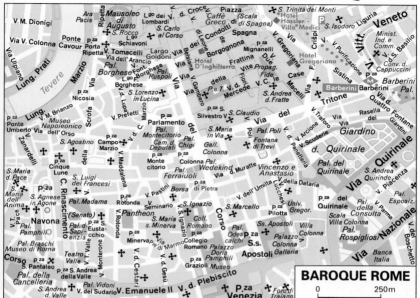

BAROQUE ROME

0   250m

perience which is of paramount importance.

The interior of the church holds fewer surprises from an architectural standpoint; but it's filled with fine sculptures and paintings. Among these are Raphael's *Sibyls* of 1514 (over the arch of the first chapel on the right) and (in the chapel opposite) a delicate fresco by Baldassare Peruzzi, depicting the Madonna with St Bridget and St Catherine, accompanied by Cardinal Ponzetti. The sacristy leads to a superb two-storey Renaissance cloister with a rectangular ground plan. Built in 1504, it was the first work undertaken in Rome by the great architect Bramante.

From there, a semi-circular portico leads us back to the piazza. The grille which surrounds it and shuts it off from the square was added in 1979, after a poor vagrant, who had made the monument into his permanent abode, was burnt alive in his sleep just because a couple of youths wanted to create some "excitement." to liven up a boring evening.

Just beyond the northwest corner of the little piazza house number 20 is the church of Rome's German community, **S. Maria dell Anima.** Its sumptuous interior, modelled on German hall churches by an anonymous North European architect, contains several richly decorated tombs, among them one for Pope Hadrian VI of Utrecht (in the sanctuary on the right), a masterpiece by Baldassare Peruzzi. It is also worth going back into the Via di Tor Millina to admire the elegant and simple three-story Renaissance façade as well as the remarkable campanile, with its colorful majolica decorations.

The house on the left next to the church, built in 1508 to accommodate German pilgrims, bears an inscription on the façade, observations by Julius Caesar and the historian Tacitus about the Germanic peoples: *Ab parvulis labori student* (They are accustomed to studying from childhood on); *Hospites sanctos habent* (They hold guests in great honor); and *Victus iter hospites comis* (The vanquished feels like a friend among his

hosts). On the other side of the Piazza Navona we come to the **Corso del Rinascimento**, a wide but characterless street which wasn't laid out until 1938. Here stands the **Palazzo Madama**, the seat of the Senate, a building in which the exuberance of Baroque has already fossilized into mere mannerism. It derives its name from Margaret of Austria, the daughter of Charles V, who lived here; she was liked and respected by the people who affectionately called her simply *Madama*.

The Via San Salvatore brings us to the **Piazza S. Luigi dei Francesi**. The church here is dedicated to the canonized king Louis IX of France, who died in Tunisia of the plague on the eighth crusade. The main attraction in this church are three marvellous paintings by Caravaggio dating from between 1597 and 1602; you'll find them in the fifth chapel of the left-hand aisle. The three paintings tell the story of St Matthew. In the first picture, he is depicted with his evangelical symbol, the angel: the work is notable for the unusual way the figures are painted. The second work, Matthew's *Calling*, demonstrates the painter's mastery in arranging pictorial elements; while the third, the *Martyrdom*, conveys a dramatic sense of dispair. The theatrical play of light and shadow confers a sense of spiritual as well as physical depth.

Going back to the Corso del Rinascimento, we see on the left, next to the Palazzo Madama, the severe façade of Giacomo della Porta's **Palazzo della Sapienza**. Until 1935, this building housed the old university, which was founded in 1303 by Boniface VIII. The magnificent inner courtyard contains the domed church of **S. Ivo**, built in 1660 by Borromini and notable for its unusual spiral tower.

Borromini was one of the architects most committed to the idea of replacing the architectural rules of the Renaissance

Above: The Piazza della Rotonda and the Pantheon. Right: Inside the Pantheon.

with the developing formal vocabulary of the Baroque; he was also one of the most brilliant of Baroque artists.

In no other building in Rome, except perhaps S. Carlino, another of Borromini's works, does the Roman Baroque reach such heights of revolutionary invention. The design of the lantern, which stands out so boldly from the dome, imparts to the stone a feeling of movement, which no one had known how to convey before.

The Corso del Rinascimento runs into the Corso Vittorio exactly opposite the impressive façade of **S. Andrea della Valle**. The construction of this church took more than 70 years and the services of four different architects. The last two, Carlo Maderno and Carlo Rainaldi, can be credited with its present appearance: Maderno designed the dome and Rainaldi the façade. After a long course of restoration to remove the layer of black which heavy car traffic had deposited on the stone, the façade can finally be seen again in its original white splendor.

The interior is opulently decked out with gold and marble, while impresive frescos adorn the light and airy vaulting. The marvellous tombs of the Piccolomini popes, dating from the 15th century, are located above the last arcades of the nave; while the steep-sided dome rising above the center of the transept is, after St Peter's, the second largest in Rome. The apse is decorated with important frescos by Domenichino, and the left side of the transept is dominated by an impressive Baroque altar.

In front of the church, in a corner of the Piazza Vidoni half hidden by parked cars, stands another "speaking statue," that of an abbott, **Abate Luigi**. An inscription on the pedestal recounts in verse the great deeds and vicissitudes of this man's life. In spite of the optimistic note on which the strophe ends: *Ma qui (ho) vita novella e alfin sicura* (But here I have at last a new and safe life), his trials and tribula-

tions seem far from over, however, since every now and again someone steals the statue's head.

Passing along the Via Monterone, which runs parallel to the Corso Rinascimento, we come to the **Piazza di S. Eustachio**, which is named after its church. Weddings can never be held here, because there is a stag's head hanging above the tympanum, and they say that a marriage which is solemnized beneath the animal's massive antlers does not promise to be a happy one.

AROUND THE PANTHEON

We now come to the **Piazza della Rotonda**, the name given in the Middle Ages to the **Pantheon**. In the days of the Empire, this magnificent Roman building was dedicated to all the gods (the meaning of the word "pantheon"); in Christian times, it commemorated all martyrs.

The huge portico is supported by 16 Corinthian columns, and the inscription

under the gable includes the name Marcus Vipsanius Agrippa, son-in-law of the emperor Augustus, the consul who had the Pantheon built in 27 BC. The gable was once covered with gilded bronze tiles, but Pope Urban VIII Barberini had them melted down and used for the baldachin in St Peter's. Pasquino commented on this in his famous epigram: *Quod non fecerunt barbari, fecerunt Barberini* (What the barbarians did not do, the Barberini did).

The interior of the Pantheon, both majestic and harmonious, attests to the outstanding ability of the Roman architects. Most impressive of all is the huge dome, rising up to culminate in the circular opening at the top.

The Pantheon isn't only for gods: it contains the tombs of Raphael, King Victor Emmanuel and his son Umberto. The

Above: "Il pulcin della Minerva" – Bernini's elephant with the obelisk. Right: Caravaggio as interpreted by a pavement artist.

building could also have been the last resting place of Emperor Charles V, if a member of the Crescenzi family had had his way. After presiding over the wanton destruction that accompanied the Sack of Rome in 1527, Charles paid a visit to the Pantheon and, curious, bent over to look through the opening in the top of the dome. The Crescenzi stifled his urge to give the Emperor a push, only to be reproached by his father later for his failure to do so.

In the piazza there is a pretty fountain with dolphins which supports an Egyptian obelisk that came to light during excavations for the building of the nearby monastery **S. Maria sopra Minerva**. The church derives its name from the fact that it was built on the remains of an ancient temple dedicated to Minerva. This temple was the source of a second obelisk, which bears hieroglyphics referring to Hophrah, the last of the pharaohs, (6th century BC). This obelisk can be seen on the back of an elephant in the center of the piazza.

Il pulcin della Minerva (Minerva's chick), as the elephant is still known in Rome, dating from 1667, is a product of Bernini's Baroque imagination. It is a graphic illustration of the maxim of Alexander VII, carved on the pedestal, that a strong spirit is needed to bear great knowledge.

Over the centuries stones have been mounted on the church's simple façade, showing the various water levels reached by the Tiber's frequent, and disastrous, floods. These were not controlled until stone embankments were built in the 19th century. Since then the Tiber has been tamed – but enclosed in 6 1/4 miles (10 km) of travertine stone walls, the river has also lost its intimate relationship with the city.

S. Maria's Gothic interior was completely ruined by a disastrous restoration in the 19th century, but still contains a wealth of magnificent paintings and

sculptures. Among these are the beautiful frescos by Filippino Lippi in the Cappella Carafa (in the right-hand transept) and the famous statue *Christ The Redeemer* by Michelangelo (also in the transept, to the left of the altar). Among the numerous tombs in various parts of the church is that of Urban VII, whose pontificate is the shortest on record: it lasted just ten days.

From the church we turn to the left down the **Via Pie di Marmo**, so called after the marble foot on the corner of the Via S. Stefano di Cacco, – all that remains of an ancient Roman statue. The street runs into the **Piazza del Collegio Romano**: on the right, you can see the unadorned façade of the Palazzo Doria; on the left, the building which gives the piazza its name. This imposing brick building forms the south side of a complex that belonged to the Jesuits: here they lived, built their church and held their seminars.

Today, the **Collegio Romano**, ten of whose students later became popes, houses one of the best public high schools in Rome; the Palazzo Doria, on the other hand, contains the beautiful **Galleria Doria Pamphili**, home to one of the most valuable collections of paintings in the whole city.

From the Piazza del Collegio Romano, the Via Lata leads to the Corso. On the left hand side, shortly before you reach the intersection, is the **Fontanella del Facchino**, which features a statue of a 16th century water-seller carrying a barrel. He is believed to have been a historical person named Abondio Rizio, who died (according to an inscription which has since disappeared), while carrying one barrel of wine on his shoulders and one in his belly.

Returning to the Via del Collegio Romano and turning left into the Via del Caravita, we come to the **Piazza S. Ignazio,** a masterpiece created by Filippo Raguzzini. To appreciate fully the grace and charm which the 18th century architect conferred upon this little piazza, stand on the top step of the church and survey the

Gregory XV in the chapel to the right of the apse.

The Via di Burrò brings us to the **Piazza di Pietra** and the eleven Corinthian columns of the Temple of Hadrian. From here, the Via dei Bergamaschi leads to the **Piazza Colonna**. The gigantic column in the center of the piazza was erected between 180 and 186 AD to commemorate Marcus Aurelius's victory over the Germanic tribes and the Sarmatians. The deeds of the victorious Roman legions are immortalized in reliefs on the column's 28 drums of marble, and run in a spiral sequence up to the top, upon which the original statue of the emperor was replaced by the present one of St Paul in 1588.

Four different architectural styles are represented on the four sides of the piazza. On the north side is the plain Baroque façade of the **Palazzo Chigi**, now the official residence of the Italian prime minister, while on the south side, at the corner of the Corso, is the 16th-century **Palazzo Ferraiuoli**. To the west is the elegant neo-classical **Palazzo Wedekind** (built in 1838), while the **Galleria Colonna**, to the east, dates from the late 19th century.

harmonious scene. The façades and curved edges of three small *palazetti* combine to form a veritably theatrical backdrop, the wings of which are formed by two identical buildings.

Turn now towards the church of **S. Ignazio**, whose magnificent Rococo façade provides a foretaste of the richly decorated interior. The vaulted ceiling is covered with a huge *trompe l'oeil* fresco dating from 1685. The best place from which to view these 13-meter-high paintings is the center of the nave; from there, you can appreciate the illusion of depth the painter, the Jesuit Andrea Pozzo, managed to create, particularly in the depiction of a wholly imaginary dome. At either side of the transept, two richly decorated altars emphasize the church's sumptuous character, which achieves its highest expression in the monument to

Crossing over and bearing to the left, you'll come to the Bernini façade of the **Palazzo Montecitorio**, where the Italian parliament, the Chamber of Deputies, holds its sessions. Begun in 1650 at the behest of Innocent X Pamphili and not completed until 1696, the palace was used as law courts until 1871. When parliament moved in, the building was expanded to the rear and a second façade added in a florid style, certainly one of the most unfortunate examples of the architecture of the period immediately following the unification of Italy.

The interior of the palace can only be viewed with special permission. In lieu of this, you can look at the stately obelisk which has adorned the piazza since 1792; before this the obelisk, broken into five

Above: The Piazza Colonna and the Columns of Marcus Aurelius. Right: There is always a good crowd on the Spanish Steps.

pieces, lay around for years in the courtyard of a house which no longer exists.

The Via della Missione, which leads past the palazzo on the left, brings us to the **Piazza del Parlamento**. From here we turn into the Via dei Prefetti, and then turn right down the Via della Lupa, to the piazza which bears the name of one of the richest Roman dynasties: the **Piazza Borghese**.

Paul V, the only pope from this aristocratic family, acquired the palace which dominates the piazza at the beginning of the 17th century, and had it remodelled into the magnificent building you see today. It is nicknamed *Il Cembalo*, ("the harpsichord"), because of its unusual shape.

The "keyboard" – that is to say the façade – is a work of genius by the architect Flaminio Ponzio, and once formed part of the backdrop to the beautiful Tiber harbor Porto di Ripetta, which was demolished when the Tiber embankment was built. Inside there is a splendid arcaded courtyard and a nymphaeum with statues and fountains, the so-called *Bagno di Venere* (Bath of Venus).

THE PIAZZA DI SPAGNA

The Via Fontanella Borghese leads to the Largo Goldoni; on the opposite side begins the Via Condotti, one of Rome's most elegant streets. Immediately on the right is the Baroque façade of the church of **La Trinità dei Spagnoli**, while the street is lined with the windows of the capital's most expensive stores.

The famous **Caffé Greco**, founded in 1760 and once the meeting place for foreign intellectuals and artists in Rome, is at Nr 86. It was frequented by Goethe, Gogol – who wrote part of his *Dead Souls* here – Berlioz, Wagner, Stendhal and Baudelaire, among others. Today the café is still filled with statues, mirrors and old furniture, but it has completely lost its intellectual atmosphere. These days the clientèle of this once illustrious rendezvous is comprised of mainly tourists and the *nouveau-riche*.

At Nr 26 stands the 18th-century house where the poet John Keats lived. He, together with Shelley and Lord Byron, are more likely to have spent their afternoons at **Babington's English Tea Rooms**, also still going strong. A later customer may well have been Robert Browing, who lived round the corner in the Vicolo del Lupo.

The Via Condotti gives onto the **Piazza di Spagna,** one of the most famous squares in the world and what might be described as the " front parlor" of the Italian capital. Shaped like two triangles joined at their apexes, the piazza is dominated by the magnificent **Spanish Steps**, constructed in the 18th century by Francesco de Santis.

At the foot of the steps is the **Fontana della Barcaccia** by Pietro Bernini, father of the more famous Gianlorenzo. It is said that the fountain was modelled on a

Above: The Piazza di Spagna and the Fontana della Barcaccia by night. Right: Outside the Antico Caffé Greco.

boat found in the middle of the piazza when the waters receded after one of the Tiber's many floodings.

The famous steps rise in broad curves punctuated by terraces and balustrades; from the top one has a great panoramic and photogenic view of Rome. In the center of the picture stands an obelisk; behind it, the slim towers of Carlo Maderno's church, the **Trinità dei Monti**, soar skywards.

Always full of life, the Spanish Steps are the meeting place and hunting-ground of Rome's Latin lovers, known as *pappagalli* (parrots), who come here to chat up the foreign girls. These are not to be confused with *paparazzi*, the photographers who ruthlessly pursue royalty and celebrities.

Leading left off the Piazza Trinità dei Monti, the street of the same name brings us to the **Pincio**, once a place for romantic walks. On the way, you pass the simple façade of the **Villa Medici**, built in 1540 and bought by Napoleon in 1801 to house the French Academy in Rome.

A little further along on the left stands the dramatic monument to the Cairoli brothers, who lost their lives fighting beside Garibaldi. Finally one comes to the part of the hill closed to automobile traffic, and to the neo-classical **Casina Valadier**, now an exclusive restaurant. The terrace above the Piazza del Popolo affords a splendid view over the domes of Rome, particularly at sunset.

Back in the Piazza di Spagna, we see on the right the column and statue of the Virgin, which Pius IX had erected when he pronounced the dogma of the Immaculate Conception in 1856. The **Palazzo della Propaganda Fide,** with its pleasing brick façade by Bernini, forms the far side of the piazza.

A second façade to the right of the palace is by Bernini's arch-enemy Borromini. Because these two bitter rivals created these two masterpieces only a few meters apart, you can compare their different styles and understand something of the different temperaments that produced them: Bernini's façade is harmonious and classically elegant, while Borromini's demonstrates an imaginaive architecture that, with its curves and projections, its rising or abruptly interrupted lines, is almost revolutionary.

Since Bernini lived right on the corner of the Via di Propaganda and the Via della Mercede, Borromini hit upon the idea of decorating the windows in the top story with unusual friezes which resemble a donkey's ears. Bernini promptly responded with a plaster figure which, although stylized, is reminiscent of nothing so much as a phallus of remarkable proportions.

The rivalry between the two great artists is expressed somewhat more temperately in the two beautiful figures of angels beside the apse of the church of **S. Andrea della Fratte** at the end of the Via Propaganda. The two statues were actually meant for the bridge opposite the Castel Sant' Angelo, but were replaced by copies.

Note the dramatic expression of the angel holding the Crown of Thorns and the graceful sweeping movement of the angel with the inscribed tablet, who looks as though he is about to soar into the air. Inside the church, in the third of the side-chapels, can be found the so-called **Madonna del Miracolo**, an image with miraculous properties which evidently succeeded in converting Alphonse Ratisbonne, a leading member of the Jewish community in France, to Christianity on 20th January, 1842.

An inscription informs us that he entered the church an "obstinate Jew," and left it a Christian. For years before this, the Jews in the ghetto had been forced to listen to the priests' sermons, but not a single one of them had ever converted. (It is said that they plugged their ears with wax).

PIAZZA BARBERINI

Walking from the church up the **Via Capo di Case**, you can gain a new per-

ton blows a powerful jet of water into the air through a conch shell. The coat-of-arms carved in the fountain indicates the proximity of the **Palazzo Barberini**; from the piazza you can glimpse this palazzo on the other side of the Via delle Quattro Fontane. Its splendid façade is made up of a central section by Bernini and two wings by Maderno.

Borromini, not yet then as famous as he was to become, (and only earning a tenth of his rival's fee), was responsible for the sections linking the main elements of the façade, into which he incorporated some very beautiful windows. He also designed the graceful winding staircase inside the palace on the right, while the equally fine staircase which leads up to the Galleria d'Arte Antica is Bernini's work.

This collection of pictures is certainly worth a visit, if only to see the impressive portrait of Henry VIII by Holbein, Caravaggio's *Judith and Holofernes* and the delicate portrait which Raphael painted of his beloved Margherita Luti, known as *La Fornarina*. The ceiling of the great hall is painted with the *Triumph of Divine Providence* (1639) by Pietro da Cortona, a Baroque masterpiece glorifying the Barberini family.

spective on the dome and bell tower from above; both are by Borromini, but unfortunately he never completed them. As in S. Ivo alla Sapienza, the great architect combined harmony and bold, rhythmic lines in this building. And while the architecture of S. Ivo derives its "movement" only from the spiralling lines of its bell tower, the tower here moves in a much more literal sense. This masterpiece of the maestro sways quite visibly when the bells are being rung; in three centuries, however, it has not yet fallen down.

From the Via Capo di Case the Via Fransesco Crispi leads to the Via Sistina. From here, turn right into the **Piazza Barberini**, where traffic roars around Bernini's magnificent **Triton Fountain**. Four splendid dolphins support the coat-of-arms of the Barberini family, while Tri-

Opposite the palace is the start of the steep **Via Rasella**. On March 23, 1943, thirty-three members of the German SS were killed here in an attack organized by the Resistance. The SS reacted immediately and mercilessly: the following evening 323 Italian prisoners and twelve foreigners were shot in a trench close to the Via Ardeatina; 73 of the victims were Jews, one was a priest, and one a 14 year-old boy. None of them had been involved in the attack.

A little further down is an intersection with four fountains, one at each of its four corners; these give the **Via delle Quattro Fontane** its name. They represent the rivers Tiber and Arno, and the goddesses Diana and Juno.

Above: A street near the Piazza Barberini.
Right: You will nearly always see this fellow in the Piazza Barberini .

If you stand in the center of the intersection on a Sunday in August very early in the morning, when traffic is light, you can fully appreciate why the town planners had the streets intersect at this particular point. To the north, to the west and to the south you can see the three obelisks of Trinità dei Monti, the Quirinal and the Esquiline, while to the east stands Michelangelo's splendid fortified city gate, the **Porta Pia**.

In the Via del Quirinale you can again witness the rivalry between Borromini and Bernini, first in the curving façade of Borromini's **S. Carlino**, and a little further on in the splendid oval interior of Bernini's S. Andrea.

Borromini worked on S. Carlino and its adjoining monastery in the early years of his career, and again at the end of his life, before he killed himself in a final outburst of rage and frustration by falling on his sword.

There is no need to describe the church, it's enough simply to look at it. Be sure not to miss the charming little inner courtyard with its elegant lines; the fountain (for which Borromini prepared a total of twelve designs); or the delightful variety of shapes in the little columns of the balustrade. In the church itself, you can admire the columns which sweep boldly up to the magnificent ceiling.

Only a few steps away is Bernini's response – the church of **S. Andrea**. An elegant portico leads into the center of the oval, where everything radiates harmony. It involves a critical confrontation with the standards of classical architecture and, as far as possible, a departure from its established rules.

Take, for example, the large window that interrupts the perfect oval of the ceiling. It allows a flood of light – that ultimate object of Baroque architects' desire – to penetrate in and illuminate the radiant statue of the saint to whom the church is dedicated.

From here, it is only a short distance to the **Piazza del Quirinale**. In the center stand the Dioscuri, the "Heavenly Twins" Castor and Pollux, Roman copies

of two Greek statues which once stood in the Baths of Constantine. The statues were restored over the centuries and embellished with the obelisk and attractive granite basin; the latter was used as a cattle trough until 1818.

The northeastern side of the piazza is bounded by the **Palazzo del Quirinale**, which was commissioned by Pope Gregory XIII in 1574 and took more than a century to complete. Bernini was one of the architects who worked on it, and Maderno was responsible for the fine portal decorated with two columns.

The palace was originally the summer residence of the popes. In the hot season when the city's lower-lying areas, which included the Vatican, were vulnerable to outbreaks of malaria, they took refuge here. In 1870 it became the residence of the Kings of Italy; since 1947, it has been the official home of the President of the Republic.

On the right, next to the palace, is the dazzling white **Palazzo della Consulta** designed and built by Ferdinando Fuga (1739). It was formerly the seat of the Santa Consulta, the supreme court of the Papal States, and now houses the Constitutional Court of the Italian Republic. To the left, its broad terrace affords a fine view of the dome of St Peter's and the city of Rome.

AT THE TREVI FOUNTAIN

Descending the steps in front of the Quirinal Palace, you come to the Via della Dataria; turn off into the Via S. Vincenzo. This leads to the **Piazza Fontana di Trevi**, the end of our walk. Before losing yourself in contemplation of Nicola Salvi's masterpiece, take a look at the church to the right of it, **S. Vincenzo ed Anastasio**.

The façade is decorated with ten columns in its lower storey and eight col-

Above: The square in front of the Palazzo del Quirinale. Right: A "must" for every tourist – the Fontana di Trevi.

umns in the upper one, so many in fact that the church is called *il canneto* (the reed-bed). But its oddest feature is an interior one: piled in the apse are the embalmed entrails of all the popes from Sixtus V (d. 1590) to Leo XIII (d. 1903). This macaber custom was finally abolished by Pius X.

Turn, finally, to the focal point of the square, the fountain which is probably the most famous in the world. At the center of a huge basin, Neptune stands in a seashell chariot drawn by two seahorses. On either side of him are the figures of Health and Abundance.

Above these are two bas-reliefs: one depicts the girl who, according to legend, led thirsty Roman soldiers to the spring which still feeds the fountain today; while the other shows Agrippa examining the plans for the building of the aqueduct.

Strange as it may seem, the fountain, in spite of its many figures, loses its whole appeal if the water is not flowing. The water is the true protagonist of the piece.

It is no coincidence that the basin is below street level; you have to be able to see the water so that it can confer some of its movement upon all the figures which make up the complex Baroque tableau.

Take a seat and watch the modern actors who perform on the edge of Salvi's beautiful stage. There are Japanese who bow and smile before the flashes of their cameras. There are groups of retirees who have arrived at the long-awaited tourist mecca, following the brightly colored umbrella of their guide. There are soldiers off duty. There is a street vendor selling horrible plastic reproductions of St Peter's (including the colonnades) and of the fountain itself. And there is also the inevitable *pappagallo*, with his shirt unbuttoned down to the navel, casting come-on glances in the direction of the female tourists. Still, before you pass on, perhaps you should throw the obligatory coin in the fountain and wish to return to Rome – even if you know the coin will later be fished out by a little boy with a magnet.

PAPAL ROME

Sightseeing

The beautiful **Piazza Navona** is dominated by the **Fountain of the Four Rivers,** the **Palazzo Pamphili** and the church of **S. Agnese**.

In the Via della Pace stands **S. Maria della Pace** and next to it the church of the German community in Rome, **S. Maria dell'Anima**.

In the Corso del Rinascimento you will find **Palazzo Madama** and the **Palazzo della Sapienza** with its church of **S. Ivo**. Where the Corso Rinascimento joins the Corso Vittorio, you will come upon the church of **S. Andrea della Valle**. In the **Piazza di S. Eustachio** you can drink an excellent espresso coffee in the **Eustachio** bar.

The **Pantheon** in the Piazza della Rotonda is open Tue-Sat, 9am-2pm and Sun, 9am till 1pm. Around the square there are pleasant little pavement cafés, and round the corner in the **Tazza d'Oro** you can buy the best coffee in the whole of Rome, either in packets to take away, or to drink at the bar. Tel: 6789792 and 6792768.

In the Piazza della Minerva you will find the church of **S. Maria sopra Minerva** and Bernini's enchanting elephant, carrying a small obelisk on its back. In the area around the Piazza della Minerva there are many shops selling clerical clothing, and liturgical articles.

If you walk from the **Piazza del Collegio Romano** towards the Corso, you will pass the **Fontanella del Facchino**.

Alternatively, if you take the Via del Caravita, down from the Via del Collegio Romano, it will bring you to the Baroque jewel of the **Piazza S. Ignazio** with Filippo Ragùzzini's church of the same name.

Around the **Piazza Colonna** and its Columns of Marcus Aurelius there are various palaces, among them the seat of the Chamber of Deputies, the Palazzo Montecitorio.

The **Palazzo Borghese** in the piazza of the same name, is interesting on account of its unusual "hapsichord" shape. The arcaded courtyard is also beautiful.

After so much history and so many illustrious names, you should fortify yourself at the **Caffé Greco**, Via Condotti 86, Tel: 6782554, or in **Babington's English Tea-rooms** in the **Piazza di Spagna**, Tel. 6786027, before climbing the **Spanish Steps**, and perhaps you should end the walk with a view over the city from the **Pincio**. If you have any energy left, (and it is not too late – remember, the churches close at 6pm), you should walk along the **Via Sistina** to the **Piazza Barberini** and the fine **Triton Fountain.**

Passing the **Palazzo Barberini** you follow the Via delle Quattro Fontane to the two churches of **S. Carlo alle Quattro Fontane** and **S. Andrea al Quirinale**, with which the great Baroque architects, Bernini und Borromini, endeavored to outdo each other. From here it is a short distance to the **Palazzo Quirinale**, and at the famous **Fontana di Trevi**, after a quick look at the church of **S. Vincenzo ed Anastasio**, you can abandon yourself to the enchantment of the place. And don't forget, your coin must be thrown into the water over the left shoulder!

Shopping

The most exclusive shopping street in Rome, the **Via Condotti,** and the little streets in the neighborhood extend an open invitation to window-shoppers. Represented here are practically all the great names of Italian and international haute couture. To give a few examples: **Giorgio Armani**, Via del Babuino 102; **Laura Biagiotti**, Via Borgognona 44; **Cucci**, Via Condotti 67; **Fendi,** Via Borgognona; **Givenchy**, Via Borgognona 21; **Gucci**, Via Condotti 8; **Max Mara**, Via Condotti 45 und Via Frattina 38; **Missoni,** del Babuino 96; **Valentino**, Via Condotti/ Mario dei Fiori; **Versace**, Via Borgognona 29. In the **Via Sistina** there are some attractive little shops, especially for shoes and dresses.

Restaurants / Ice-cream parlors

Al Moro, Vicolo delle Bollette 13, Tel: 6783495, book ahead; closed Sundays and all of August.

Al 34, Via Mario del' Fiori 34, Tel: 6795091. **Chez Albert**, Vicolo della Vaccarella, Tel: 6565549, sophisticated Nouvelle Cuisine. **Da Mario**, Via della Vite 55, Tel: 6783818, Tuscan specialities, closed Suns and all August. **L' Eau Vive**, Via Monterone 85, Tel: 6541095, international, book ahead for the evening. **Girone VI**, Vicolo Sinibaldi 2, Tel: 6542831, book ahead; closed lunchtime, Suns and 14th Dec. to 8th Jan. **Il Buco**, Via Sant'Ignazio 8, Tel: 6793298, Tuscan specialities, closed Mons and 15–31 Aug.

Il Falchetto, Via dei Montecatini 12/14, Tel: 6791160, closed Fridays and 5th–20th August. **La Tavernetta**, Via del Nazzareno 3/4, Tel: 6793124, closed Mondays and all of August. **Papà Giovanni**, Via dei Sediari 4, Tel: 6565308, really top class restaurant. **Piccola Roma**, Via Uffici del Vicario 36, Tel: 6798606, closed Sundays and all of August. **Trattoria del Pantheon**, Via del Pantheon 55, Tel: 6792788, closed Sundays and 15th–31st August. **Tritone**, Via dei Maroniti 1, Tel: 6798181, closed Saturdays, 5th–15th February and 10th–20th August.

Ice-cream parlors: **Giolitti**, Via Uffici del Vicario 40. **Tre Scalini**, Piazza Navona 28.

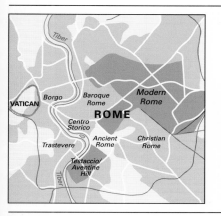

CAPITAL OF THE NATION

**THE NATIONAL MONUMENT
VIA NAZIONALE
PIAZZA DELLA REPUBBLICA
BEYOND THE AURELIAN WALL
SAN LORENZO
ALONG THE TIBER
TESTACCIO AND AVENTIN**

"It was a time when the dark doings of demolition men and building contractors were flourishing on the soil of Rome. Together with the clouds of dust arose a kind of crazed pursuit of profit, like a storm of evil blowing through the city... All decency had been lost, respect for the past abandoned. The fight for profit was carried out with unremitting tenacity, without restraint: its weapons were the pickaxe, the mason's trowel, and dishonesty." Thus lamented Gabriele d'Annunzio in his 1895 novel *Le Vergini delle Rocce.*

He was looking back at the first 25 years of the Kingdom of Italy, Rome's being made capital of the young monarchy had effectively set the seal on the process of Italian unification. The capital of the Papal States and center of world Catholicism, the "salon in which all Europe whiles away its time," as the French journalist P. Rey dubbed it, was to grow into a great metropolis over the next few decades. But it was a capital city without a hinterland: the Roman *campagna,* described by Gregorovius as a "great

Classical idyll" and by Reymont as a "huge cemetery in the midst of which stands the giant tomb of Rome," was deserted. Malaria had depopulated the countryside along the coast and in the hills around the city. In Rome itself, on the other hand, the population was swelling as people flocked to the new capital. In 1871 it was about 250,000; by the turn of the century it had doubled to 500,000, and by 1930 it had already passed the million mark.

In 1870 only a quarter of the area encompassed by the 12.5 mile (20 km) Aurelian Wall around the city, which formed the boundary between city and country until into the 20th century, was actually populated; the rest of the land was taken up by villas and parks standing side by side with classical ruins and gardens, vineyards and cow pastures. One obvious answer, therefore, to the question of how to accommodate the growing population was to develop this area within the walls.

The dissolution of many of the church's administrative bodies meant that the Romans had lost much of their financial support. They had to get used to the lira instead of the papal *scudi,* as well as to new systems of weights and measures, rising prices, a serious housing shortage, increased taxes, and military service, as

Previous pages: Rome – city of pigeons. Fountain of the Naiads in the Piazza della Repubblica. Left: S. Maria in Aracoeli and the National Memorial.

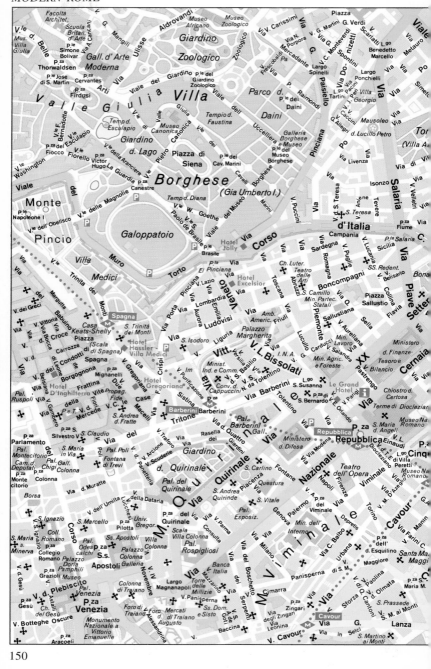

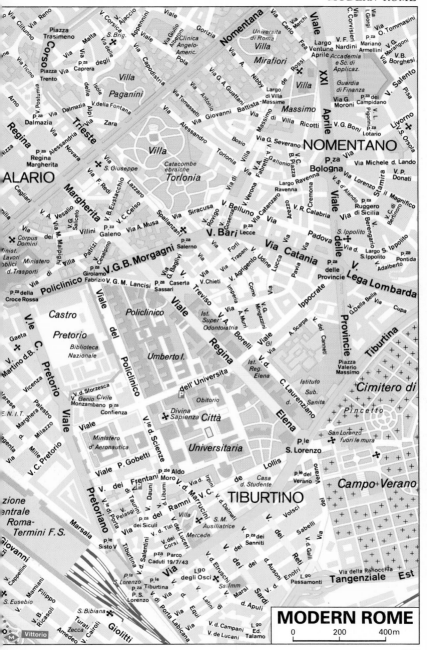

MODERN ROME

0   200   400m

the papal mercenaries had been disbanded. The "Black Aristocracy" remained loyal to the Holy See, while the newly-arrived nobility owed their allegiance to the royal court.

The city's rapid expansion into a capital meant a frenzy of building activity and speculation. North Italian, French, Belgian and British banks and corporations seized upon every potentially profitable investment.

The real estate market was booming: between 1870 and 1885, the price for a plot of land rose by anything from ten to a hundred times. The construction industry was also enjoying a boom and was able to support its speculations on the *allegra finanza,* or financial recklessness of the moneylenders. The rustic character of the city on the Tiber quickly became a thing of the past.

Above: The Carabinieri on parade in the Piazza Venezia. Right: The National Monument, nicknamed "the typewriter."

The city that a French writer once compared to "a huge farmstead amidst broad fields of grain" began to take on a more urban stamp. But as late as the 1860s farmers driving their cattle, sheep or goats through the city streets were still a normal part of the city's life.

With the advent of the Savoy monarchy, the pomp of the Papal State also disappeared. Nuns and priests in habits, coifs and cowls became increasingly rare. And the "monsignori, treading the streets...followed by solemn servants who returned on their behalf the bows of the lesser citizens" were disappearing, as the novelist Henry James noted with concern. On the Pincio, which had once been a popular meeting place for Eminences and Excellencies strolling with fellow Romans, their Royal Highnesses had taken over.

THE NATIONAL MONUMENT

The **National Monument to Vittorio Emmanuele II** became a symbol of the

new order. In order to make room for it, the medieval buildings on the north slope of the Capitoline Hill were demolished, and the "eighth hill of Rome" was created – "financially the most extravagant as well as the largest national monument of the 19th century, the total cost of which amounted to the then princely sum of 50 million lire," as the historian Jens Petersen later recorded.

Twenty-six years in the building, the monument still towers over the Piazza Venezia. Despite the fact that its figures and carvings were meant to represent a synthesis of Roman and Italian history, the edifice's dimensions, and the gleaming whiteness of its Brecca marble, make it a completely alien element in Rome's building landscape, which is dominated by the ochres, golds and burnt sienas of stucco and tufa, travertine and brick.

For its harsh whiteness, which not even the work of a hundred years has been able to veil with a more flattering patina, the then-prime minister was held accountable. Rumor had it that he hailed from Brescia, and the terms of the contract by which he arranged to have marble delivered from his home town secured his tenure in office for many years.

This "altar of the fatherland" became the butt of many jokes. Silvio Negro used to describe it as a "sugar mountain," the British soldiers of World War II called it the "wedding cake," and the locals' ironical term for it is the "typewriter" because of its shape.

As it is such a prominent feature of the skyline, however, it is a useful landmark for visitors to Rome trying to find their bearings. On one occasion the gilded equestrian statue of Vittorio Emmanuele was even the scene of a typical Roman *spaghettato*, an opulent pasta dinner featuring an ample supply of wine from the *campagna*. The guests climbed up a ladder into the belly of the king's horse, which, unlike its Trojan forbear, did not contain any Greeks – just a well-laid table.

On the first terrace the Eternal Flame burns beside the **Tomb of the Unknown**

153

Soldier. Members of the different armed services are responsible for mounting the guard-of-honour. The belly of this white "beast" contains not only water tanks for the various fountains, but also a police station. Few visitors, however, find their way to the museum and archives of the Institute for the History of the Risorgimento.

While most government ministries were initially housed in expropriated convents and monasteries after the move to Rome, a whole new building was erected for the **Finance Ministry** with its burgeoning staff. It was built on the Via Venti Settembre, the extension of the Via Quirinale; this latter street begins at the Quirinale Palace, the former residence of the popes, which had now been taken over by the royal court. The idea was that the political and administrative center of the new Italy should develop "on the heights," as close to the royal palace as possible.

In fact, while the **Ministry of the Interior** was also built on the Viminal Hill, the **Ministry of Education** was built in Trastevere and the Department of Justice was shipped off to the Via Arenula. The senior **judicial authorities**, meanwhile, were ultimately housed in the newly built Palace of Justice on the Tiber.

VIA NAZIONALE

One of the first urban development projects was the area around the bustling shopping street **Via Nazionale**. The plan was based on a previous design drawn up under Pius IX. The Vatican's former Minister of War, Monsignor de Mérode, had laid out the streets and piazzas of the new neighborhood in the middle of the 19th century; his plan included the Via Nazionale, which followed the line of the ancient *Vicus Longus* between the Quiri-

nal and Viminal hills, and which, originally, was named for him (Via de Mérode). Along this axis, which connects the main railway station with the city center, via the Piazza della Repubblica, the head office of the Banco d'Italia and the **Palazzo delle Esposizioni** (1878-82) were built in the 1880s. Ultimately, the plan was to do justice to the capital's obligations as a cultural center by building theaters, museums and galleries. A step toward this goal was the monumental Palace of Exhibitions, designed by the architect Pio Piacentini, set back slightly from the street, which was intended from the outset to accommodate rotating art exhibitions. After many years of restoration it was reopened to the public in 1991. Works by contemporary artists are now displayed in the building's three spacious storeys.

A little further on is St Paul's Church, which serves the English-speaking Protestant community in Rome. It was the first non-Catholic church to be built in the city after the dissolution of the Papal State. Its English architect, George Edmund Street, employed stylistic elements from medieval basilicas to create a new synthesis very much in the spirit of the late 19th century. Shortly after his death, his plans for the neo-Gothic Anglican church in the Via del Babuino were also realized.

Only a few steps beyond the church is the opera house, the **Teatro dell'Opera.** It is another of the buildings from the early years of the monarchy in Rome. In 1880, the hotelier Domenico Costanzi commissioned Achille Sfodrini with the building of his own private opera house. Not until 1926 did the theater become municipal property, finally to become the City Opera House.

PIAZZA DELLA REPUBBLICA

One of the grandest squares built after 1870 is the **Piazza della Repubblica**,

formerly the Piazza dell' Esedra, at the end of the Via Nazionale.

The imposing palazzi which line the south-western side of the piazza are the work of the architect Gaetano Koch. He adapted for his Roman buildings the *portici* or arcades which are typical of the old quarter of Turin.

The layout of the buildings follows the course of the ancient *Exedra*, a semicircular stadium, presumably also used as a theater, which formed part of the Baths of Diocletian complex. Hence also the original name of the piazza – "dell'Esedra." The central building of these extensive baths, the *frigidarium*, was converted by Michelangelo into the church of **Santa Maria degli Angeli**, without altering its original character.

To the left of the church is the **Planetario**, a domed hall, restored to its original state, in which famous ancient marble and bronze statues are displayed. The center of the spacious piazza is graced by the **Fountain of the Naiads**. A circular basin by Alessio Guerrieri forms a pedestal for the opulent groups of figures by sculptor Mario Rutelli, which symbolize man's victory over the forces of nature.

Also in the baths complex is the **Museo Nazionale Romano** or **Museo delle Terme**, the Roman National Museum or Baths Museum. It occupies the premises of a former Carthusian monastery, which was built by Michelangelo in 1561 on the ruins of the baths.

The museum, which was opened in 1889, contains one of the most important collections in the world. Initially, it exhibited the many classical relics which were unearthed during the active period of construction after 1870. To these were added the classical treasures of the Museo Kircheriano and the Ludovisi Museum. The cloister and surrounding rooms contain a unique collection of frescos and mosaics, sarcophagi and sculptures.

Parts of the museum have been under restoration for years, so that the collection can at last be presented in a truly appropriate setting. Today, the main attrac-

tions are finally on display once again: the Ludovisi throne of the 5th century AD, as well as the *Apollo from the Tiber* and the *Niobide*, both dating from 460 BC. And Livia's Garden Room from her villa at Prima Porta is also again open to visitors. In order to make space for the treasures kept in store, exhibits of the Roman Imperial period have gradually been being transferred to the restored **Collegio Massimo**, situated to the right of the train station and destined to become part of the National Museum, since 1988.

Rome's main station, the **Stazione Roma Termini**, is only a few steps away on the Piazza del Cinquecento. In 1863, seven years after the opening of the first railroad to Frascati, the decision was made to build a station by the Baths of Diocletian. Until its opening, there was a

temporary station at the Porta Maggiore, where the Aurelian Wall had been breached for the sake of the railroad tracks leading into the city from the southeast.

Gregorovius gives the following description in his *Roman Diaries*: "Yesterday the Lazio railroad was opened; the Pope was noticeably absent. The temporary station at the Porta Maggiore had been transformed into a festive scene; the yellow and white flags were flying above pictures of the globe, and both the locomotive and the carriages were elaborately decorated. In the grandstands sat the most senior clerics, the general staff and the diplomatic corps. Gregory XVI called the railroad an invention of the devil, but could do nothing to resist its progress." Soon after this Rome was connected by rail with all the large cities in Italy.

The railroad station in its present form was begun shortly before the beginning of World War II to a design by Angiolo Mazzoni del Grande, and was finally completed in 1950 with the addition of its

Above: A busy scene outside the Stazione Roma Termini. Right: Taking time out in the Via Veneto.

front section. A broad, well-lit concourse leads travellers to the platforms; underground, a Metro station gives access to Rome's subway system. In 1955, a few years after the station was completed, the Columbian Nobel Prize winner Garcia Marquez, who was travelling through Europe as a journalist at the time, described it as the most beautiful station in Europe.

The *febbre edilizia*, or building craze ushered in with the arrival of the monarchy, didn't only devour the villas and their park-like grounds at the city center; the ring of villas to the northeast, on the other side of the Piazza della Repubblica, also fell into the greedy hands of the speculators.

A phenomenon described by Goethe shortly after his arrival in Rome in 1786 was carried over into modern times: "One finds traces," the poet wrote, "of a splendor and a destruction of such magnitude that they are beyond our comprehension. What was left standing by the barbarians has been laid waste by the builders of the new Rome." The grounds of the Villa Ludovisi, 50 acres (20 ha) in area, belonging to Cardinal Ludovisi, were described by writers from Goethe to Gogol as one of the finest examples of garden design in Europe, yet were sold as building land by a descendant of the Pope. It became the elegant Ludovisi quarter, where reputable architects built spacious palazzi for the Roman bourgeoisie.

When the **Via Veneto** was extended, this upper middle-class district also got its showpiece boulevard. It was here, in the 1960s, that the legend of Rome's *Dolce Vita* or "sweet life" was born, soon world-famous through Fellini's film of the same name.

Along this street, which is reached from the Piazza della Repubblica by going down the Via E. Orlando and Via L. Bissolato, there is a series of grandiose buildings, nearly all bearing the stamp of the architect Gaetano Koch.

The **Palazzo Margherita**, together with a smaller palazzo, was built in 1886-90 in

the Renaissance style. Once the residence of Queen Margherita of Savoy, it serves today as the United States embassy, and its fine rooms are used to entertain Italian officials. The **Hotel Majestic**, whose façade, at least, does justice to its name, is another work of Gaetano Koch.

BEYOND THE AURELIAN WALL

The Via Veneto ends at the **Porta Pinciana**, a gate in the Aurelian Wall. If you take a 490 or 492 bus from here along the Corso d'Italia, you'll come to another city gate, the **Porta Pia**. This gate, the last building Michelangelo designed, has a particularly intimate connection with the history of the unification of Italy.

In the early hours of September 20, 1870, the people of Rome were awakened by the thunder of cannons. Windowpanes shook throughout the city,

Above: In the Piazza Mincio. Above right: One of Rome's roasted-chestnut sellers.

even in the Vatican itself; the papal mercenaries were trying to beat back an attack by the Piedmontese troops at the Porta Pia. Their efforts were in vain, of course; in the face of the Bersaglieri's superior strength, their resistance was more symbolic thn anything else.

Even today, "The Nobles of His Holiness," otherwise known as the Pope's "Black Aristocracy", meet here every year on the anniversary of this event for a service to commemorate the fallen, and to wallow in nostalgic dreams of a restoration of the Papal State.

Close to the Porta Pia, a memorial on the outer side of the Aurelian Wall recalls this traumatic defeat. Shortly after the capture of Rome, the diplomatic corps assembled one last time in the Vatican to attend a Papal Mass. An illustrious procession then made its way to the Villa Albani, the headquarters of General Cadorna. Their proud Excellencies strutted through the debris around the Porta Pia in ceremonial uniform, three-cornered hats and buckled shoes, to the amusement of

158

the Bersaglieri, who greeted them with an ironic salute.

One of the strangest piazzas in Rome is the **Piazza Mincio,** to the north of the Porta Pia. A huge, dimly lit candelabra adorns the entrance to the piazza; while the houses around the square seem seem to have sprung straight from the pages of a storybook.

With this group of homes commissioned by a non-profit housing society, the Florentine architect Gino Coppedé perfectly suited the taste of the *nouveaux riches* of the early 1920s. Elements of Mannerism, Liberty and Art Deco are reflected in the aesthetically overburdened façades. One *villino*, a small villa with a garden reminiscent of a medieval tower house, is even decorated with Dantesque frescos.

The piazza itself is laid out in the classical Roman tradition, with a turtle fountain splashing in the middle. This piazza is a last, excessive reflection of all of the variety of Roman architecture through the centuries, before the advent of the sober, four-square buildings of the Fascists.

Not far from here, in the Via Nomentana, Benito Mussolini's private hideaway, the Villa Torlonia, was destroyed by a terrorist bomb in 1946. Its gardens are now a public park, beneath which are some 3rd century Jewish catacombs. On the site of the villa itself, the modern **British Embassy**, designed by Sir Basil Spence, was completed in 1971.

Note that there is another building named **Villa Torlonia**, set in spacious gardens beside the Via Salaria, to the north of the Porta Pia. This was built in 1760 and originally named the Villa Albani after the cardinal who commissioned it. Today, the building houses a valuable collection of classical sculpture, originally arranged by Winckelmann. Many of the pieces were removed by Napoleon but have since been replaced by others.

Princess Alessandra Torlonia bought the villa in 1866; you can only visit it by sending a written request. (To make matters still more confusing, there is also a *Museo Torlonia* in Trastevere, which contains another large collection of classical sculpture.)

The **Via Salaria**, one of the oldest roads in Rome, dates back to the early Republic; its name indicates that it was used for the salt trade. Along it are the entrances to many catacombs, most of them unfortunately closed to the public. However, the **Catacombs of Priscilla**, at Nr 430, may be visited with a guide, who can show you some interesting murals dating from the 2nd or 3rd century AD. The original purpose of the catacombs is still uncertain.

SAN LORENZO

At the beginning of the 20th century, the Giolitti government, by making credit more easily available, effectively promoted the construction of public housing for the first time. For the most part, it was building co-operatives which realized the concept of low-cost housing, usually in the form of working-class housing estates in newly opened-up areas. Thus, whole new neighborhoods with their own infrastructure sprang up at Testaccio, San Saba, and, extending eastwards from the main railroad station, the district of **San Lorenzo**. The university and the Policlinico group of hospitals were also located here.

"We will not erect any shapeless façades consisting of nothing but glass and iron or boring, grey concrete, like those being constructed these days in northern Europe. Instead we will place spacious, elegant entrance halls as the central focus of our buildings. In other words, they will be typically Italian, indeed typically Roman." This was the proud boast of the architect Marcello Piacentini in 1933. The year before, Mussolini had commis-

sioned him to undertake the planning and construction of the **Città Universitaria**.

Under his direction a team of young architects worked on designs for the university institutes, library, Aula Magna, museums and student accommodation. Functionalism dominated, and decorative elements were largely eschewed. At the same time, these flat-roofed buildings incorporated the very latest in technology. The Botanical, Physics and Mathematical institutes were regarded at the time as something entirely new in architecture. Beside the buildings of the various faculties are the administrative offices with the university library known as the *Alessandrina*, founded in 1670 under Pope Alexander VII, and transferred from the old La Sapienza university to the new one in 1935. Next to these is the modern church of **Divina Sapienza**, also designed and

built by Piacentini, and consecrated by Pope Pius XII in 1948.

On the other side of the Viale dell' Università, to the north of the university, are the adjacent university clinics and the **Policlinico Umberto I**. When it was built between1886 and 1903, this extensive hospital complex was the pride and joy of the young capital city. The modern pavilion-style buildings of the separate medical departments, set in a large area of gardens, are connected by bridges which, because structural steel could be used for the first time in their construction, seem to swoop effortlessly over the open spaces. The hospital complex has of course been repeatedly expanded and updated since its construction. Today it has more than 3,000 beds.

The macabre jokers among the Roman population claim it's no accident that right next to the hospital, which unfortunately suffers from a dubious medical reputation, is the city's biggest graveyard. This is the **Campo Verano**, *Il Verano* for short, an extensive old park

Above: The stillness of the Campo Verano.
Right: Typical Roman funeral niches in the Campo Verano.

which at the end of the 19th century was turned into what is now the largest cemetery in Rome. The monumental entrance, built in 1874 by Virginio Vespignani, is guarded by the four massive figures of Silence, Charity, Hope and Meditation. Passing through it we come to a quadruple portico which ends in the chapel of **S. Maria della Misericordia**. Numerous graves in the *fin-de-siècle* style stand in rows in the park-like cemetery grounds. A circular war memorial recalls the men of Rome who fell in World War I.

Outside the cemetery is the **Piazzale di San Lorenzo** with the bronze statue of St Lawrence by Stefano Galletti (1865) at its center. The basilica of **San Lorenzo fuori le Mura,** situated directly on the piazza, is one of the oldest churches in Rome, and one of the city's seven pilgrimage churches. It was the only church in Rome to have been badly damaged by bombing in World War II, but with much skilful restoration work it has been returned to its original condition and can be appreciated again in all its simple beauty.

Admittedly, it's not a flawless example of an early Christian basilica, since, originally, it actually consisted of two churches. According to tradition, the original Constantinian building was erected here in 330 AD over the grave of St. Laurentius.

In the 5th century, Pope Sixtus III built an adjacent church dedicated to the Virgin, and it wasn't until the 13th century that Honorius III joined the two buildings. Ionic columns support the nave and two side aisles; the mosaic floor is Cosmatesque work from the 13th century; while the mosaic inside the triumphal arch, depicting Christ enthroned on the orb of the world, dates back to the 6th century. The throne in the apse is exclusively reserved for the Pope.

In the older basilica, which wasn't unearthed until the 19th century and lies lower than the rest of the church, are

preserved the relics of St Laurentius, St Stephanus and St Justus.

THE BANKS OF THE TIBER

One of the great works of construction around the turn of the century, which fundamentally altered the face of Rome, was the building of embankments along the Tiber. In 1859, the historian and painter Friedrich Pecht spent six months in Rome; his description of the Tiber's banks is of an idyll which was soon to be lost forever. "In the foreground, you can see a mill of which there were many to be found along the Tiber, close behind it the columns of the enchanting little temple of Vesta and beyond that the jumble of houses lining the narrow streets of the Ghetto."

In the course of Rome's history there were many projects for controlling the flow of the Tiber – some of them quite absurd – all designed to prevent it from bursting its banks, as it did regularly twice a year. The worst floods were in

1598 and 1870. On both occasions the water flooded St Peter's Square and even reached the Piazza di Spagna on the left bank of the Tiber, where the **Barcaccia**, the fountain in its center, shaped like a boat, recalls these disastrous floods.

Not until 1871 did a committee of experts finally draw up concrete plans to regulate the river. Even then, it was 1877 tbefore Gregorovius was able to report: "Work on the Tiber has begun. The banks are being cut away in several places, so that the picturesque appearance of the river is lost. Half of the garden of the Farnesina is being removed... The Ponte Sisto is at present being widened, and houses are being pulled down on the Trastevere side... A society is to be formed to recover the antiquities which it is hoped will be found in the Tiber."

By the time the works were completed, shortly before World War One, the river,

which had been the heart and soul of Rome, had more or less vanished from the cityscape. This vital artery, which for thousands of years had supplied the Romans with goods, was enclosed within embankment walls fourteen to sixteen feet (4 m-5 m) high and thus hidden from the eyes of the city's residents.

Streets were built along the embankments and these developed into broad traffic corridors known as *lungotevere*. This mammoth undertaking, which by 1900 had already cost the vast sum (for those days) of 100 million lire, had swallowed up the picturesque appearance of the riverbanks with their original buildings, as well as the harbor called Ripetta, which had stood there since Baroque times. Today the buildings along the embankments face a new threat in the form of steadily increasing traffic, while the many attempts to reincorporate the Tiber in the life of the city have all failed.

Experts of the period generally considered that regulation of the Tiber was a necessary prerequisite for developing the

Above: The Tiber may have been tamed, but Rome's anglers can still enjoy it.

TESTACCIO / AVENTINE

0   150m   300m

Prati, the marshy meadows behind the Castel Sant'Angelo, into the built-up city district that stands there today. No less an expert than Baron Haussmann, the designer of modern Paris, gave the Romans technical help and advice.

The area, much of which was owned by the church, was particularly at risk from flooding. It was considered damp and unhealthy and, what is more, impossible to build on, because the nature of the subsoil meant that any building erected on it was liable to subsidence. A prime example is the case of the Palace of Justice.

THE PALACE OF JUSTICE

One day in 1971 officials and visitors in the Palace of Justice were alarmed by a heavy thud. A block of stone weighing several hundredweight had detached itself from the vaulted ceiling of a corridor and crashed to the floor. All over the walls, cracks and bulges began to appear; at first, people thought that an earthquake had struck. Experts were summoned, and ordered the immediate evacuation of the building. In the ensuing chaos quite a few files went missing, and the Roman newspapers were hardly sympathetic. "La guistizia sta crollando", trumpeted the headlines: "Justice is crumbling."

What had happened? The monumental building, Guglielmo Calderini's greatest work, built on the right bank of the Tiber between 1889 and 1910, had become the victim of its own great weight. The three-storey edifice, which was originally supposed to be a storey higher, constructed from outsized blocks of travertine, was sinking deeper and deeper into the Tiber bank's sandy soil.

A relatively minor change in the water table was responsible for finally triggering the disaster, which necessitated years of restoration work. This "architectural monstrosity" had always been a thorn in the Romans' side; after this incident, it was a running joke in the city to compare the tottering Palace of Justice, built on sand, with its neighbor, the Castel Sant'

163

Angelo, which had stood for 1500 years on its solid foundations.

MONTE TESTACCIO AND THE AVENTINE

A little further downstream is a man-made hill, the **Monte Testaccio** (Potsherd Hill"). Since classical times, when the old harbor with its commercial docks and market halls were located here, this mound of *amphora* or pottery fragments rose to a height of 131 feet (40 m).

Today the hill affords an unusual perspective of the city; from here, you can see not only the historic parts of the city, but also the less scenic suburban districts. One example is the traditionally working class district of **Testaccio** at the foot of the hill, which in recent years seems to have become an "in" place to live, in spite of its gasometer, visible from miles

Above: Rustic idyll in the Testaccio. Right: The Pyramid of Cestius.

around, and the old, abandoned slaughterhouse.

To the south you can see the EUR (Esposizione Universale di Roma) with its characteristic "square Colosseum," to the east are the Protestant Cemetery and the Pyramid of Cestius, to the north the Aventine and to the west, on the other side of the Tiber, the residential area of Monteverde.

A few junk dealers live around the foot of the hill; wine is stored in the cool "caves" carved into the pottery mountain's side; and more and more "in" bars are opening in the area, many of them offering excellent music, making Testaccio a popular spot in Rome's night life.

Testaccio itself has a genuine working-class Roman atmosphere. As if to remind one of the proximity to the former slaughterhouse, countless local trattorias serve excellent dishes made from offal, so typical of traditional Roman cooking.

When the famous English poet, Percy Bysshe Shelley, had to bury his small son in the new **Protestant Cemetery**, he found it so beautiful that he wrote: "It might make one in love with death to think that one should be buried in so sweet a place." And in fact when he drowned three years later, his ashes were brought here for burial.

Until the end of the 18th century, non-Catholics could not be buried in a Catholic cemetery or a Catholic church. Their interments, furthermore, had to take place under cover of darkness, by torchlight, and protected by the Roman police. The papal authorities had therefore made available the area outside the Porta San Paolo, directly alongside the Aurelian Wall, as a non-Catholic cemetery. In 1748 it appeared for the first time on a map of the city (by Giambattista Nolli) with the description: "Place where the Protestants are buried."

In a manner of speaking, the first grave on the site was the **Pyramid of Gaius Cestius**, a brick pyramid faced with marble which is the striking memorial to a Tribune of the People who died in 12 BC. From a 72 ft (22 m) square base it rises to a height of 89 ft (27 m).

The first graves of common folk were in the open on the *Prati del popolo romano*, the meadows of the Roman people. Originally this was a scene of much merry-making since the city of Rome owned two wine cellars beneath the Testaccio hill, and numerous taverns had sprung up around them. There were frequent drunken brawls, and the unprotected graves lying in the middle of the *campagna*, grazed on by sheep during the day, were often desecrated at night.

In 1803 the eldest son of the Prussian envoy Wilhelm von Humboldt died in Rome; his younger brother followed four years later. Both were buried outside the walls in a nocturnal funeral, and their father put up two gravestones which in those days had to be protected by a fence.

In 1821, when the English Romantic poet John Keats died of consumption in his house at the foot of the Spanish Steps

at the age of 26, negotiations about setting up a walled cemetery were in progress. The Papal Secretary of State, Cardinal Consalvi, acceded to the request of the diplomatic representatives of Prussia and Russia, and the cemetery was fenced in – at the expense of the Holy See, no less.

In 1894 the German Embassy bought another acre (0.4 ha) of land, to add to the existing cemetery grounds. Four years later the simple but dignified funeral chapel was built at the end of the avenue of cypresses.

Until 1870 every inscription on a gravestone or monument had to be submitted to a papal commission for approval, and no crosses were allowed on the graves. With the dissolution of the Papal State these intolerant regulations also came to an end.

But it wasn't until 1921 that the current guidelines for this burial ground were established. According to these, it is stated that the cemetery is open to all foreign states who have Protestant and Orthodox

citizens." In 1953 the term "citizens of the Protestant or Orthodox faith" was replaced by "non-Catholic citizens."

More than 4,000 people have found their last resting place here; it has a special attraction for visitors to Rome as a "cemetery of poets and thinkers." In addition to Keats and Shelley (who drowned while sailing in 1822), there are many English literary figures including the historian J. Addington Symonds (d.1893) and the novelist R.M.Ballantyne (d.1894).

Goethe's son August, who died in Rome in 1830, is buried here. Goethe himself presumably also toyed with the idea of making this his last resting place, since he enthuses in his *Roman Elegies*: "O how happy I feel in Rome!...Tolerate me, Jupiter, to come here, and later, Hermes, lead me gently past Cestius' monument, down to Hades."

Among the important political figures who are buried here, the name of the co-

Above: The tombstone of the poet Keats.

founder and spiritual leader of the Italian Communist Party, Antonio Gramsci, has particular resonance. After spending twenty years in prison as an "enemy of the state," he died from the effects of his incarceration. To prevent his grave from becoming a place of pilgrimage for his supporters, the Fascists buried him furtively under cover of darkness in the Protestant Cemetery.

Between Monte Testaccio in the south and the deep inroad made by the Circus Maximus, which separates it from the Palatine, lies the quiet, green **Aventine Hill**. Climbing it from the direction of the Circus Maximus, up the Via Sabina, one passes the **Roseto di Roma**, the municipal rose garden, which starting in June opens into a mass of blossoms. A little further up on the right, behind an old brick wall, a lovely orange grove gives off an intoxicating scent, especially in winter. It reaches down to a terrace right on the bank of the Tiber, from where one has a superb view of the city.

Close by the orange grove is one of the most beautiful early Christian churches in all Rome, **S. Sabina**. This early Romanesque basilica was built in the 5th century over the house of a Roman convert to Christianity named Sabina; in 1222 Pope Honorius III presented it to the Dominican monks as a home. The main door, as old as the church itself, has remarkable carved-wood panels with biblical scenes, including one of the oldest known representations of the Crucifixion. The nave is supported by 24 Corinthian columns taken from a 2nd-century temple. Next to the church is a convent with a fine Romanesque cloister.

The Via S. Sabina continues as far as the **Piazza dei Cacalleri di Malta**, which was designed by Piranesi and decorated with mysterious esoteric symbols. In the garden door of the **Villa del Priorato di Malta** is a keyhole; anyone who peeps through is rewarded with a unique view of the dome of St Peters.

THE BIRTH OF MODERN ROME

Sightseeing

Between Piazza Venezia and Porta Pia: One of the most questionable monuments of turn-of the-century Rome is the **Monumento Nazionale a Vittorio Emanuele II** (National monument to Victor Emanuel II.) in the Piazza Venezia. Located in the eastern wing of the monument is the **Museo Centrale del Risorgimento** (for history of the Italian Risorgimento; information, Tel: 6793598); and also the **Museo Sacrario delle Bandiere della Marina Militare** (museum of naval memorabilia) open daily 9am-1.30 pm).

In the **Via Nazionale**, a wide thoroughfare linking the train station with the city center, stands the **Palazzo delle Esposizioni**, Via Nazionale 194, (10am-9pm, closed Tue, changing exhibitions of contemporary art). You can find a diary of events in the **Trovaroma** supplement to the Friday edition of the daily newspaper *La Repubblica*, or in the same paper under the heading *giorno & notte Roma*. In the Via di Firenze, a sidestreet off the Via Nazionale, is the **Opera House** (Teatro dell'Opera), Tel: 461755. This is worth a visit, despite the rather mediocre productions, because of its beautiful decor, and because any opera performance in Rome is a social event. The **Piazza della Repubblica** is known to the Romans as the Piazza Esedra. In the middle of the square stands the **Fountain of the Naiads**, and on the east side the church of **Santa Maria degli Angeli**, which Michelangelo built inside the Exedra of the ancient **Baths of Diocletian. The Baths Museum (Museo Nazionale Romano oder Museo delle Terme)** contains the most important collection of ancient works of art in Rome. Tue-Sat 9am-1.30pm, Sun 9am-1pm; since spring 1993 the exhibition rooms in the **Collegio Massimo** have been open to the public. The railroad terminus building, **Stazione Termini**, is well worth seeing from an architectural standpoint. In the **Via Veneto** you will find relics of 19th century grandeur, expensive shops, magnificent hotels, elegant bars and restaurants. A taste of the macaber: the burial-place of the Capucines in the church of **Santa Maria della Concezione** (Via Veneto 27). Near the **Porta Pia** at the end of the Via XX Settembre one can see the breaches in the city wall, made by the Italian revolutionary troops in 1870.

Outside the Aurelian Wall

The **Piazza Mincio** (well worth seeing!) is not far from the park of the **Villa Torlonia** (Via Nomentana) and the villa, where Mussolini once lived. One can walk to the **Campo Verano**, a park-like area with interesting gravestones. Next to it is the patriarchal basilica of **San Lorenzo fuori le Mura**, with a beautiful cloister. *Bus:* 11, 63, 65, 71, 109, 111, 163, 309, 311, 411, 415, 490, 492; *Streetcar*: routes 19, 19b, 30, 30b.

Testaccio and the Aventine
Transport connections

To the **Testaccio**: *Bus*: Routes 95 and 57. *Metro*: Line B (to Piramide station). From the Piazzale Ostiense one can get to the Pyramid of Cestius and the Protestant Cemetery and then on to the Tiber. To the **Aventine**: *Bus* Nr.94.

Sightseeing

At the foot of the "Hill of Potsherds" one should cast a glance over the area where the abbattoir used to stand. Domestic animals roam around here freely, and in the evenings the drivers of the horse-dawn carriages return home. If you climb the hill (entrance on the corner of Via Galvani and Via Zabaglia), you can look down the other side on to the **Pyramid of Cestius** (tomb of the praetor Caius Cestius, erected in 11 BC) and next to it the **Cimitero degli Inglesi** or **Cimitero Accattolico**, (non-Catholic Cemetery), entrance Nr 6 Via Gaio Cestio (open daily 8am-11.30am and 3.20-5.30pm in summer and 8-11.30am and 2.20-4.30pm in winter).

If you are in Rome in June, visit the **rose-garden** on the slope of the Aventin Hill. **The church of Santa Sabina** (Piazza Pietro d'Illiria) is one of the most beautiful early Christian basilicas in Rome. The Via S. Sabina ends in the **Piazza dei Cavalieri di Malta**. Look through the keyhole of the entrance to the Knights of Malta: you get a very unusual view of the dome of St Peter's!

Restaurants / Nightlife

In the little restaurants and trattorias of the district you find good Roman cooking. The music scene is well established on the Testaccio.
RESTAURANTS: TESTACCIO: **Checchino dal 1887**, Via Monte Testaccio 30, Tel: 5746318, typical Roman cooking. **Er Burino Molisano**, Via N. Zabaglia 25, Tel: 5742317. **Grottino – Da Rino**, Viale Aventino 40, Tel: 5750497. **Il Piccolo Angoletto Due**, Via Magazzini Centrali 8/B, Tel: 5744882. **Turiddu al Mattatoio**, Viale Galvani 64, Tel: 5750447, by the old abbattoir.
NIGHTLIFE: VIA VENETO: **Café de Paris**, Via Veneto 90, Tel: 4885284. **Harry's Bar**, Via Veneto 150, Tel: 484643.
TESTACCIO: **L'Alibi**, Via Monte Testaccio 44, Tel: 5748448, gay disco. **Alphe'us**, Via del Commercio 34/36/38, dancing, cabaret. **Spago**, Via Monte Testaccio 35, Tel: 5744999.

FROM FASCISM TO THE PRESENT

P. AUGUSTO IMPERATORE
PIAZZA DEL POPOLO
PIAZZA MAZZINI
FORO ITALICO
OLYMPIC VILLAGE
EUR / CINECITTÀ
THE BORGATE

(See map on pages 6/7)

PIAZZA AUGUSTO IMPERATORE

The Piazza Augusto Imperatore lies at the end of the Via Ripetta, between the church of S. Carlo al Corso and the Tiber embankment. The large, rectangular square is surrounded on three sides by grand, colonnaded marble buildings, while on the side facing the Tiber rises the Ara Pacis Augustae. The whole square is a typical example of the Fascists' determined, sweeping city planning: all the houses which had previously stood in the shadow of the **Mausoleum of Augustus** were demolished, to be replaced by the usual Fascist neoclassical buildings which surround the mausoleum today. Work started on the project in 1936; by 1940 nearly 7 acres (2.7 ha.) of residential space and whole networks of streets had disappeared. The circular mausoleum once stood 144 ft (44 m) high, was planted with cypresses and crowned by a statue of the emperor Augustus. It was his last resting place, together with his wife Livia, sister Octavia, and nephew Marcellus, as well as the emperors Tiberius, Claudius and Nerva.

Previous pages: Going home after a very tiring day. Left: Crowds in the Via Condotti.

The obelisks once flanking the entrance today stand in the Piazza del Quirinale and the Piazza dell'Esquilina. At that time, the whole monument was clad in white marble.

Near the banks of the Tiber, inside a protective glass-walled structure, stands the **Ara Pacis Augustae**, an altar which the emperor Augustus had erected some time between 13 and 9 BC, in order to commemorate peace after his campaigns in Spain and Gaul. The altar is surrounded by a high balustrade carved with wonderful reliefs depicting the imperial triumph and various allegories. This magnificent work wasn't rediscovered until excavations beneath the Palazzo Fiano in the Via del Corso uncovered it in the 19th century. Apart from the few pieces which are displayed in the Louvre and the Villa Medici, and have been copied, all the fragments assembled here are original. Some of the reliefs are very badly damaged; others were carefully restored in 1983. On the plinth of the glass cover enclosing the altar, on the side facing the mausoleum, you can read the testament of Augustus (*Res Gestae Divi Augusti*), in which the emperor gives an account of his political and military enterprises, in bronze lettering.

PIAZZA DEL POPOLO

If you walk along the Via Ripetta in a northerly direction, you will come to the **Piazza del Popolo**. This square is one of the most beautiful and impressive in Rome. It was originally laid out by Manetti in 1538 for Pope Paul III, but was remodelled by Valadier at the beginning of the 19th century, and is now a perfect example of neoclassicism in Roman architecture. The ground plan is in the shape of an ellipse, enclosed by two semicircular walls decorated with statues and sphinxes. At the center of the square stands the 80-ft-high (24 m) **obelisk** which Augustus had brought from the

Egyptian Temple of the Sun in Heliopolis and erected, at first, in the Circus Maximus. Valadier placed it on a fountain in the piazza; around it, at the four points of the compass, he placed four marble lions spitting out jets of water.

Above the eastern semicircle of the Piazza del Popolo lies the **Pincio** with its viewing terrace, also designed by Valadier, which offers the most beautiful view of the sun setting over Rome. The Pincio is said to have been the site of the fabled gardens of the Roman epicure, Lucullus.

To the north, the square is bordered by the Aurelian Wall and the Porta del Popolo. Here begins the **Via Flaminia**, an ancient road which led through Rimini to northern Italy, and along which, for centuries, pilgrims and other travellers from northern Europe headed for Rome. To the right of the Porta Flaminia stands the

Above: The twin Baroque churches in the Piazza del Popolo. Right: The Piazza del Popolo by night.

church of **S. Maria del Popolo**, built atop the tombs of members of the Domitian line, including, so it is said, the tomb of Nero, although his ashes had been scattered to the winds. Originally it was only a small chapel, but was later enlarged and finally, under Pope Sixtus IV in the 15th century, received its present Renaissance form, which was later altered slightly by Bernini. The church contains many works of art: frescoes by Pinturicchio, including the *Adoration of the Child* above the high altar; two masterpieces by Caravaggio, *The Conversion of St Paul* and *The Crucifixion of St Peter,* as well as the octagonal **Chigi Chapel**, designed by Raphael between 1513 and 1516 for the wealthy banker Agostino Chigi, and the mosaics in the dome, also based on designs by Raphael.

If you stand with your back to the Porta Flaminia and look out over the square in front of you, you'll see what was for many travellers from the north the very first impression of Rome. Even outside the wall they were overpowered

by one of the finest views in the city, the so-called *Tridente*, formed by the three streets radiating out from the Piazza del Popolo. In the middle, the **Via del Corso** runs straight as a die for nearly a mile (1.5 km), as far as the Piazza Venezia. In Roman times this street was called Via Lata and was, among other things, a place where horse races were held. At Nr 18 you will find the Goethe Museum, in one of the apartments where the famous poet stayed during his time in Rome.

On the right, the **Via Ripetta** leads diagonally down to the Tiber. Because of the risk of flooding and the proximity of the docks, it has always been rather more rustic and less exclusive than the other two streets. Today, the Academy of Arts is situated here, along with many small shops selling art books and postcards. To the left of the Via del Corso, the rather more fashionable **Via del Babuino** leads along the side of the Pincio Hill and through what is known as the "English quarter" to the Piazza di Spagna. The Renaissance palaces along this avenue now house art galleries, antique-dealers and fashion boutiques. Their roof-gardens offer views over the park of the Villa Borghese. Halfway along this boulevard stands the Babuino: a statue so covered with moss as to be unidentifiable, which the Romans have therefore irreverently dubbed "the baboon."

At the point where the three streets enter the Piazza del Popolo, one is struck by two almost identical Baroque churches: **S. Maria di Montesanto** and **S. Maria dei Miracoli**. Both were designed by Rainaldi and completed by Bernini. The difference between them lies in their ground plans: the left-hand church is elliptical; the right-hand one, circular.

The *Tridente* was laid out by the Renaissance popes and is a typical example of the conception of city planning current at that time. Other equally straight and noteworthy streets of this period are the **Via Sistina**, right above the Spanish Steps; the **Via di S. Giovanni** on the Celio; and the **Via Giulia** in the Field of Mars.

PIAZZA MAZZINI

To the north of the Castel Sant' Angelo lies the *della Vittoria* quarter, also known as the Mazzini quarter, since it's oriented toward the Piazza Mazzini, a circular, tree-lined piazza with a fountain in the middle. It was laid out in 1919 to a design by a German architect, and its style sets the tone for the whole area. This is, in fact, one of the rather rare instances in Rome of planned urban development. Streets built in concentric circles round the square are crossed by a total of eight other streets which radiate out from the piazza like a star. The most important of these is the **Viale Mazzini**, a broad boulevard with a strip of lawn down the middle, which runs from the Monte Mario to the Tiber.

Today the entire quarter is a residential district favored by senior executives and

Above: Peace and tranquility on the Pincio.
Right: The muscle-men of the Stadio dei Marmi.

professionals. The streets are lined with trees and filled with solid, well-built houses. Originally, the pavilions for the 1911 World Exhibition stood here. A similar development was realized around the Piazza Bologna, in the east of the city.

FORO ITALICO

Between the northward bend of the Tiber and the Monte Mario lies the **Foro Italico**, which was built by the Fascists between 1929 and 1937 and was originally named *Foro Mussolini*. At the entrance, facing the Duca d'Aosta Bridge over the Tiber, there's still an obelisk bearing the inscription *Mussolini Dux* (Mussolini the Leader).

Side by side are two large sports stadia: the **Stadio dei Marmi**, built under the Fascists, which is decorated with 60 marble statues of athletes around the perimeter; and the **Olympic Stadium**, designed by Paolo Nervi and completed in 1960 for the Olympic Games of that year. The latter seats 85,000 spectators and was renovated and partially roofed in for the 1990 soccer World Cup. The soccer fans of Rome make a pilgrimage here every Sunday to cheer one of the two local teams, AS Roma or Lazio.

The Foro Italico complex also includes the Academy of Physical Education, the indoor Olympic swimming pool, the open-air pool with a grandstand, the fencing hall, and a large number of tennis courts. The whole area is planted with tall, shady umbrella-pines. In the middle is the **Fontana del Globo**, a large fountain with a round basin decorated with mosaics and a great marble sphere in the center. Above the sports grounds rises the **Monte Mario**, one of the last remaining green spaces within the city limits. From the lookout terrace (which has a bar) there is a beautiful view over the Tiber and northern Rome.

THE OLYMPIC VILLAGE

Almost opposite, on the far bank of the Tiber, and enclosed by its northern bend, lies the so-called "Olympic Village," a development with 1,348 apartments built for the 1960 Rome Olympics. Originally, there was a little *borghetto* on the site, a hamlet called Campo Parioli. According to the zoning plan, the area should have been a public park area. What was actually built there were a number of square buildings made of concrete and cement blocks, arranged in rows and "soaring" on concrete pillars. They were designed by a group of architects (Cafiero, Libera, Luccichenti, Monaco and Moretti) and were formally opened in 1960 as accommodation for the athletes and their entourage. Today, the Olympic Village affords housing exclusively to employees of the state.

The 1960 Olympics were the impetus for a number of other building projects in northeastern Rome. Among the sports facilities in the immediate vicinity is the **Palazzetto dello Sport**, designed by

Nervi and Vitellozzi, a round, tent-shaped concrete building with reinforced concrete supports arranged in a star formation around it, which has a seating capacity of 5,000. A little closer to the Tiber is the Stadio Flaminio, which can hold 45,000 spectators and includes a swimming pool, fencing hall, three gymnasia and training tracks. Another important construction project was the **Via Olimpica**, which was to have linked the northeast of Rome with the EUR district in the southwest, where further sports facilities are located. However, it remained unfinished, and not until the World Cup in 1990 was it connected up with the ring road and motorway network. Another of Nervi's projects, completed in 1969, is the overpass of the **Corso Francia**, which sweeps over the Olympic Village on concrete stilts and links the two banks of the Tiber. The Olympics were also an excuse to build underpasses at the Porta Pinciana and along the Tiber. However, the Tiber underpasses, intended to accelerate and facilitate the flow of traffic

175

through the city along the whole length of the river, were never completed.

The Olympics also saw the completion of the **Leonardo da Vinci Airport** on the coast at Fiumicino. But it was another five years before a motorway was built linking it with the city; and train connections took another 30 years to complete.

These ambitious construction projects and interventions in city planning were jointly financed by the state, the municipality and the Italian Olympic Committee. They radically altered the appearance of the city in the 1960s and were realized without any regard for previously existing plans for the city's development.

A comparable situation arose in 1990 on the occasion of the soccer World Cup. Such periods make all too clear the prevalent pattern of Rome's urban development: uncontrolled and illegal building, unrestricted speculation, an astronomical rise in land prices, and only occasional intervention by the authorities. Countless development plans were consistently ignored and used only as a topic for discussions in the Schools of Architecture.

EUR

The modern district known as the EUR lies southwest of Rome, between the city and the coast. Since 1950 there has been a Metro connection between the EUR (Fermi station) and the Stazione Termini; until 1979, in fact, this was Rome's only Metro line. (There are now two). The arrow-straight **Via Cristoforo Colombo,** a ten-lane highway, runs through the EUR and on to the coast. This neighborhood was conceived, planned and laid out for a World Exhibition (**E***sposizione* **U***niversale* **R***oma)* to be held in Rome in 1942 in commemoration of the twentieth anniversary of Mussolini's march on the city. Construction work was interrupted during the Second World War, and not

Right: The "Colosseo quadrato" in the EUR.

taken up again until the early 1950s. What resulted was a modern residential and office district, with tower blocks, government offices, company headquarters and luxurious villas, as well as a church and several museums.

The layout and architecture of the whole district, based on an original design by Piacentini, Pacano, Rossi, Piccinato and others, are a faithful reflection of the pompous rhetoric of Fascism with their arcades, hemicycles, fountains, columns and pillars. Everything is clad in white marble; and to top it all off is the "square Colosseum," where the World Exhibition was to take place, and which was intended to recall the classicism of imperial Rome. Originally the EUR was planned over a pentagonal area of over 1,000 acres (420 ha.). Some of its most striking buildings are described below.

The **Palazzo della Civiltà del Lavoro** (Palace of the Nobility of Labor), more commonly called the "square Colosseum," rises to a height of 223 ft (68 m) with a square floor plan, and is surrounded on all four sides by a massive flight of steps. Each side is six storeys high, with nine arches. The **Palazzo dei Congressi** is a huge cube, with a high entrance hall, and surmounted by a large cross-vaulted roof. It is equipped with all the facilities of a modern conference center. On the **Piazza Guglielmo Marconi**, which forms the central focus of the area and is dedicated to the inventor of wireless telegraphy, stands a 148-ft-high (45 m) obelisk of white Carrara marble – a further example of the monumental style of the EUR. Also striking is the church of **SS. Pietro e Paolo**, a cube-shaped building with four side-apses and a dome; its dominating position is emphasized by a long flight of steps leading up to it. Among the museums on the Piazza Marconi is the **Museo delle Arti e delle Tradizioni Popolari**, with displays about Italian country life, folk art, costume, dance, and other customs.

Further to the south lies an artificial lake; beyond this, the **Palazzo dello Sport** was another Nervi design, forming part of the sports facilities for the 1960 Olympics. The building is circular, with completely glassed-in sides and a dome 330 ft (100m) in diameter. It seats 15,000; today, it serves as a venue for the few rock concerts held in Rome. The 1960s saw the opening here of the famous **Luna Park**, an all-year-round amusement park with a Ferris wheel and other rides, but these days its charm has become rather tawdry.

CINECITTÀ

On the Via Tuscolana, at the terminus of the Metro line A, lies the movie city of **Cinecittà**. This area was once the property of Princess Torlonia. In 1936, under the Fascists, this 1.5-acre (6000 sq. m) complex was designed by Roncoroni and built as a studio for the production of films for the regime: in 1940, 85 films were made here, and in 1941, no fewer than 89. But as the fortunes of war turned against Italy, production declined and finally dried up altogether. After July 25, 1943, the German army used the studios as a barracks, and they later served as a refugee camp. But as early as 1945 work began on rebuilding the film industry, with the United States serving as the main investor; it was thus that the Roman Hollywood came to be, which was to launch the great successes of the Neo-Realist directors in the 1950s and 1960s. The output in the 1970s chiefly consisted of so-called "spaghetti Westerns;" since the 1980s, the studios have been on the decline, and today are sometimes used for television or theatrical productions.

Since 1989, "Film City" has had a companion across the Via Lamaro, a large, two-storey shopping center that goes by the name of **Cinecittà 2**.

THE BORGATE

The Italian word *borgata* means a suburb, specifically and exclusively a suburb

of Rome. It was first coined in 1924 to describe a newly built district in the drained swamp around Acilia, 12 miles (20 km) outside Rome. Since then, all the suburban developments which have shot up all around the city more or less overnight are *known as borgate*. These are not *borghi*, or townships in the true sense, but a sub-species of them, without infrastructure, without schools, in fact only provided with the bare essentials of water and electricity: in effect, huge dormitories left to their own devices.

At the beginning of the 20th century immigrant laborers, drawn to the growing city to work on construction, began to form spontaneous, informal settlements. During the Fascist period, the suburbs that had grown up in this way became part of a deliberate planning policy: its goal was the destruction of the old, organic heart of the city, which would

Above: Hardly an idyll of suburban life. Right: The Palazzo dei Congressi in the EUR.

make it easier to isolate the great monuments of antiquity, and appropriately display their grandeur. In the process, the district around the Capitoline Hill was flattened, as were the area between the Capitoline and the Colosseum, the Borgo quarter before the Vatican, and the houses which stood in the way of excavations on the Largo Argentina. The people who had lived in these demolished areas had to be resettled; new housing, therefore, was quickly built for them, of the very poorest quality. Fifteen years of this "bulldozer policy" created the *borgate* of Acilia, San Basilio, Prenestina, and Gordiani; in the next five years (from 1935 to 1940), the borgate of Trullo, Tiburtino III, Pietralata, Tufello, Val Melaina, Primavalle, Tor Marancio and Quarticciolo also sprang up.

The residents of these new suburbs were given their own name: *borgatari*. They played a significant role in the films of the Italian Neo-Realist school, and later in the novels and films of Pier Paolo Pasolini, such as *Accattone*, *Mamma*

Roma and *La Ricotta*. The Fascist state's deliberate policy of social and geographical segregation was followed in the post-war years by so-called spontaneous development, or, more accurately, the policies of the relevant "independent authorities," who worked independently of any kind of urban planning, as well, even though they were the local authorities for public housing and housing cooperatives. The results: the city's uncontrolled, haphazard expansion along the old consular roads and deep into the countryside, right beside the newly-built industrial zones; suburban apartment blocks built taller and taller, packed more and more closely together; poor transportation links with the city; and often a lack of even the most basic social amenities: no schools, no hospitals, no parks, no sports facilities, and so on.

In the mid-1970s a comprehensive plan for the improvement of the *borgate* was finally set in motion. The much-needed infrastructure (water, electricity, sewers, local public transport) was established; schools and health centers were built, parks laid out and proper access roads constructed. The scattered estates were finally linked up with and incorporated into the city itself. In the meantime, however, new housing developments, known as *borghetti*, have sprung up, and the whole process has begun all over again: private and unauthorized building is followed by the systematic, intense, and equally unauthorized construction undertaken by building speculators. When everything is finished, the city authorities are forced to provide the necessary infrastructure. And so it goes on, with no planning or control.

The last twenty years

Rome is certainly a city which continually develops, at least in the sense of urban expansion; recently, there's been building even beyond the *Gran Raccordo*

Anulare, the orbital motorway which was intended to enclose the entire built-up area of the city. But the city has also developed in terms of its demographic features: the average age of the population is increasing, there are more and more immigrants from developing, Third World countries; and until the birth-rate began to decline in 1979 there was a continuous growth in population. Habits, traditions, and lifestyles in the city have also changed; more and more people are living alone, which means that more and more apartments have to be built.

For the past two decades Rome has been divided up into 20 *circoscrizioni*, each one as large as a medium-sized Italian city, which take over a variety of functions and are supposed to help decentralize the city.

Recently, giant supermarkets and shopping centers have been built around the periphery; newspapers, insurance companies, advertising agencies, software producers and other industries which aren't dependent on a particular

location have established their offices away from the center of Rome.

This economic development was characteristic of the 1980s, but since the beginning of the 1990s the effects of the recession have been as noticeable here as in the rest of Italy. One important economic factor in Rome is the tourist trade, and this, in recent years, has experienced a serious decline. Far too many potential visitors have stayed away, avoiding the high prices, fearing the Mafia and the rising crime rate, believing that the city is allowing its cultural heritage to decay, and tired of facing the locked doors of yet another museum or gallery which is *in restauro* for an indefinite period.

The task of coming up with a new and comprehensive direction for the city's future urban development has been entrusted to Japanese architect Kenzo Tange, creator of the "Park of Peace" in

Above: Restoration is going on everywhere. Right: In the Via dei Fori Imperiali. Following pages: A Roman knife-grinder.

Hiroshima. Tange's plan envisages three major city centers: the historic center, which is to be developed into an "Archaeology Park" and become the cultural focus of the city; the EUR, which will be the site of administrative offices and corporate headquarters; and a new center in the east of the city for banks and government ministries. These three complexes are to be linked by a Metro network and underground tunnels. To counteract the stream of people and traffic into the historic center, which is directly linked to the concentration there of ministries and businesses, Tange proposes not only moving these institutions out to the city's periphery, but also introducing a greater concentration of improved communications and data-transmission technology, to facilitate the exchange of information between different administrative centers and make it unnecessary for employees to move so often from place to place.

The law *called Roma Capitale*, passed at the end of 1990, provides a ten-year financing scheme to support the measures so badly needed to keep the city alive, as well as other projects designed to relieve the center of the burden of commuter and transit traffic.

Despite the improvements to the infrastructure which were carried out in time for the World Cup in 1990, Rome continues to suffocate from the effects of the private car (1.8 million cars are licensed in Rome; an average of 800,000 of these are believed to be in use on any given day). Air pollution has reached such alarming proportions that the *centro storico* is now closed to private cars for eight hours every day.

A Utopian "Archaeology Park"

The **Via dei Fori Imperiali** is a typical example of Fascist urban planning: of tearing down, that is, entire neighborhoods dating from the Middle Ages or Renaissance in order to isolate and set off

ancient monuments from the built-up areas around them. When it was first built, the street was named Via dell' Impero (referring, of course, to Mussolini's "empire"). It ran straight as an arrow from the Colosseum to the Piazza Venezia, and was originally intended as a triumphal avenue for Fascist processions. Even to this day annual military parades on Republic Day still take place along it.

The construction of the Via dei Fori Imperiali meant levelling an entire district of the city. What is more, the avenue covers an area of excavations which comprises about 84% of the original Forum Romanum. What we see today, therefore, is only a fraction of all the Fora which still lie undiscovered in the valley between the Quirinal, Capitoline and Esquiline Hills. Today the street is an important traffic artery as well as being a kind of runway from which to view the massive ruins of the Fora.

The *Roma Capitale* legislation will support the creation of an "Archaeology Park" beside the Via Appia Antica. When this plan is eventually realized, a wedge-shaped area of green park-land will run from the Via Appia Antica up to the slopes of the Capitoline Hill, that is, into the heart of the city. It is hoped thus to restore the city's relation to the surrounding Campagna, today threatened by the city's uncontrolled expansion and the illegal building of suburban estates.

The "Fora Project" was inaugurated in 1978. However, the excavations which are supposed to connect the different parts of this archaeological zone have unfortunately thus far only achieved the limited result of removing the *Via della Consolazione*, which ran underneath the Senatorial Palace and separated it from the Forum Romanum.

Excavations of the Via dei Fori Imperiali, on the other hand, tentatively begun in 1983, soon ceased again, not least because of a forceful campaign in the press, which had more to do with the political whims of the moment than with any real considerations of practical urban planning.

THE ROME OF THE LAST 50 YEARS

Sightseeing

From the **Piazza Augusto Imperatore** to the **Foro Italico**: There was not a great deal of building in Rome during the Fascist period, but there was certainly great destruction. Fine old buildings were demolished, to make way for Mussolini's grandiose projects, through which he wanted to be seen as a successor to Augustus.

By demolishing entire blocks and city districts the ancient monuments were exposed, as for example the **Mausoleum of Augustus** in the **Piazza Augusto Imperatore** (For information about opening-times, Tel: 67102070) and the **Ara Pacis Augustae**, open Tue-Sat 9am-12.30 pm and 3.30-5.30pm; Sunday and Monday 9am-12.30 pm.

If you walk from **Piazza Augusto Imperatore** to the **Foro Italico**, another of the *Duce's* grand projects, you can follow the **Via Ripetta** (Academy of Fine Arts; many art bookshops) to the **Piazza del Popolo**. Passing the church of **Santa Maria del Popolo** you continue up to the **Pincio**, from the **terrace** of which there is a wonderful view over the square and the domes of the city. Two of these border the piazza on the left-hand side; they belong to the twin churches of **S. Maria di Montesanto** and **S. Maria dei Miracoli**. Between them, three streets radiate out to form the famous *Tridente*: the **Via del Babuino** (antique and fashion shops and art galleries), **Via del Corso** (a busy shopping-street) and the Via del Ripetta, along which you have come. Also worth seeing is the **Obelisk** in the middle of the square and the **Porta del Popolo**, once the city gate leading to the north. The two famous cafés, the **Rosati**, Piazza del Popolo 5a, Tel: 3225859 and 3611418, and the **Canova**, Piazza del Popolo 16, Tel: 3612231 and 3612227, offer an Espresso or a snack in elegant surroundings.

Passing the **Palace of the Navy Ministry**, you cross the Ponte Mateotti over the Tiber to **Prati** and the **Piazza Mazzini**. The **Foro Italico** provides a fine view of the **Monte Mario**.

Sport / Leisure

Large areas of green space surround the two stadia, **Stadio dei Marmi** and **Stadio Olimpico**. Here you will find one of only two (!) public swimming pools in the whole of Rome: the **Piscina del Foro Italico** (indoor and outdoor pools), open daily 9am-9pm. The second swimming-baths is the **Piscina delle Rose**, Viale Oceania, open daily, 9am-7pm (June to September only).

In the **Sports stadium** you can see soccer matches (for informationt: Tel: 3966733; *Bus:* 32,

48, 391). If you want some exercise, you can book a **tennis court** in the Foro Italico (Tel: 3619021), although your chances a slim because of the enormous demand for courts.

Restaurants

Some top-class restaurants around the Piazza del Popolo: **Casina Valadier**, Via Valadier, Tel: 6794189, Pincio, marvellous view, fancy prices. **Hassler Villa Medici**, Piazza Trinità dei Monti 6, Tel: 6782651, a very chic address, with prices to match, superb food, unforgettable view over Rome. **Ranieri**, Via Mario dei Fiori 26, Tel: 6791592, has a long tradition (founded in 1865 by a Neapolitan, who was once *Queen Victoria's* head chef).

IN THE EUR

Sightseeing

The EUR (*Metro:* Line B to the terminus, EUR-Fermi) not only contains a number of interesting museums, but is also worth visiting for its archticture and urban design.

From the mushroom-shaped viewing tower (Fungho) you get a good overview of the district. Important buildings: the **Palazzo della Civiltà del Lavoro** ("square Colosseum"), the **Palazzo dei Congressi**, the **church of S. Pietro e Paolo,** and the **Palazzo dello Sport**.

Museums

Museo del Alto Medioevo, Via Lincoln 3, Tel: 5915656, open daily 9am-1.30pm, Sundays and holidays 9am-12.30pm. Admission free. Modern museum of the Middle Ages.

Museo della Civiltà Romana, Piazza G. Agnelli 10, Tel: 5926135, open 9am-1.30pm, Sun 9am-1pm, Tue and Thu also open 4pm-7pm. Admission 4000 lire. The history of Rome is presented with the help of models and reconstructions. Didactically well planned, and particularly interesting for children.

Museo Nazionale delle Arti e Tradizioni Popolari, Piazza Marconi 10, Tel: 5926148, open 9am-2pm, Sundays and holidays 9am-1pm. Admission 4000 Lire; visitors under 18 and over 60 yeras old are allowed in free. Customs and daily life of the Italian people at the beginning of the present century. Also recommended for children.

Museo Nazionale Preistorico Etnografico L. Pigorini, Piazza Marconi 14, open 9am-1.30pm, Sundays 9am-1pm. Admission 6000 lire; visitors under 18 and over 60 years old are allowed in free. A large museum with prehistoric exhibits from different continents. On the second floor is a display of finds from the prehistory of the Italian peninsula.

THE EXPERIENCE OF ROME

Villas and gardens

If there were a map of Rome showing the city as it was before the unification of Italy, you could see that in and around the Aurelian Wall there were still many open green park areas. You would read names like *Villa Altieri*, *Villa Ludovisi*, *Villa Patrizi* and others – tracts of parkland which were all sacrificed to the building boom that took off as soon as Rome was named capital of Italy. More than anything, it was the speculators' greed which ultimately turned Rome into a city with fewer parks than any other major city in Europe. Every one of these parks has disappeared, and they would have vanished from human memory altogether had not traces of them survived here and there in the name of a street or in an old rustic

Previous pages: On the Piazza Navona. Above: Sunday in the Villa Pamphili. Right: Amore in the Villa Borghese.

manor house which miraculously managed to escape the pickaxe and today suffocates in traffic fumes. Yet it is open to question whether the Romans appreciate even the few patches of green that the city still calls its own. The ancient parks are neglected and are suffering from vandalism which, thanks to the indifference of the local authorities, has become virtually routine.

You should walk at least once up the steep Gianicolo to the Piazza Garibaldi: from the terrace you can look over the wonderful domes and church spires of the Baroque city all the way to the gentle outline of the distant Alban Hills. But if you turn your gaze from this impressive panorama and look down at the green slopes of the Gianicolo, you will see, among the weeds, innumerable bits of waste paper and garbage of all kinds. And should you be seized by a desire to stroll through the park, between the busts of Garibaldi's comrades-in-arms which are scattered along the so-called *passeggiata*, you will see that these poor heroes

who died for their fatherland have become a favorite target for vandals, whose graffiti scrawls are executed in indelible paint, making them virtually impossible to remove.

If you walk a few yards beyond the Porta S. Pancrazio along the street of the same name, you'll come to the largest public park in the city, the 45-acre (18 ha.) **Villa Doria Pamphili**. Yet even here, despite the beauty of the park and the elegant architecture of Algardi's fountain and pretty little 18th-century summer-house (unfortunately not open to visitors), you can't help but be annoyed at the defacing of the many statues which surround the so-called *giardino segreto*. Not a single one still has its head; of the Venus who used to stand in the wall surrounding the little palace, and for whom the fountain is named, only the legs remain. The vandals didn't even spare the statue of the Madonna, erected in memory of the French soldiers who fought against Garibaldi's volunteers in the year 1849.

Things are not quite so bad in the **Villa Sciarra**, which lies on the same hill. The statues here were brought from an unknown villa in Lombardy and set up in the park by its last owner, an American millionaire named Wirtz. So far they have by and large escaped the hooligans' mania for destruction, probably because they are not made of marble and therefore present less of a temptation. Take a look at this park before these gray, slightly weathered stone statues have been ruined like the others.

Even where there hasn't been any nocturnal desecration, the paths and flower beds where Rome's patrician families once frolicked have been disfigured with dirt and litter. This is the case in the **Villa Borghese**, the best-known and most visited public park in the capital. The Villa Borghese was built in the 17th century by Cardinal Scipione Borghese; in the 18th century one of his descendants, Prince Marcantonio Borghese, brought the Scottish gardener Jacob More in from Edinburgh to lay out the gardens. These

187

were expanded in the early 19th century, and in 1902 were bought by the state and opened to the public. Today, apart from the fact that many of the statues here, too, are headless, the paths and vegetation could do with much more attention, especially the centuries-old trees, in whose hollow trunks rubbish often collects. And perhaps one day the poor old Mephistopheles on the Goethe Monument should be given back his nose and, even more important, his horns.

Perhaps, also, the old **Zoo** on the north side of the Borghese park should be given a new home. Admittedly, the Zoo is still worth a visit: not for the cramped cages in which the animals are housed, but for the attractive buildings which were erected in the 1930s in the colonial style. The most successful examples of this are the *Museo Africano*, the restaur-

ant, and especially the pretty entrance to the zoo itself.

It is a great pity that one is forced to make such negative observations about all these places, which under different circumstances would be really enchanting; and that one is confronted time and again with the litter left by indifferent visitors, or with the dilapidation of the buildings, such as the neoclassical **Villa Torlonia**, on which restoration work has finally started. There is only one public park which can be unequivocally recommended: the **Botanical Garden**, laid out in the former gardens of the Palazzo Corsini, for which you have to pay admission to enter. Sad to say, it's perhaps the fact of having to pay that has made the Romans really respect this place.

Museums and galleries

In the course of its history, the whole city of Rome has itself become a work of art of massive proportions. Built with the wealth of great Roman families, who thus

Above: The bust of Constantine the Great in the Capitoline Museums. Right: Cultural treasures in the Vatican Museums.

influenced the overall look of the city with their own personal and varied notions of taste, the facades of its palaces and churches open up a new world of impressions of the cultural history of the West to the visitor. Many of the museums and galleries housed in these buildings were not originally intended for the eyes of the public, but were the private collections of these Roman families. Therefore they fill out, in effect, the overall picture of the city's history.

Hardly another city in the world boasts as many art treasures as Rome. It's open to question whether the Romans truly appreciate the value of this cultural heritage. From their opening times to their presentation and display, the organization of the museums leaves a lot to be desired. After all, it's a bit unusual that the museums and art galleries of a major world capital should normally close for the day at 2 pm. It is only since 1992 that the new Minister of Culture has been endeavoring to make radical changes, which involved disputes with regional politicians as well as the trade unions. Today there are indications that a complete reorganization of the museums and will soon bring them up to the standard of those in other European capitals.

As a way of familiarizing yourself with ancient history, we recommend that you begin with the **Museo Nazionale della Civiltà Romana**, even though it contains no original objects. Its explanatory style of presentation and manageable size combine to make it an excellent place in which to gain an overview of Roman antiquity. Like a picture book, it unfolds aspects of the crafts, agriculture, warfare, legal system, manners, and customs of daily life in Ancient Rome. Of special interest is the model of the city as it looked in the 4th century AD, built to a scale of 1: 250. This is a good museum for children; after a visit here, they'll be able to make more sense of the ruins of the imperial Fora.

A visit to the **Capitoline Museums** is also indispensable to a better understanding of antiquity. The private collec-

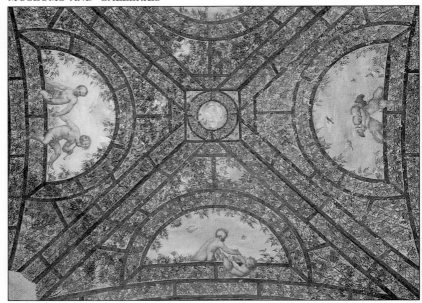

tions of ancient works of art in the **Museo Capitolino** and the **Palazzo dei Conservatori** on the Capitoline Square were presented to the Roman people as a gift by Pope Sixtus IV in 1471, which makes them one of the first known public art collections of modern times. They contain a wealth of classical sculptures of the Roman period and excellent copies of Greek originals.

In the *Sala dei Conservatori* of the Palazzo dei Conservatori stands the original statue of the she-wolf suckling the twins Romulus and Remus. Another famous statue is *Boy Plucking a Thorn from his Foot* (*Spinario* in Italian); while in the inner courtyard you can see the massive remains of the colossal statue of the emperor Constantine, which once stood 40 ft (12 m) high.

The museum also has an adjacent picture gallery, which was founded in 1748 by Pope Benedict XIV, comprised of

Above: A magnificent painted ceiling in the Villa Giulia.

items from the former Sacchetti collection. On display here are paintings by Titian, Tintoretto, Lotto and Velasquez, among others.

Anyone interested in the pre-Roman culture of the Etruscans should be sure to visit the **Museo Nazionale Etrusco** in the Villa Giulia. This villa originally served as a summer residence for Pope Julius III, who commissioned its design from the architect Vignola and had it built in 1551-1553. It was first opened to the public as a museum in 1889. Displayed here are many extremely interesting Etruscan finds from Latium, Tuscany and Umbria.

A short way east of the Villa Giulia, in the Via Gramsci, is the British School at Rome, designed by Lutyens, with a façade based on that of St Paul's Cathedral. A study center for archaeology and the fine arts, it is frequented by many British students who come on scholarships.

An important feature of Rome's museum landscape are the numerous galleries which house the collections of rich patrician families. Predominant among these is the **Galleria Borghese** in the Villa Borghese, surrounded by one of the largest parks on what was once the edge of the city, outside the ancient walls. The gallery was founded in 1615 by Cardinal Scipione Borghese; in 1902 both the villa and its park came into public ownership. Today, it is one of the most valuable art collections in all of Rome, with sculptures which can be numbered as among the most beautiful in the world, including the first statues of Bernini, whose talent had early been recognized by Cardinal Borghese.

The marvellous sculpture of Paolina Borghese lying half-naked on a divan, carved in white marble by Antonio Canova (1757-1822), can also be seen on the ground floor of the villa. Paolina was the sister of Napoleon and was married to Prince Camillo Borghese. Her nearly nude statue created a major scandal at the time, and was therefore kept under lock and key for many years. The painting collection on the upper floor is closed at the moment for extensive restoration.

Following the example of those wealthy noble families who indulged their passion for collecting art, other galleries were created in Rome. One such is the **Galleria Doria Pamphili**, in the center of the city. The collection, started by the sister-in-law of Pope Innocent X in the mid-17th century, is still privately owned and so is not always open to the public. Then there is the **Galleria d'Arte Antica** in the massive Palazzo Barberini, where, among other things, you can look at Raphael's celebrated *Fornarina*.

Also in central Rome is the **Galleria Spada** in the palace of the same name, which houses several important works of the Italian Mannerist school. On the upper floor there is a small, valuable collection of paintings, including works by Domenichino, Titian, and Sebastiano del Piombo. When here, don't neglect to notice Borromini's optical illusion, the small colonnade which he designed to look much larger than it really is.

Very close by, in the Palazzo Farnese, now occupied by the French Embassy, is the **Galleria Farnese, but it's far from easy to get permission to visit it.** If you would like to see the **spectacular frescoes of the Galleria Caracci,** you should submit an application in writing before setting off on your trip.

In the Palazzo Braschi, near the Piazza Navona, the **Museo di Roma** is worth a visit for anyone interested in the history of Rome from the 18th century onwards.

The subject of Italian unification is covered by the **Museo del Risorgimento**, which contains historic documents from the period. More historical detail is provided by the **Museo Napoleonico**, where you can even admire a marble replica of the breasts of Napoleon's sister Paolina. The museum has only recently been reopened and displays furniture and various other items from the collection of Count Primoli, a distant relative of the Bonaparte family.

You can round out your knowledge of Roman antiquity by visiting the little **Museo Barracco**, where Baron Barracco's collection of classical sculptures of various cultures is displayed; the museum has been open to the public since 1902. Modern art is represented by works from the period 1900-1950 in the **Galleria Nazionale d'Arte Moderna**, though even this building is only partly open to the public.

Among the specialized museums in Rome are the **Goethe Museum**, where memorabilia and drawings dating from Goethe's sojourns in the city are displayed; the **Keats and Shelley Museum** on the Spanish Steps, where you can see the room in which the poet John Keats died at the early age of 26; and the quaint **Museo delle Anime del Purgatorio**, the Museum of Souls in Purgatory, whose small collection contains what is claimed to be evidence of reincarnation.

Shopping and markets

To begin with, let it be plainly said: Rome is expensive. With the exception of public transportation, everything in Rome, be it eating in restaurants, buying clothes, or going to the cinema, carries a hefty price tag. A tourist might well think that he had landed in a city of millionaires when he sees how full the restaurants and cinemas always are, and seldom will he come across a Roman who is not impeccably dressed, usually in the very latest fashion.

But in fact, Rome is not a particularly wealthy city, at least in comparison to Milan, Bologna or other industrial cities in the north. It's just that it's easy to "make arrangements" here, that is, somehow to secure a supplementary source of income. Regular salaries are often rather low. So you will frequently find a civil servant working as a janitor on the side, a

Above: In one of the many street markets in Rome.

teacher who gives extra private lessons, or a housewife selling cosmetics and detergents to her women friends. In short, in Rome – indeed, all over Italy – almost everyone manages by the end of the month to have picked up one or two extra 100,000-lira notes, which enable him or her to enjoy a better standard of living. Of course, there are a great many rich people, especially in the business community. (In many of these cases, great wealth is not so much a reflection of business success as of one's ability to get around the tax authorities; but this subject is a chapter unto itself.)

Food: Before you clothe your body, you have to fill your belly – preferably well and without spending an inordinate amount. The cheapest markets are of course the delightful open-air ones.

There are a great many markets in Rome, which are more or less expensive depending on the districts in which they happen to be situated. The little market in the Via della Croce, near the Piazza di Spagna, for example, is more expensive than the formerly "proletarian" market in the Via Andrea Doria. Similarly, the picturesque, oh-so-typical Roman market on the Campo dei Fiori is, precisely because it is so picturesque and typically Roman, no longer very reasonably priced (if it ever was); nevertheless, it can be recommended because the produce, and especially the fish, is particularly fresh here. Long live the markets, we say: note, however, that the choicest goods are kept back for the regular customers, and that a foreigner or a tourist is never served with quite the same attention.

Be particularly careful with fruit (you are not allowed to select your own), and when you buy cold cuts, make sure that the wrapping paper isn't weighed and included in the price. Electronic scales, which are compulsory these days, make it possible to subtract the allowance for wrapping. Unfortunately, many merchants forget this, in which case it does no harm to remind them.

In summation, one can say that it is still cheaper to do your food shopping in the much-despised supermarkets, although that you run the risk of going in to buy a quarter pound of ham and come out with a fully loaded shopping cart. Unless you are an inveterate consumer, don't hesitate to cross the threshold of one of these food palaces. You may not find such a wide choice, or even such a high quality, as in the markets, but you will certainly find the prices lower, and will not pay for more than the net weight.

Usually, the most blatant manifestation of Italian chauvinism is the Italians' claim that you can eat better in Italy than anywhere else in the world; but one result of this is that it can be difficult in Rome to buy international products. One little shop in the Via della Croce, called Ercoli, did use to offer a wide choice of foreign delicacies, from German *weisswurst* to peanut butter; but even this shop has now closed. However, if you look around in the neighborhood of the Piazza di Spagna, you'll probably be able to find one or two "exotic" products. And if you fancy drinking a good wine to accompany the fruits of your shopping labors, we can recommend one very special address: the *Enoteca Trimani* at Via Goito 20, very near the central railway station. The store has an enormous selection of wines, and the staff are always courteous and ready to advise you.

Clothes: The center of Rome, as the center of any other great European city, has become one huge display window to showcase all manner of goods, and not always of the highest quality. One by one, the old antiquarian booksellers and artisans' shops have disappeared, and even the fashionable clothing stores where you could buy camels-hair jackets or silk shirts are becoming increasingly difficult to find.

The street which has suffered the most from this change is the Via del Corso: within the last twenty years, it has been transformed from a boulevard for well-to-do residents of the district into a noisy playground for a new kind of crowd from the suburbs.

If you want to get your hands on jeans and sportswear at prices at least 30 % lower than those in the Via del Corso's boutiques, get on the Metro and ride out to the suburbs where the kids you see hanging around on the Piazza di Spagna come from. If you get out at the Giulio Agricola station, for example, and stroll along the Via Tuscolana, you will find exactly the same selection of goods on sale, but for significantly lower prices.

However the shops may differ in other respects, they all, unfortunately, have one thing in common: the unwelcome persistence of the salespeople. The bad manners of Roman shop assistants, which is in any case certain of its place in the annals of history, reaches particular heights in the expensive shops along the Via Borgognona and the Via Condotti. The sales staff there can spot at twenty paces

whether or not a customer plans to spend real money; those who don't are treated with the patronizing arrogance of an aristocrat toward a commoner.

If you prefer to do your shopping in peace and quiet, pick out your clothes for yourself, and use the salesperson at most as a source of unbiased opinion, then you should go to the *Rinascente*. In Rome there are two of these up-market department stores: one in the Piazza Fiume and the other in the Via del Corso. They aren't exactly cheap, but the quality is first-class, and you can browse at your leisure without having to disentangle yourself from an eager salesperson's clutches.

Another good address for customers of maturer years is 158 Via del Corso – an old, genteel store with modest window displays (something pretty rare in the Via del Corso) which goes by the name of *Schostal*. Here you can buy pullovers, shirts, towels and linen of excellent quality at reasonable prices. You will be extremely politely served by ladies in simple blue suits, and when you get to the cash register (to which you are always obligingly escorted), your change will be given in crisp, new bills, one of the shop's nice customs. One might almost think one was somewhere other than in Rome...

Porta Portese: No chapter on shopping in Rome would be complete without a word about this Sunday flea market in Trastevere. Unfortunately, the best purchase here is the one you don't make, since it's impossible to find anything in the Porta Portese that is really worth the price being asked for it. Probably the only things that come into question are the so-called "modern antiques," objects from the 1950s and 1960s; but even those are far from cheap. Porta Portese is always fun to stroll around, but it's not a place to shop. Don't, however, go there later than 10 am; after that, you will be crushed by the huge crowds. And always keep a sharp eye on your purse!

Above: What's keeping that bus?

VILLAS AND GARDENS

Villa Ada, Via Salaria; a beautiful park for solitary walks. **Villa Borghese**, beyond the city wall, outside the Porta Pinciana, including the **Zoological Garden**, open daily 8am-6.15pm, in winter till 5pm (closed on 1st May). Children and senior citizens are admitted free. In theVilla Borghese you will also find the **Casino Borghese** with its **museum** and **picture gallery**, open Tue-Sat, 9am-2pm, Sun 9am-1pm. At present only the lower floor can be visited because of renovation work.

Villa Celimontana, between the Colosseum and the Baths of Caracalla, entrance in the Piazza della Navicella. **Villa Corsini** (Botanical Garden), Largo Cristina di Svezia 24. Mon-Fri 10am-6pm (in summer till 7pm), Sat 9am-1pm; Admission: 2000 lire.

Villa Doria Pamphili, Via Aurelia Antica; the largest and most beautiful park in Rome, with broad green spaces and shady pines. **Villa Sciarra**, Via Dandolo, attractive small park dating from the 18th cent., in the Gianicolo area. **Villa Torlonia**, Via Nomentana, lovely, quiet park with the **Palazzo Torlonia**, built at the beginning of the 19th century, and currently being renovated.

MUSEUMS AND GALLERIES

The opening hours of museums and picture galleries change so frequently, that you should enquire about times by telephone before your visit. Museums that are not listed here can be found in the text of the relevant chapter.

Antiquarium Forense, Piazza S. Maria Nova 53, Tel: 6790333, daily except Tues, 9am-6pm, in winter 9am-3pm. Finds from the Forum Romanum.

Musei Capitolini, Piazza del Campidoglio, Tel: 6782862, daily except Mon, 9am-2pm, Tue and Thu also open 5pm-8pm; Sat, also open 8.30pm-11pm, Sun 9am-1pm. The world's oldest public museum, with a collection of ancient art. In the Pinacoteca Capitolina there are paintings from 15th-18th centuries.

Museo Barracco, Corso Vittorio Emanuele 168, Tel: 6540848. Tue-Sat 9am-2pm, Tue and Thu, also 5pm-8pm, Sun 9am-1pm. Closed August. Sculptures from various cultures.

Museo d'Arte Ebraica, museum illustrating the history of Roman Jewry, Lungotevere Cenci, Tel: 6864648, open Mon-Fri 10am-2pm, and 3pm-6pm, Sun 10am-12 noon, closed Sat.

Museo della Civiltà Romana, Piazza Agnelli 10 (EUR), Tel: 5026135,Tue-Sat 9am-1pm, Thu also 4pm-7pm, Sun 9am-1pm. Models and re-constructions from the history of Rome, e.g. of ancient Rome in the 4th century AD. At present a number of rooms are closed for rebuilding.

Museo delle Cere, Piazza SS. Apostoli 67, Tel: 6796482, daily 9am-9pm. Wax figures.

Museo delle Mura, Porta S. Sebastiano, Tel: 7575284, summer: Tue-Sat 9am-12 noon, Sun 9am-1pm, winter: Tue-Sa 10am-5pm, Sun 9am-1pm, history of the Aurelian Wall.

Museo di Goethe, Via del Corso 18, Tel. 3613356. Collection of drawings and memorabilia from Goethe's stays in Rome. Currently closed for rebuilding.

Museo Francescano dei Padri Cappuccini, Via V. Veneto – Chiesa di S. Maria della Concezione, daily 9am-1pm and 3pm-7pm.

Museo Keats-Shelley, Piazza di Spagna 26, Tel: 6784235, daily 2.30-5.30pm, closed Sat, Sun.

Museo Nazionale delle Arti e Tradizioni Popolari, EUR, Piazza Marconi 10, Tel: 5911848; Tue-Sat 9am-2pm, Sun 9am-1pm. Italian folk-arts.

Museo Nazionale di Castel Sant'Angelo, Lungotevere Castello 1, Tel: 6875036, daily 9am-2pm, Sun 9am-1pm, closed Mon.

Museo Nazionale Etrusco di Villa Giulia, Piazzale di Villa Giulia 9, Tel: 3601951, Tue, and Thu-Sat 9am-2pm, Wed 9am-6pm, (in summer 3pm-7.30pm), Sun 9am-1pm. Collection of artefacts from the Etruscan culture.

Museo di Palazzo Venezia, Piazza Venezia 3, Tel: 6798865, daily 9am-2pm, Sun 9am-1pm closed Mon.

Museo di Roma (Palazzo Braschi), Piazza San Pantaleo 10, Tel: 6865562, Tue-Sat 9am-2pm, Tue and Thu also open 5pm-8pm; Sun 9am-1pm. The museum itself is currently closed because of renovation, but the rooms of the palace are open for exhibitions.

Galleria Colonna, Via della Pilotta 17, Tel: 6784350; open Sats only, 9am-1pm.

Galleria Comunale d'Arte Moderna, Piazza S. Pantaleo 10, Palazzo Braschi, 9am-2pm.

Galleria Doria Pamphili, Via del Corso/Piazza Collegio Romano, Tel: 6794365; Tue, Fri, Sat, Sun, 10am-1pm; guided tours 10am-12 noon.

Galleria Nazionale d'Arte Antica, Via della Lungara 10 (Palazzo Corsini); Tel: 6542353. Mon, Sat 9am-2pm, Tue-Fri 9am-7pm, Suns and holidays 9am-1pm.

Galleria Nazionale d'Arte Moderna, Viale delle Belle Arti 1331, Tel: 3224151, daily except Mon, 9am-2pm, Sun 9am-1pm.

Galleria Spada, Piazza Capo di Ferro 3, Tel: 6861158, Tue-Sat 9am-2pm, Sun 9am-1pm, closed Mon, private collection, 17th century.

ROME BY NIGHT

Eating out

Here's a piece of useful advice: avoid the restaurants that have been done up to look oh-so-typically Italian! Whenever you see old farm-carts, saddles and other bits of rustic nonsense, you can be pretty sure that the bad taste is not limited to the decor – it will extend to the food as well. Don't trust restaurants that call themselves *Ostaria* (the correct term for an inn or tavern, even in Roman dialect, is Osteria), much less *Hostaria* (people stopped pronouncing the H even before the age of Augustus).

Another piece of advice: walk in the other direction if you see tables laid with lace-edged tablecloths and crystal glasses. A candle on every table is a particularly bad sign; worse still are pictures on the walls by some artist evidently attempting to reinvent Western art. Dinner here is likely to consist of a few bites rather than a hearty meal; all that's likely to be hefty is the bill, which reflects the services of the interior decorator rather than those of the chef.

And a third piece of advice: don't trust a restaurant that has been recommended to you by one of your fellow-countrymen. Since the days of Goethe, every traveller has felt compelled to make some kind of amazing discovery in Rome; but all too often, this "discovery" is some inferior *osteria* which no Roman would be seen dead in, and which is full of tourists taken in by the proprietor's inviting smile and folksy patter.

If you want to be sure of finding a place where you can eat well without paying too much, your very best bet is to ask a passer-by in the street for the name of a good and not-too-expensive restaurant. He will go to some trouble to think of an address for you, which you can later pass on to others with a clear conscience. Don't worry if you can't understand Italian too well: your informant will make extravagant use of gesture in telling you how to find the place.

Here the question arises of what kind of meal it is you want: Italian or Roman? Don't make the mistake of thinking these are the same. They are not. Just because you are in Rome doesn't mean you will automatically be given Roman food. Quite the contrary: the Romans themselves hardly know the cuisine of their own city; and most of what they do know, they don't much like. Just try putting a nice plate of *rigatoni* with *pagliata* in front of a Roman. Most of them would react by making a face. They have no idea what they're missing! This dish is one of the most traditional culinary delicacies of the Papal City: short pasta in a marvellous sauce of tomatoes and a piece of intestine from a suckling calf – a marvellous combination of ingredients which harmonize brilliantly with one another. Who first came up with the idea of making a sauce from ingredients which are usually regarded as waste? What gastronomic genius was inspired to mingle the noble *pomodoro* (literally "golden apple") with the tender innards of a young animal, full of the pure cow's milk which the creature had drunk and digested a short time previously? Don't say you are turning up your nose as well! In that case you probably will not want to try any other Roman delicacies. If you're intimidated by such a delicious dish as the *pagliata*, you will never have the pleasure of tasting a hearty *coratella* (a blend of fried liver, kidneys and artichokes). And if your palate is so sensitive (and unenterprising), how will you ever enjoy the divine cow's udder, or tasty *torciolo* (pancreas) or delicious *granelli* (bull's testicles – yes, really!). You have no idea of the pleasures you're forgoing!

Previous pages: The Fountain of the Four Rivers in the Piazza Navona. Right: An evening meal in the Trattoria Lilly.

And I haven't even mentioned *trippa* (tripe), or the wonderful *coda alla caccinara* (ox-tail).

How, you may ask, can a city which contains such masterpieces of art and architecture within its walls possibly have such a coarse, earthy cuisine? But however many domes, fountains and obelisks may have surrounded them, the ordinary people of Rome were poor, and obliged, generation after generation, to keep coming up with ways to survive and even to add a bit of "spice" to their bleak existence. The same genius which was able to combine the language of the Tuscan stonemasons who came to Rome in the 16th century with the local patterns of speech to create one of the most colorful dialects in the whole country is the driving force which lay behind devising an excellent cuisine from the unwanted offal of the slaughterhouse. Unable to treat themselves to steak, the Romans of previous centuries satisfied themselves with the innards and even the skin of various animals, creating from them such thoroughly tasty dishes as, for example, *fagioli con le cotiche,* an excellent concoction of pig's skin and white beans.

The Roman Campagna, where sheep and cattle grazed, was the fabled land of Arcadia, in which imaginary bucolic trysts took place between shepherds and shepherdesses, as tender and charming as the porcelain figures of Capodimonte. But the real living conditions of the poor herdsmen were quite different: all year round they were exposed to the vagaries of the weather and ran the risk of being stabbed to death by the many robbers who roamed the valleys and ravines of the hilly countryside of Latium. It was shepherds such as these who developed the dish which most typifies Roman cuisine: the *abbachio* or weaning lamb, so named from the blow of a heavy stick (*abbacchiatura*) with which they were killed. Also the invention of the shepherds are the two delicious, but very different, types of cheese which play such an important role in Roman gastronomy. What would Roman cooking be without

the creamy *ricotta,* which you can either mix with *maccheroni* or use in fillings for delicious sweet cakes? And, equally, what would it be without a plate of *spaghetti alla carbonara*, or a helping of *bucatini alla amatriciana,* generously sprinkled with grated *pecorino* cheese?

But the poor Campagna didn't restrict itself to providing Rome with nourishing main courses; it also came up with tasty side dishes, which harmonize perfectly with the good, honest cooking. When you're eating in a restaurant, order an arugula salad, but please call it a *rughetta*, and only dress it with oil and salt (vinegar is unnecessary, and would destroy the balance). Is the taste too strong for you? Then you may switch to an ordinary mixed salad – but only as long as it's brightened up with a few leaves of *mentuccia*! If you did like the rughetta, however, you should also try the delicious *puntarelle* with anchovies, or *cicoria* (en-

dive) which has been fried in a pan with garlic, olive oil and *peperoncino*.

There are many other dishes we could recommend; but unfortunately, many of the original Roman specialties are almost impossible to find these days. For instance, whatever happened to *spaghetti con le lumache* (snails), which used to be served on the Feast of San Giovanni? And there are only a few people left in Rome who still know how to make a *giuncata*, a heavenly dessert made of milk, for which someone in the last century, so the poet Belli tells us, actually risked his life by daring to venture into the bandit-ridden Campagna in search of the delicacy. And you don't see *copiette* any more. What's become of these strips of horse- or donkey-meat that had been dried in the sun and were served, sprinkled with *peperoncino, in osterie* to accompany a glass of wine?

Incidentally, which wines should be served with these various Roman specialties described above? A spontaneous answer to this question is Frascati, a dry

Above: Dining at the Piazza Navona.

white wine which is a perfect accompaniment to even the most flavorful *coratella* (although some would insist that a red wine is a better beverage for this dish). Ah yes, Frascati. If only there *were* such a wine! If only one could find it! You can read the name everywhere. Every supermarket offers a wide variety of bottles bearing the Frascati label. But the contents of the bottles give one cause for doubt. If all the wine that is sold in Italy under the name Frascati actually came from Frascati, then that attractive little town would be completely smothered under all the grapevines. Strictly speaking, however, it's not quite true that genuine Frascati can't be found. Certainly it can be found. But only in Frascati. And most of it is drunk by the people who make it. So when it comes to wine, just choose whatever catches your eye. If you like, you can ask the wine-waiter for advice, but you can be quite sure he'll recommend the most expensive bottle.

One can't really talk about Roman gastronomy without mentioning the exceptional Jewish cuisine which is an important element of the city's culinary tradition. But be careful only to eat Jewish specialties when you're in the Ghetto. Don't, therefore, order the most famous dish, *carciofi alla giudia* (artichokes Jewish style) unless you're somewhere near the Portico d'Ottavia. And if you are in this district, don't miss the opportunity to stock up on some of the sweet cakes and pastries from the *pasticceria* there, the smallest and best in all of Rome – and certainly the only one where, all year round and not just at Christmas time, you can buy the delicious baked goods which are so much a part of Roman and Jewish tradition. Located opposite the Piazza delle Cinque Scuole, where the Via del Portico d'Ottavia becomes the Via S. Maria del Pianto, this tiny shop offers its customers the most delectable marzipan pastries, as well as inimitable *mostaccioli* made from honey, almonds, raisins and candied fruit; these last are so heavy that after a couple of them you won't need to eat for the rest of the day.

Yes, if you know where to look in Rome, you can eat blissfully well. There's even a time-honored folk proverb that sums up the Romans' love of good food: *tanto guadagno, tanto me magno* (Whatever I earn, I spend on food). Similarly, the folk song *La cena della sposa* (The Bride's Dinner) enumerates what the wife is able to eat on twelve consecutive evenings, in order to fill herself with the following foods: a strawberry, half a baby lamb, a salad, two pieces of puff-pastry, a cake, three pigeons, four tomatoes, five pigs, six chickens, seven eels, eight endives, nine jugs of wine, ten olives, eleven boxes of sweets and – *dulcis in fundo* – twelve little sugar cakes.

Nightlife

Only ten years ago, Rome still had more cinemas than almost any city in Italy. If you opened a newspaper to the page with the entertainment and cultural schedule, you were faced with a choice between countless movie-palaces, whose exotic names recalled the most celebrated colonial conquests of the Fascist period. In those days, going to the cinema usually meant that you simply wanted to kill a few hours before dinner, or before it was time to go to bed.

In the cinemas at the edge of the city (the so-called *pidocchietti*, most of which have since been turned into blue-movie houses) some members of the audience were there not so much to watch the film as to give a loud running commentary on it. Some people were so enchanted by the quick-witted humor of these commentators that they left their comfortable middle-class homes in the evening and went to these cinemas, simply to be entertained by the spontaneous wit and anarchic fantasy with which these self-ap-

pointed comedians commented on the dialogue and action on the screen. Slowly but surely, however, television has drawn audiences away from this kind of movie theater. Today, people sit on the sofa in their comfortable flats and watch the same films – with the advantage of being able to switch from channel to channel whenever their interest starts to flag or the film is interrupted by commercials.

These days, in Rome (and Italy in general), people no longer go to the movies just to while away the time. This has certainly had a positive effect on the quality of the films shown, but it has also led to a steep increase in the price of tickets, which by now cost about the same as a pizza and a half-carafe of wine (albeit in a fairly modest pizzeria). Nevertheless, the habit of commenting on the action has persisted, even though the remarks are less witty than they used to be. A general buzz of conversation has

replaced the lewd comments about the leading lady's physical endowments that once echoed through the auditorium. It can be very difficult, especially on Saturdays and Sundays, to watch a film in peace; one is constantly forced to listen to the chatter of the people beside, in front of or behind you. This is true even of the cinemas, grown increasingly rare, that show a full program; the comments there may perhaps be less crude, but they are just as distracting.

Theater audiences, on the other hand, are generally more disciplines. It is true that in recent years there haven't been any more of the attempts that the city's various Ministers of Culture used to make to persuade people to go to the theater more often. This is chiefly because the Roman theater-going public are hard to win over for really innovative cultural enterprises. Just by looking at the programs of the various theaters, you can see that the same authors have their works performed year after year, and new authors and plays can be counted on

Above: Dinner in the Campo dei Fiori. Right: Commedia dell' Arte by Dario Fo.

the fingers of one hand. In this regard, the **Teatro Vittoria** shows genuine courage, since, for the past few seasons, it has been the only theater that has tried to offer a really original program every year, presenting not only works by new authors, but many different forms of entertainment, ranging from one-man shows to musical comedy, from pantomime to puppet theater.

Rome's nightlife, of course, isn't limited to cinema and theater. A short stroll through the Centro Storico will be enough to demonstrate this fact to you. The Roman *movida* begins around 9 pm and finishes in the gray light of dawn, after what are known as the *quattro salti* (four jumps) in a disco. The rule-book for night owls requires them to spend the whole night moving from one disco to the next.

The discothèques in Rome are quite expensive; anyone who frequents them should be careful not to consume anything more than what is included in the price of admission. However, if you have enough money and time, you could start by warming up at the **Follia**, an elegant spot in the rather unexciting Prati district. After that you can look in at the **Dipsodia** in Parioli, where you can familiarize yourself with a very specific social type: the chic and arrogant offspring of the wealthy residents of this area.

It is a pity that the scandals and court-cases of the last few years have wiped out another social type (actually it would be more correct to speak of a political type), once also *sui generis*: what the Italians call a *rampante* (climber), the political arriviste who appeared in the 1980s under the banner of the then-omnipotent Socialist party. The most glittering figure among the politicians of this party was the former Foreign Minister, Gianni de Michelis (who will certainly be known to posterity as the author of a little book about nightlife in the discos of Rome). He habitually frequented what is probably the most exclusive discothèque in the whole city, the **Gilda** in the Via Mario de' Fiori. Always accompanied by

an impressively-sized – and mainly female – retinue, he liked to hurl his bulky figure around the dance floor, to the delight of photographers and of his entire party, since their progressive policies and – what did they call it again? Oh yes – *transgressività,* a willingness to flout established conventions, were amply demonstrated by his cavorting.

To end the evening on a respectable note, you could go a few yards further on to the old and renowned **Piper**, which was the very first disco in Rome. However, if you are hoping for a nostalgia trip back to the Sixties, you can save yourself the money: for the last few years this has been more a hangout for eighteen-year-olds than a rendezvous for fifty-somethings in search of their lost youth.

For anyone with "special" tastes, or, in simple English, for the gay community, there are two main nightspots in the Eter-

Above: A popular gay rendezvous on the Testaccio. Right: Gilberto Gil at a concert durring the Estate Romana.

nal City: the **Angelo Azzuro** (Blue Angel) and the **Alibi.** The latter has traditionally been the disco most frequented by Rome's gay jet-setters. It's not, however, a pick-up bar; the central railway station remains the place where rent-boys can be picked up. And there, late at night, you can also see the gangs of youths who roam the streets, the *ragazzi di vita,* about whom Pier Paolo Pasolini wrote his novels and films. It was one of these who killed him in the autumn of 1975.

Should you go in search of the images captured in Fellini's *La Dolce Vita*, and go out along the **Via Veneto** looking for excitement, you are in for a disappointment. Today, this wide street is nothing more than a chaotic traffic artery leading from the affluent neighborhoods of Parioli and Via Salaria into the Centro Storico. Every evening, thousands of cars drive through the arches of the Porta Pinciana, under the hopeless misapprehension that they will find a parking space as close as possible to the bars and dives around the Piazza Navona and the Pantheon. On the Via Veneto, along the sidewalks where the celebrities of the Sixties used to stroll and do their shopping, not even the hookers are managing to do much business any more.

To the sorrow of nostalgia freaks and the displeasure of the shopkeepers who sell neckties for the price of a complete suit, the glory days of the Via Veneto are indeed over. The only people who are still willing to believe in the seductive attraction of the street are Japanese tourists; they are also the only people who still take photos of it, and the only dupes who allow themselves to be tempted by the Slavic charms of a rather ageing hostess and naively follow her into the last surviving night-club on the street.

Believe it or not, the nocturnal activity that you see between the Porta Pinciana and the Porta S. Paolo is a relatively recent development. It was born of an initiative in the late 1970s, which aimed at

giving the Romans back the historic heart of their city; thereto, it was a place where people walked around by day, and was virtually deserted at night. The *Estate Romana* (Roman Summer), as the initiative was called, was the inspiration of the architect and popular playwright Renato Nicolini, who at the time was the cultural spokesman on the left-wing municipal council. The whole thing was a titillatingly provocative experience, whatever your views of it. Crowds and spectacular events filled the streets. The magnificent courtyards of the Baroque palaces were transformed into concert-halls, the piazzas became stages, the historic parks were dance floors, the Forum Romanum and later the Circus Maximus were turned into gigantic cinemas under the stars. The experiment lasted about ten years, although it may have lost some of its original zip towards the end; yet it continued to provide the few people who remained in the city during the summer months with an opportunity to relax and have fun.

The *Estate Romana* came to an end with the local elections in 1985, when the Communist party was defeated. The series of cultural events which are held under the same name today have absolutely nothing to do with the concept which was realized in the late 1970s and early 1980s. But even without the stimulus of the *Estate Romana*, the nightlife of the capital has taken a few steps forward in recent years. Some would say, perhaps, too many.

The music scene

The Testaccio has had a remarkable history. It started as a huge pile of refuse in the age of imperial Rome; went on to become an open-air circus where bullfights were often held in the Middle Ages; later turned into the slaughterhouse district; and, a few years ago, made the final transformation to its current status as a place of nightly pilgrimage for intellectuals and music buffs. It is, furthermore, the red-and-yellow heart of the city

(red and yellow being the colors of the AS Roma football team); and some Romans would say this is its most important attribute of all.

Its musical significance began only fifteen years ago with the founding of the now-legendary music school **Scuola Popolare di Musica di Testaccio**. This institution was the brainchild of a cooperative of musicians, who were more motivated by an urge to bring music to the people than to make money (those were still the days of great social movements and ideals). They met, at first, in a few bars at the foot of the "Potsherd Mountain." But the school, which was a rapid success, was eventually transformed into a cultural center and finally the most important place to go to hear the Roman brand of jazz, which has since become the best anywhere in Italy. The reputation

Above: Astor Piazzolla at a concert on the Capitoline. Right: A Verdi opera performance at the Teatro dell' Opera.

of the *Scuola di Testaccio*, and the crowds of students and fans who came to hear the jam sessions, obviously had an impact on the local geography. Thus was founded the **Caffé Latino**, where you can hear both Roman and international jazz, although you'll probably have trouble finding a seat (not surprisingly, given the club's terrific atmosphere).

A bit less intellectual than the Caffé Latino, but just as atmospheric, and even trendier, is a club with the odd name of **Spago** ("string," whence *spaghetti*, little bits of string). Admittedly, the music played here is more traditional piano-bar fare, but it's presented with such elegance and style that this place has become another of the city's most popular nightspots.

If you prefer softer music with a Latin-American beat – which incidentally has become all the rage in Rome over the last few years, just as it has in the rest of Europe – then the club directly above the Spago is the place for you. Its name – the **Caruso Caffé Concerto** – is more remi-

niscent of an aristocratic salon at the end of the 19th century than of the driving rhythms of Afro-Cuban music which is the club's usual repertoire. The Caruso is more or less the opposite of the Spago. You can see immediately which visitors are heading for which bar: those who go into the Spago are dressed rather smartly, whereas the Caruso clientele is clad more in the "underground" mode.

If you happen to be in the Testaccio during the day – but only during the day! – then don't neglect to take a look at the rather down-at-heel area around the old slaughterhouse. If you're there at night, and simply want to spend a few hours in pleasant company, having a quiet conversation and maybe sipping at a good cocktail, then the right place for you is the **Aldebaran**: elegant, pleasant, quiet. The only catch is the usual problem: it is difficult to get a table.

It's a truism that all Italians have good voices and are willing to prove this at any time, at the top of their lungs. In fact, the musical life of the Italian capital, seen at close quarters, gives little cause for rejoicing. In relation to the size of its population, the city has extraordinarily few music venues; great conductors and soloists are fairly rare and the performances rather lackluster; what is more, there is not a single theater with acoustics that can stand comparison with the theaters in other European countries.

Still the city's best venue for musical events is unquestionably the **Accademia di Santa Cecilia**, which offers a rich and varied program from November to June in the rooms of the auditorium in the Via della Conciliazione. Admittedly, it is rather difficult to get hold of tickets, and downright impossible to acquire a season-ticket, since these are handed down like family jewels from father to son.

The **Teatro Olimpico** also offers a good program of concerts, though it changes less frequently than that of the Accademia di Santa Cecilia. The chorus and orchestra of the city's Italian Radio (RAI) given regular concerts in the auditorium of the **Foro Italico**.

207

*Above: Entrance to the Teatro dell' Opera –
Rome's opera house.*

When it comes to opera, one thing you have to understand right away is that Rome is not Milan and the **Teatro dell'-Opera** in no way matches up to La Scala. Nor is the tradition of opera in Rome among the world's greatest. In the early 19th century, for instance, when prima donnas like Malibran and Giuditta Pasta were already making great names for themselves all over Europe, in Rome *castrati* were still singing in public. Nevertheless, the Roman Opera is frequently mentioned in the press, albeit less for its artistic performance than for other reasons. One often reads that there has been a strike by the make-up artists, orchestra players, members of the chorus, or one of the other groups which contribute to the staging of an opera, and which are all organized in their own tiny trade unions, any one of which is capable of putting a stop to any production it chooses. It's not that the workers are underpaid; quite the

contrary. Any permanent employee of the Opera di Roma takes home a very respectable salary every month. But that's the way it goes. If by striking the workers stand a chance of adding a few lira to their salaries or securing some additional privilege, then it's always worth a shot. And when the performance finally does take place, the critics usually keep their enthusiasm well under control, not to say hidden altogether. This doesn't mean that *all* the presentations of the Teatro dell' Opera are worthless; far from it. Now and then the theater manages to put on a truly successful production. But when it does succeed, it is more often the determination and professionalism of the leading singers or the director that are responsible, rather than a co-operative effort of the opera company as a whole. This means that memorable productions are rather the exception than the rule.

The opera season at the Teatro dell'Opera ends at the beginning of the summer, and is then continued in the magnificent setting of the **Baths of Caracalla**. Gradually, it must be admitted, people are beginning to wonder just how long these ruins can stand up to the annual summer onslaught of thousands of spectators before they finally collapse. It is in any case doubtful how much longer tourists and Romans are going to continue to be thrilled by the sight of horses and elephants in *Aida*, or by the choreography in *Carmen* or *Don Quixote*. It may well be that the historic concert of Pavarotti, Carreras and Domingo will remain the last great musical event that these ancient walls had to witness. It is, after all, possible to make superb music without such a grand backdrop.

Speaking of open-air concerts, it has to be noted at this point that unfortunately, even today, Rome doesn't have a single really suitable venue for staging the major rock concerts which, in other cities, always attract tens of thousands of young people.

ROME'S NIGHTLIFE

If you want to find out what entertainment is on offer during your stay in Rome, get hold of the Friday edition of the daily newspaper *La Repubblica*. In the **Trovaroma** supplement you will find everything you need to know.

Restaurants

TOP-CLASS RESTAURANTS: **Alberto Ciarla**, Piazza S. Cosimato 40, Tel: 5818668. Famous for fish dishes. **Alfredo all' Augusteo l'Originale**, Piazza Augusto Imperatore, Tel: 6878734/6878615. The real Alfredo himself is the king of *fettuccine*. **Casina Valadier**, Villa Valadier, Pincio, Tel: 6794189. Marvellous view, place where the top people meet. **Chez Albert**, Vicolo della Vaccarella 11, Tel: 6565549. *Nouvelle Cuisine*. **El Toulà di Roma**, Via della Lupa 29, Tel: 6873498/ 6873750. One of the best restaurants in Rome. **Hassler Villa Medici**, Piazza Trinità dei Monti 6, Tel: 6782651, superb view over Rome. **Leon d'Oro**, Via Cagliari 25, Tel: 8551900/8551847, fish dishes. **Mario's Hostaria**, Piazza del Grillo 9, Tel: 6793725, fish. **Papà Giovanni**, Via dei Sediari 4, Tel: 6565308, (near Piazza Navona). **Ranieri**, Via Mario dei Fiori 26, Tel: 6791592. A restaurant with a great tradition. *GOOD VALUE:* **Da Alfredo e Alda**, Via dei Banchi Vecchi, Tel: 6864219/6864519. **Alfredo alla Scrofa**, Via della Scrofa 104. **Al Vicario**, Via degli Uffici del Viacario 31, Tel: 6840447. **Antica Pesa**, Via Garibaldi 18, Tel: 5809236. **Bafetto**, Via del Governo Vecchio 114, Tel: 6861617. Very good pizza. **Il Bistechiere**, Via dei Gigli d'Oro 2/3/4, Tel: 6542104. Open till 2.30 in the morning. **La Bruschetta**, Via Ancona. Good, simple cooking. **Cannavota**, Piazza S. Giovanni in Laterano, Tel: 775007. Good pasta dishes. **L'Eau Vive**, Via Monterone 85, Tel: 6541095. Favorite with priests and churchgoers, the waitresses are ex-missionaries. **Fiaschetteria Beltramme**, Via della Croce 39. Very good food, friendly atmosphere. **Mastro Stefano**, Piazza Navona 94, pretty terrace. **Meo Patacca**, Piazza dei Mercanti 30, Tel: 5892193. Touristy, but fun even so. **Settimio**, Via del Pellegrino 117, Tel: 6789651, nr Campo dei Fiori. *ROMAN CUISINE:* **Capanna del Negro**, Via Portuense 45, Tel: 5816054. Terrace above the Tiber. **Checchino dal 1887**, Via Monte Testaccio 30, Tel: 5746318. Speciality: offal. **Da Fieramosca**, Piazza dei Mercanti 3a, Tel: 5890289, in Trastevere. **Er Faciolaro**, Via dei Pastini 13 and 123, Tel: 6783896 and 6793797. Speciality: beans. **Gino**, Vicolo Rosini 28, fish soups, Tel: 5803403/5806226. **Romolo**, Via Porta Settimiana 8, Tel: 5818284. Beautiful garden. **Taverna Trilussa**, Via del Politeama 23, Tel: 58118918. Bohemian rendezvous. **Trattoria Lilly**, Lungotevere Tor di Nona 31.

Nightspots

Aldebaran, Via Galvani 54, Tel: 576013. **L' Alibi**, Via di Monte Testaccio 44, Tel: 5748448. **Alien**, Via Velletri 13-19. **Angelo Azurro**, Via Cardinal Merry del Val 13, Tel: 5800472, disco. **Caffé Caruso**, Via di Monte Testaccio 36. **Caffé Latino**, Via di Monte Testaccio 96. **Casanova**, Piazza Rondanini 36, Tel: 6547314. **Club 84**, Via Emilia 84, Tel: 4751538. **Easy Going**, Via della Purificazione 9, Tel: 4745578. **Gil's**, Via dei Romagnosi 11a. **Gilda**, Via Mario dei Fiori 97, Tel: 6784838. **Il Dito al Naso**, Via del Fiume 4, Tel: 3612389. **Jackie O'**, Via Boncompagni 11, Tel: 461401. **La Makumba**, Via degli Olimpionici 19, Tel: 3231178. **Magic Fly**, Via Bassanello 15 b, Tel: 3668956. **Piper 90**, Via Tagliamento 9, Tel: 854459.

Cabaret and cocktails

Le Cabanon, Vicolo della Luce 4. **Le Cornacchie**, Via del Pozzo delle Cornacchie 53. **Fantasie di Trastevere**, Via di Santa Dorotea 6.

Opera and concerts

Teatro dell'Opera, Piazza Beniamino Gigli. **Terme di Caracalla**, Via delle Terme di Caracalla (from July till mid-August). **Accademia Filarmonica Romana**, Via Flaminia 118. **Auditorio del Foro Italico**, Piazza L. de Bosis. **Auditorio di Santa Cecilia**, Via della Conciliazione 4, Tel: 6833242. **Basilica di Massenzio**, Via dei Fori Imperiali. **Concerti a Villa Giulia**, summer concerts, information Tel: 6790389.

Theaters

Teatro Parioli, Via G. Borsi 20, Tel: 8083523. **Teatro Piccolo Eliseo**, Via Nazionale 183, Tel: 4882114. **Teatro Quirino**, Via Marco Minghetti 1, Tel: 6794585. **Teatro Sistina**, Via Sistina 129, Tel: 4826841. **Teatro Valle**, Via del Teatro Valle 23, Tel: 6543794. **Teatro Vascello**, Via G. Carini 72, Tel: 5809389. **Teatro Vittoria**, Piazza S. Maria Liberatrice 8, Tel: 5740170. **Teatro delle Arti**, Via Sicilia 59, Tel: 4818598. **Teatro Argentina**, Largo Torre Argentina 52, Tel. 6544601. **Teatro Belli**, Piazza S. Apollonia 11/a, Tel: 5894875. **Teatro della Cometa**, Via del Teatro Marcello 4, Tel: 6784380. **Teatro delle Muse**, Via Forli 43, Tel: 8831300. **Teatro Flaiano**, Via S. Stefano del Cacco 15, Tel: 6796496. **Teatro Ghione**, Via delle Fornaci 37, Tel: 6372294. **Teatro Manzoni**, Via Monte Zebio 14/c, Tel: 3223634. **Teatro Nazionale**, Via A. Depretis 51, Tel: 485498.

THE ENVIRONS OF ROME

The bucolic image of the Campagna populated with goatherds, shepherds and shepherdesses, wandering the green hills between the ancient ruins, has been passed on to us from paintings of the 18th and 19th centuries, when Rome and Lazio (ancient Latium) were compulsory stages on the Grand Tour through southern Europe. Although this landscape is becoming increasingly built up today, it has managed to preserve much of its former charm.

The Via Appia

The Via Appia, which led out from Rome into the Campagna, was one of the great consular roads of the Roman republic and empire. It got its name from the *censor* Appius Claudius Caecus, who or-

Above: A paved road, over 2000 years old – the Via Appia Antica. Right: The Villa Aldobrandini in Frascati.

dered its construction in 312 BC. The road was originally intended to link Rome with Capua; later it was continued southward to Benevento and, in the time of the Gracchi brothers (2nd century BC), it was built as far as Brundisium (modern Brindisi). It starts near the Circus Maximus and runs through the Porta San Sebastiano, past numerous ancient villas, aqueducts and tombs, for twelve Roman miles, as far as Boville.

Shortly before the Porta San Sebastiano (the ancient Porta Appia) lies the **Tomb of the Scipios**, an almost square building that contained the sarcophagi of this patrician family which had such a profound influence on Roman history. Today, the sarcophagi and original inscriptions are housed in the Vatican Museums. Just beyond the mighty gateway stands the famous **Temple of Mars**, which was probably built in 388 BC. It is followed by a series of tombs and buildings from different epochs.

The **Catacombs of Saint Calixtus** (named after the Pope who died in an uprising in 222 AD) are considered to be the most important subterranean Christian burial chambers in Rome. The archaeological complex of S. Sebastiano, on the other hand, was known even in Antiquity as the "memoria apostolorum" because it was connected with the then-contemporary cult of the apostles Peter and Paul; not until a later century was the cemetery named after the martyr who was buried there. A little further on, you come to the **Villa and Circus of Maxentius**, named for the son of the emperor who built them in 309 AD; the circus, restored in the 1970s, is the best preserved in Rome. Nearby is the **Tomb of Cecilia Metella**, dating from the reign of Augustus, and also very well preserved.

At the fifth milestone, which traditionally marked the border between Rome and Alba Longa, lie two circular burial-mounds, which even today are wrongly called the **Graves of the Horatii and the**

Curiatii, legendary families of early Roman history. A little further on stands the magnificent **Villa of the Quintilii**, the largest outside Rome. It was built in the middle of the 2nd century AD and is particularly noteworthy for its extensive gardens and race course.

The Via Appia then continues past the remains of buildings and tombs, numerous stelae and inscriptions, fragments of statues and columns, ruined medieval towers and the arches of aqueducts. Beyond the 11th milestone it joins the Appia Nuova, which leads to Frattocchie. Here one is already in the depths of the Campagna Romana. The next item on the itinerary is a tour of the Alban Hills.

The Castelli Romani

This is the name given to Frascati, Grottaferrata, Marino, Castel Gandolfo, Albano, Ariccia, Rocca di Papa, Genzano, Nemi, Velletri and several other towns in the **Alban Hills** (Colli Albani), where popes and noble Roman families built themselves castles and fortresses in the Middle Ages. In the Renaissance and Baroque eras, superb villas were added as summer residences for the aristocracy. The whole region has its own ancient culture: the site where Castel Gandolfo stands today was once taken up by the legendary *Alba Longa*. The Latin tribes were then subjugated by the Romans, and the region took on the role which it still fulfils today: it became the farmland which provided food for the constantly growing city. The beauty of the landscape with its gentle hills, green woodlands and blue lakes, not to mention its archaeological and architectural treasures, make the Castelli the perfect destination for excursions. The old *trattorie* serving traditional dishes and the famous Castelli wines are further attractions.

Most famous of the Castelli Romani is **Frascati**. Its very beautiful location made this little town the favorite summer resort of the popes (the official papal summer residence was here before it moved to Castel Gandolfo), and the no-

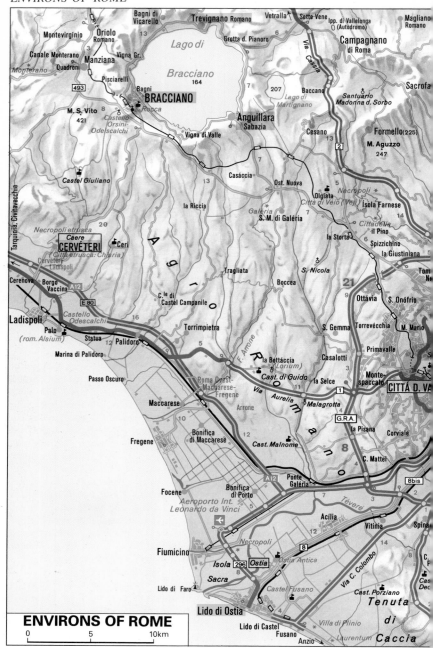

ENVIRONS OF ROME

0   5   10km

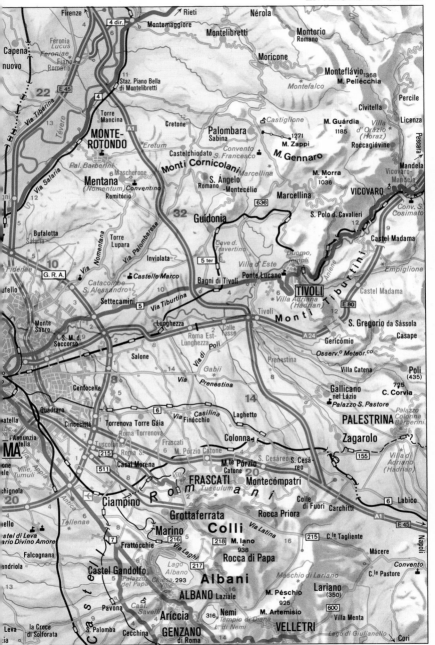

bility of Rome built their finest villas here. You can see the grand houses of the Lancellotti, Falconieri and Mondragone families, dating from the 16th century, as well as the magnificent villa Aldobrandini, designed around 1600 by G.B. Della Porta and completed by C. Maderna and G. Fontana; the latter also built the very beautiful fountains in the gardens. However, Frascati really owes its reputation to its wines, which you can sample in the town's old wine cellars.

Albano Laziale lies on the lake of the same name, one of the old crater lakes of volcanic origin which are to be found in the Alban Hills. The town was founded by the emperor Septimius Severus and became an episcopal seat in the 6th century. In 1697 Pope Innocent XII acquired it for the *Camera Apostolica*. Among the sights here are the Chiesa della Rotonda (the former *nymphaeum* of the Villa of

Above: Nemi, one of the Castelli Romani.
Right: Roast sucking-pig is a great speciality in Ariccia.

Domitian), the ruins of the Villa of Pompey, the 5th-century catacombs of the Madonna della Stella, and the villas of the Altieri, Doria and Venosa, as well as the Palazzo Corsini.

Castel Gandolfo is one of the most frequently visited of all the Castelli towns. Not only do many tourists come here, but also Romans on summer vacation. Beside the lake, where according to legend Ascanius founded *Alba Longa*, a village grew up in the 13th century around the castle of the Gandolfi family. In the *consistorium* of 1608, the town was declared the inalienable property of the Holy See, and thenceforth was the summer residence of the popes. As well as the Papal Palace, built by Carlo Maderna at the beginning of the 17th century, you can see the church of San Tommaso di Villanova, designed by Bernini, the Palazzo Torlonia (in the Roman neoclassical style, with sculptures by Thorvaldsen), the Villa Cybo with the Vatican's own astronomical observatory, and the Villa Barberini, in whose gardens

the ruins of the ancient Villa of Domitian are still visible. The Villa Cybo, the Villa Barberini, and the Papal Palace form a single large complex, which belongs to the Vatican.

In **Ariccia**, where Bernini's great influence on the layout of the town and the building of its monuments is plainly evident, you will have a chance to sample the delicious and justifiably famous *porchetta* (suckling pig). In **Nemi**, on the other hand, strawberries are the chief gastronomic attraction. This little town lies on the Lago di Nemi, a small volcanic crater filled with water, which is of archaeological interest because the remains of an ancient temple dedicated to Diana Nemorense can be found on its eastern slope; because of this temple, the lake was once known as "Diana's Mirror." In the years 1929-31, two Roman ships, probably dating from the reign of Caligula, were recovered from the lake; but these were destroyed by fire in the Second World War, and only the bronze parts survived (today, they are displayed

in Rome). Two scale models of the ships can nevertheless be seen in the Nemi museum. Characteristic of the area around Nemi is also the cultivation of flowers, from which derives the tradition of the *infiorata* of **Genzano**: in this town, which lies between the Via Appia and the Lago di Nemi, every year in June images, people, and current events are depicted on the streets through the medium of flower petals.

The last of the Castelli Romani beside the Via Appia is **Velletri**. The wine cultivated in this town is so excellent that its praises are even sung in folk songs and poetry.

One place you should definitely visit is **Cori**, south of the Alban Hills. This fine old town is situated on the north-western slopes of the Monti Lepini. Here you will find the massive remains of Bronze Age walls; a Roman temple of Hercules and one dedicated to Castor and Pollux; the medieval church of Santa Oliva, with additions dating from the Renaissance and Baroque periods, as well as a beautiful monastery built around the end of the 16th century.

Lago di Bracciano

The Lago di Bracciano was formed from extinct volcanic craters in the Monti Sabatini. On the shores of its waters, which are full of fish, lie the villages of Anguillara, Trevignano and Vicariello – and, of course, the small town after which the lake is named. The most important monument in **Bracciano** is the Orsini-Odelscalchi Castle, built in the 15th century on a polygonal ground plan by Napoleone Orsini. Its interior is decorated with frescoes by Antoniazzo Romano, paintings by Zuccari and sculptures from the school of Bernini.

Tivoli and Palestrina

In the 1920s, if you drove out of Rome along the *Tiburtina* or *Prenestina* highways to Tivoli or Palestrina, you passed through an almost unspoiled landscape, dotted with the ruins of ancient buildings grown over with vines and bushes. Nowadays, however, the same route presents nothing of the same atmosphere, nor the same contemplative stillness. For Rome's rapid expansion eastwards along the old consular roads has created new suburbs which lack even the slightest aesthetic pretensions and were often built illegally. Nonetheless, an expedition to Tivoli or Palestrina is a must if you want to get to know the most important areas around Rome and at the same time acquire some idea of the ancient city's remarkable culture and civilization.

The Tivoli of today was the ancient *Tibur*, which the Romans captured in 338 BC. It then became a summer retreat for wealthy patrician families, who built their villas there. One of these villas was

Right: Beside the Canopus in the grounds of Hadrian's Villa, near Tivoli.

built by the emperor Hadrian early in the 2nd century AD; its majestic ruins can still be seen today. A visit to **Hadrian's Villa** (Villa Adriana) is perhaps of greater archaeological than aesthetic interest, since, throughout the Middle Ages the magnificent imperial residence had to serve as a quarry for building materials. The archaeological finds made in later centuries were, little by little, taken to museums in Rome; as a result, there is no longer a great deal of the villa left to see, but what does remain is still sufficient to enable one to picture it in its former glory. *The Canopus* alone, its basin still ornamented with a few of the statues which once stood all around its edge, conveys some idea of the villa's past. There are many other buildings on the grounds copied from various originals which the emperor had seen on his travels throughout the world. But perhaps most impressive are the ruins of the villa itself, bearing testimony to a massive complex which is thought to have once covered an area of more than 120 acres (50 ha).

Any excursion to the town of Tivoli should certainly include a visit to the famous **Villa d'Este**. Starting in 1550, this edifice was built, enlarged and decorated by Cardinal Ippolito d'Este and his successors, until it became a complex which included one of the most beautiful gardens in Italy and a magnificent palace fitted out with priceless furnishings and pictures. The terrace here affords a breathtakingly beautiful view over the garden and beyond to a broad panorama of the Campagna. In the garden itself, hidden amongst the lush vegetation, there are hundreds of fountains, large and small, displaying all manner of aquatic invention.

On the way to visit the spectacular cascades at the Villa Gregoriana, take a look at the church of **S. Silvestro** with its frescoes, on your left, and the **Piazza S. Nicola**, where there are still several interesting medieval houses which survived un-

scathed the no fewer than 22 air raids to which Tivoli was subjected when the city was a target for bombers during World War Two.

The Via del Colle brings you to the **Cathedral**, where you can see a life-sized *Burial of Christ*, a superb wood-carving from the 13th century, as well as the famous *Triptych of the Redeemer*, which admittedly you can only view on special occasions. Continuing along the Via S. Valerio and the Via Sibilla, you'll come to the two temples dedicated to Vesta and to the Sibyl of Tibur. The Temple of Vesta is a beautifully situated, elegant circular temple, with ten of its original 18 Corinthian columns still standing. In the **Villa Gregoriana** itself the River Aniene rushes down the famous waterfalls, a magnificent spectacle which one can enjoy from all the viewing points that are marked with signposts.

If you drive out of Tivoli in the direction of Rome and then turns left in Ponte Lucano, after about 12 miles (20 km) you'll come to the second stop of this excursion into the Roman countryside: **Palestrina**, called *Preneste* in ancient times. The oldest part of this little town clusters round the grim-looking **Palazzo Colonna Barberini**, which was built on part of the great **Shrine of Fortuna Primogenia.** Back in the days of the Roman republic, the great orator Cicero wrote about this shrine, not only because of its impressive size, but also because of its famous oracle, which had been consulted since as early as the 4th century BC. The area of the former temple probably stretched as far as the modern Via del Borgo, perhaps even up to the north side of the Piazza Regina Margherita, where in the adjoining *sala absidata* (a rectangular room which may have been part of a *nymphaeum*) the mosaic was found which was later displayed in the museum of the palace. This work of art, probably created in the 1st century BC, shows the entire course of the Nile from its sources down to where it flows into the Mediterranean. The map is populated with human and animal figures; the depictions

of the animals are particularly charming and lovely. In the other rooms of the museum numerous archaeological finds from the district, some very valuable, are displayed. As you leave the palace, on a clear day there is a view for miles across the rolling hills of the Campagna.

Ostia Antica and Ostia Moderna

As Ostia was the port of ancient Rome, you might expect to find the sea there. But the sea has receded; or, to be more accurate, the coastal strip has become wider and wider as the Tiber changed its course over the centuries. The river, on the other hand, once ran parallel to the town, protecting it against possible land attacks from the north; on the town's south side was a solid defensive wall. But one day in the year 1575, when the water receded after a disastrous flood, the Tiber

Above: Fountains playing in the Villa d'Este.
Right: The famous mosaic floor of Ostia Antica.

220

was found to have dug itself a new bed a hundred yards further to the north, and thus the splendid citadel, which a century earlier had been built to protect the city of Rome from attackers rowing upstream, was left high and dry, so to speak. One might well say *sic transit gloria mundi*, and this maxim is appropriate not only because it is Latin, but also because the history of Ostia, in Antiquity as today, has been one of glory interspersed with much misfortune.

In imperial times, Ostia was a city with 100,000 inhabitants, but it fell further and further into decline until in the end it was completely depopulated; its magnificent buildings collapsed and were eventually covered with earth. Pope Gregory IV's attempts to create a new settlement there in the 8th century, which, with touching modesty, he wanted to name *Gregoriopoli*, did not get very far. As recently as 1878 an English traveller, Augustus Hare, wrote that he saw only one inhabited house there. The chief problem in Ostia was malaria, and not until the beginning of the 20th century were decisive measures taken to combat it by draining the surrounding marshland. From that time on, the new city, today's Ostia Lido, grew rapidly and became the favorite seaside resort of the Romans. They began by building pretty little holiday houses here, as at other places along the coast, but then in the 1960s they started erecting tower blocks of very questionable taste. Meanwhile, the increasing and uncontrollable pollution of the coastline (bathing is strongly discouraged) has turned the one-time beach resort into a satellite city of Rome, occupied mainly by foreign workers and by all the many Romans who can no longer afford to pay the horrendous rents in the *capitale*.

The following brief guided tour through the excavated areas of **Ostia Antica** should be enough to give some impression of the splendor of this once important ancient city. You enter by the **Porta Romana**, beyond which ran the *Decumanus Maximus*, the long, straight main street, before turning left towards the sea. Along this street stood the most important buildings, including the **Baths of Neptune**, which appear on the right-hand side after a few hundred yards. You can compare the elegant mosaics of this complex with the more modest ones a little further on in the **Osteria of Fortunatus**, a tavern where a sign invites you to drink, provided, of course, *quod sitis* ("that you are thirsty").

Immediately beyond the Baths lies the large circular amphitheater; just past this is the **Piazzale delle Corporazioni**, the commercial hub of the ancient city, which included at least 70 shops. Being a cosmopolitan city, Ostia also had numerous temples dedicated to the various deities worshipped in all the different parts of the empire. Surprisingly, very little evidence of Christianity has been found.

Turning right into the Via dei Molini to the right, and then going left along the

Via Diana, you will come to the **Museo Ostiense**, which displays the most important archaeological finds from the excavations. Returning to the *Decumanus,* you'll eventually come to the **Forum**, on the south side of which are the remains of the **Temple of Rome and Augustus**. Next to that are the large **Baths**, one of the city's numerous public bath complexes, which also included the **Baths of Mithras**, in the Via della Foce, and the **Baths of the Seven Sages**; the latter have become known above all for their marvellous mosaic floors depicting hunting scenes.

Passing the baths on the left, you come to an arcade, the **Cardine degli Aurighi,** and from here you return to the *Decumanus Maximus*. Following this to the right, you'll reach the **Porta Marina**, beyond which lie the ruins of a forum and another huge public bath complex, which at one time gave directly onto the sea. However, as mentioned above, the sea receded centuries ago, leaving the city to a fate of neglect, decay and collapse.

THE ETRUSCANS

The mysterious race we know as the Etruscans settled in the Italian peninsula around 1000 BC and subjugated the local inhabitants. For centuries their power extended northward into the Po Valley and southward beyond Campania. They formed city-states, of which the twelve most powerful were united in an alliance. The decline of the Etruscan empire began in the 5th century BC. Their fleet was defeated by the Greeks of Syros at the Battle of Cumae in 474 BC, and in 396 the Romans captured the Etruscan city of Veii. Not long afterwards the entire Etruscan empire was in Roman hands. The new masters adopted the Etruscan insignia and ceremonial customs, absorbed the cultural heritage of Etruria and adapted it to their own needs.

Previous pages: Fun at the fountain. Above: A tranquil couple on an Etruscan sarcophagus. Right: Etruscan or Giacometti?

What remains of this cultural legacy today is mainly to be seen in the remains of monuments and articles found in burial complexes. In the region around Rome there are several of these necropolises, which are well worth visiting – for example Cerveteri, the ancient *Caere*, which is located about 30 miles (50 km) northwest of the capital.

The Etruscan cities of the dead were modelled on living communities, and laid out with main streets and sidestreets. As in all societies of the ancient world, the cultural, economic and political life of the living was reflected in the homage paid to the dead. The richer and grander a family was, the higher was its burialmound – an attitude which you still find today in Italy, where the grave is considered to be a status symbol.

Inside the tomb there was everything which would be required for a comfortable existence in the Valley of Death: furniture carved straight into the rock, valuable jewellery, well-designed vases and all sorts of articles for daily use. There were also highly prized weapons among the burial gifts – these also represented a status-symbol in the hereafter.

The walls of the long, corridor-like burial chambers were painted with frescoes, from which we learn that the Etruscans certainly appreciated the pleasures of their earthly existence. They show music-making and dancing, revelry and feasting, and hunting scenes, as well as themes from mythology. The women wear costly jewels and appear very sophisticated.

From images found on sarcophagi, it has been concluded that women in Etruscan society clearly had a great deal of freedom and enjoyed extensive matrimonial rights. The richer women in perticular were not only very free to enjoy the pleasures of life, they were also highly respected, were considered fully equal to men and took their full share in public life.

The wealth and power of the Etruscans were based on the mining of iron ore, copper and tin. Early in their history they possessed a merchant fleet and their closest trading partners included the Greeks and the Carthaginians.

The Greeks had a great influence on Etruscan art, particularly in the plastic arts of carving and ceramics, which the Etruscans raised to a peak of perfection never later surpassed. In the 6th and 5th centuries BC, Etruscan goldsmiths' work, exquisitely engraved hand-mirrors and bronze vessels were much sought after in export markets, and their black pottery and terra-cotta vases, which can be seen in museums today, are of great aesthetic quality.

Etruria is said to be the originator and mother of magic. The superstitious gesture, so beloved of Italians, *fare le corna* (making the horns), was already familiar to the Etruscans. They were always very anxious to discover the will of the gods, in order to use any means possible to win their favor. The title *haruspex* was given to the Etruscan priests, whose task it was

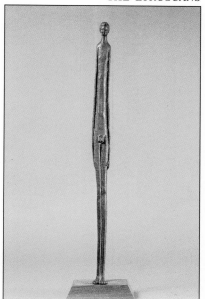

to interpret the will of the deities by examining the liver and innards of sacrificed birds. Their interpretation of lightning and other natural phenomena also had a profound influence over private and public life.

In the Archaeological Park of Cerveteri you can visit the excavations of Etruscan burial cities. The *tumuli*, in which earth is piled up over a circular base of up to 100 ft (30 m) in diameter, conceal burial chambers hewn out of the rock and designed like private dwellings. Later, the upwardly mobile middle class erected plinth tombs, which only contained a single burial chamber.

Some of the artefacts found in individual graves can be seen in the museum which was opened in Cerveteri in 1967. It is located in the palace of Prince Ruspoli and contains impressive displays of grave furnishings. Other finds are displayed in the Villa Giulia in Rome, and the most important exhibits are to be seen in the recently reorganized Museo Gregoriano Etrusco, in the Vatican.

WATER IN ROME

Water in Rome – it is the music from more than three hundred murmuring and splashing fountains, a sound which fills the squares, alleys and courtyards of the city. It is the symbol of the stylish elegance of the Romans and of their *penchant* for luxury and extravagance. No less than 450 gallons (2000 liters) of water cascade every second from the many wall fountains, pouring over the entwined limbs of tritons, lapping over sea shells into marble basins, spurting from the mouths of Baroque beasts, but also flowing, cool and refreshing, from numberless simple drinking pipes.

The water of Rome is also the Tiber, which rolls its dirty brown current lethargically and sluggishly through the city. The days are long gone when one could bathe in the river, then come out into the fresh air, just as Goethe enjoyed doing

Above: The fountains of Rome – quenching everyone's thirst. Right: ...self-service.

during his stay in Rome in 1787. It is scarcely conceivable today, that the Tiber, along with a few cisterns, provided the city with drinking water for many centuries.

With the construction of the first water conduit (in 312 BC, under the *Censor* Appius Claudius), to which others were added over the centuries, a healthy and well-watered era began for Rome. The staggering volume of 750,000 cubic meters of water was brought daily from the hills to the east and southeast, providing the population with drinking-water and to feed the gigantic thermal baths. Today, the architectural traces of this ancient hydraulic technology have left their mark on the Roman landscape. The *Acqua Marcia*, 55 miles (91.5 km) long, was the longest water conduit, running in one place for 6.5 miles (11 km) over a continuous series of arches; the Claudine Aqueduct carried water for a distance of 41 miles (68 km) and ran above ground for 11.5 miles (19 km) across arches up to 89 ft (27 m) high, which today are still a characteristic element of the landscape along the Via Tuscolana and the Via Appia.

The "hydraulic" age of Rome came to an end with the besieging of the city in 537 AD by the Goths, who destroyed the conduits and thus cut its vital artery. It was to be almost a thousand years before the Renaissance popes restored and enlarged the Roman aqueducts, thus supplying the city once again with life-giving water. But they had more in mind than simply ameliorating the shortage of drinking water and controlling the spread of cholera: by building magnificent fountains they were not only bestowing a unique splendor on Rome, but enhancing their own reputation and prestige, and giving even greater importance to the ancient and long-lost culture of water.

The first conduit to be restored by the popes was the Acqua Vergine, in 1570. Even today, it still feeds three of the most

famous fountains: La Barcaccia at the Spanish Steps, the Fountain of the Four Rivers in the Piazza Navona and, probably the best known of them all, the Fontana di Trevi. Three other aqueducts repaired by the popes are the Acqua Felice, which feeds the Fountain of Moses, the Acqua Marcia, whose waters bubble from the Naiad Fountain, and the Acqua Paola, which ends in a huge wall-fountain of the same name.

Rome's abundance of water and its rulers' desire for glory were the foundation of an age of creative activity which reached its zenith in the work of Bernini (1598-1680). The Triton Fountain in the Piazza Barberini (1637) has a unity of form which puts it among his greatest masterpieces. But other artists also created remarkable fountains, which helped to shape the Baroque city. One only has to think of the popular Turtle Fountain in the Piazza Mattei, or of the fountains in front of the Pantheon. What they all have in common is a debt to antiquity, so that the fountains bestow classic unity to the architectural design of the city. Antiquity, Renaissance, Baroque and modernism all blend, together with the carefree charm of the Romans, into a harmonious whole.

But in Rome water also meant power as manifested in the arches of the aqueducts, which celebrate their builders like triumphal arches.

It is almost like poetry to see how the water unites the marble basins of the fountains with the charm and grace of Baroque figures – poetry which the 19th century Swiss writer, Christian Friedrich Meyer, cast in these immortal lines:

The glistening jet ascends and falls to fill the rounded marble bowl/ which, veiling itself, spills over/ into a second bowl; this, too, becomes too full,/ its water surging over to a third,/ and each both gives and takes,/ is motionless, yet moves.

Many visitors succumb to the magic of Rome's water, hoping that if they throw a few coins into the Trevi fountain, its power will fulfil their wish to return one day to the Eternal City.

THE WOMEN OF ROME

The typical Roman woman is quite small, with a well-rounded figure which is shown to advantage by elegant and close-fitting clothes. She usually has wavy black or brown hair, exactly as one would imagine. Nearly every young *Romana* rides a moped or a Vespa. She will scarcely ever leave the house without make-up. On the other hand, the plump, black-clad *mamma* with dozens of children hanging round her skirt, is seldom seen any more. This is because the women of Rome now delay or avoid starting a family: in the last two years, the birth rate has declined by 14 per cent.

In Italy the proportion of women of working age who are in employment is still only just above 30 per cent. The rest, according to opinion polls "have no opportunity or interest in entering the labor

Above: Confidently riding around Rome on a Vespa or a moped. Right: Girl talk outside the Pantheon.

market." Women who decide to raise a family generally give up any thought of earning a living. It is true that every child between the ages of 3 months and 3 years is entitled to a free place in a crèche; but the crèches are suffering from a shortage of money and staff. For instance, in the summer of 1993 the gardens and play-areas of the state-run crèches could not be used: no one wanted to be responsible for clearing away the used hypodermic needles and condoms which were lying around there. This means that the crèches are only used by unmarried mothers, who have no other choice. The middle-class Roman mothers send their children to private nursery schools and continually act as their chauffeurs. Yet, it would be no surprise to learn that, in the 1970s, these same women were among the thousands of demonstrators on the streets, shouting: "*Tremate, tremate, le streghe son tornate!*" ("Tremble with fear, the witches are here") – in other words, neither whores nor madonnas, but just women at last.

The feminist movement in Rome and Italy had a great influence on Europe as a whole: venerable palazzi were occupied and turned into women's centers, with no water or electricity, but with mattress dormitories and courses in self-defense and self-examination. At that time the women's movement already benefited from a solid theoretical basis, both within and outside the political parties, and after a few years could look back on some considerable achievements: in a country where women did not get the vote until 1945 and divorce was forbidden until 1970, there has, since 1978, been a law permitting abortion within a specified period after conception. The women's movement has now set its sights on reforming the law on rape and the right to establish autonomous women's centers. In general, feminism has been out of the headlines for more than a decade; it has become calmer. But in Rome, as long as 15 years ago, the "Virginia Woolf Women's University" was set up, with its own archive on the history of the women's movement, which has already made a name for itself thoughout Europe. It is located in Trastevere, in the "Buon Pastore" women's center, formerly a juvenile reformatory attached to the famous Roman jail, the "Regina Coeli." Seminars, film-showings and other events are held there.

The new women's consciousness, which emerged in the 1970s, has still, however, not fully taken root. In the universities, women predominantly study literature, while faculties of law, business management and all the technical and scientific subjects, are three-quarters occupied by men. It is certainly true that it is easier today for women to go out alone in the evenings, without immediately being taken for prostitutes. Until ten or fifteen years ago, for Roman men as well as women, an evening out simply meant a meal, going to the cinema or to a nightclub. Only after the breakthrough of the

women's movement, did it become possible to meet in perfectly ordinary wine-bars, pubs and cafés which were not the preserve of exclusive cliques, nor a jungle for the hunter and the hunted.

Yes, the women of Rome have certainly gained in self-confidence. They greatly enjoy looking attactive and sexy, in the knowledge that no one can any longer assume the right to brand them, for this reason, as loose or immoral. The one big event which the women's movement will not allow to be taken from them is the demonstration on 8th March, International Women's Day. All over Italy, this day is celebrated with processions and slogan-shouting, when the women adorn themselves with mimosa. Yet even the character of this event has altered and become more conciliatory in the past ten years: in many Italian towns, as far south as Sicily, the local authorities have now taken over the official distribution of mimosa to all their female citizens – a form of homage paid before returning to the daily battle of the sexes.

DAILY LIFE IN ANCIENT ROME

Let us imagine a Roman citizen in the 2nd century AD, when Rome stood at the height of its power. He is a rich man, who owns *latifundia* (country estates) which are worked by his slaves. He has a house in the city and a villa in the country. He wakes early. The Roman nights are anything but quiet, since traffic is banned from the streets during the day, and so, all night long, carts rumble over the rough, cobbled streets. In the early hours one hears the lowing of cattle being driven to the slaughterhouses, and porters shout for people to make way for them. Our typical Roman washes superficially, dons his toga with the help of a slave and breakfasts on some bread and cheese.

In the meantime the mistress of the house has woken up in her own bedroom. Her morning toilette occupies a good deal of time: she cleans her teeth with

Above: A Roman lady attends to her beauty.
Right: A dinner-party in ancient Rome.

powdered horn, and gets her personal slave to pluck out any unwanted facial hairs and to arrange her coiffure. Today she might even choose a wig imported from India to adorn her head. With the help of an army of slave-girls she powders her forehead and arms white, puts on lipstick and rouge, and blackens her eyelashes and eyelids with kohl.

By now her husband is receiving his *clientes*, people from various ranks of society and professions, who appear at his house every morning, in order to receive a certain sum of money. On a private level, this is the same as what takes place between the emperor and approximately 150,000 of his subjects, who do no work but live on state support. After he has satisfied his *clientes*, the Roman citizen leaves his house. Outside he makes his way with some difficulty through the bustle of a city with a million and a half inhabitants. There is construction going on everywhere, because houses keep burning down and have to be rebuilt. The narrow streets, stinking of refuse, are thronged with people of every race and color. He heads for the Forum to deal with some urgent business and perhaps to meet some acquaintances; or he may go to the basilica to attend a friend's court case, or to find out about the numerous divorce suits that have been filed.

Meanwhile, at home, the *matrona* has been attending to domestic matters, has rewarded or punished her slaves as necessary, and made the final arrangements for the day. She now has herself carried in a litter by four strong Greeks, to the center of the city where she makes some purchases in the luxury shops. Around midday she goes to the baths, where she spends the rest of the day with her husband. First of all they do a little gymnastics, then go into the turkish bath and after that into the *caldarium*, where they bathe in hot water. When they have energetically rubbed down their skin (soap was still unknown in those days),

they head for a lukewarm room, the *tepidarium*, and from there to the *frigidarium*, to refresh themselves with cold water. Surrounded by statues and frescoes, they now take their *prandium*, a cold meal comprising meat, vegetables and fruit and a glass or two of wine, and finally go for walk through the arcades which stretch for 2 1/2 miles (4 km) through the center of Rome.

In the late afternoon they may enjoy a theater performance, or perhaps a gladiatorial contest or chariot race, before visiting a friend who has invited them to dinner. Their host receives them surrounded by a large number of slaves. In the *triclinium*, or dining-room, the majordomo shows each guest to the place to which he or she is assigned according to a strict social hierarchy. They stretch out on one of the divans arranged on three sides of the large square table. Leaning on the left elbow, the diners put the food into their mouth with the right hand. There are no forks, only knives, spoons and toothpicks. Now and then slaves pass round

bowls of scented water and towels. The meal is made up of at least seven courses, including an hors d'oeuvres, three main dishes, two light, grilled dishes and a dessert, which is usually a rich gateau or flan. A large choice of side-dishes, various sauces, vegetables and fruit from all over the world complete the meal. With it, the guests would drink several different wines and would be entertained by poets, comedians and dancing-girls. In the end the evening turns into uninhibited carousing.

On the way home through the unlit streets, accompanied by slaves carrying flaming torches, our couple tries to avoid notorious neighborhoods and to get safely past the waggons and herds of livestock which crowd the nocturnal streets. Once home, they retire to bed in separate rooms.

There have been many novels and films which have attempted to recapture the atmosphere of imperial Rome, but the only one that really succeeded was the marvellous *Satyricon*, by Fellini.

THE SALONS OF ROME

The Colosseum, the Fora, the baths, the triumphal arches, the columns and the obelisks symbolize for millions of people the Eternal City and the splendor of the Roman empire. By contrast, the palazzi bear witness to the Rome which grew up from the Middle Ages to our own day, and they show another side to the city, one with more human characteristics. Being owned by great families the palaces have an eventful history, marked by both tragedy and gaiety, by weddings and feasts, by passions and violent crimes; and the legends which are woven around these buildings make the aristocratic families who lived in them appear even more fascinating.

There are magnificent historic buildings in many other cities of Italy, but only Rome has the Palazzo Colonna, which

Above: Last-minute shopping for tonight's party.. Right: ...while the chauffeur is already waiting.

has been lived in by the same family for over a thousand years. I had the honor to be invited there on many occasions, by Princess Isabel Colonna who, at the age of over ninety, was still the First Lady of Rome. On one occasion the guests included, along with high-ranking prelates and members of the papal aristocracy, a famous journalist and director of a leading daily newspaper. But on that very evening some serious international crisis had developed, which meant redesigning the whole front page of his paper. I tried to explain this to the *principessa*, who was obviously very indignant that her guest had still not arrived. All she said was: "When one is invited to the Colonnas, one does not arrive late!"

In the numerous salons in the Rome of the last twenty years it was, of course, not always as formal as that, and in general an enjoyable custom grew up of inviting a mixture of politicians and novelists, aristocrats and film people, journalists and business tycoons, all to the same parties. When the weather got warm, the "salons"

were moved out on to the beautiful Roman terraces, where, fanned by the pleasantly cool zephyrs of the *ponentino*, one held discussions late into the night, reached agreements or set various initiatives in motion.

Even though the individuals who frequented the salons were nearly always the same, this did not prevent every salon from having its own typical guests, who usually matched the personality of the lady of the house: those invited by the Contessa Emanuela Castelbarco, whose grandfather was the great Arturo Toscanini, were lovers of classical music, and you might meet Zubin Mehta, von Karajan or Horovitz there. Maria Angiolillo, on the other hand, kept open house chiefly for government ministers and members of the ruling party. The home of Gilberte Ossola, whose husband was the Minister of Foreign Trade and prior to that, director-general of the Banca d'Italia, was a meetingplace for the world of finance, while those that foregathered at the palazzo of the Marchesa Sandra Ve-

rusio were mainly intellectuals, writers and newspaper publishers. If you were invited by Chicca Monicelli you could expect to meet filmstars like Alberto Sordi or Monica Vitti; in the Palazzo Pecci Blunt the Black Aristocracy was again represented, but the Contessa Donatella also opened her doors to the highest state dignitaries, including the chairman of the Senate, Giovanni Spadolini.

My own salon was known for being a favorite rendez-vous of politicians and liberals, and in the 1970s it served as the headquarters in the battle to secure the introduction of the divorce law in Italy. It was also always the salon of leading figures in European politics, and my guests included Walter Scheel, Simone Weil, Count Otto Lambsdorff, Catherine Lalumière, Adolfo Suarez, Emilio Colombo, Gerhart Baum, and many others.

The year 1993 was marked by economic crises and austerity, yet one must hope that a tradition that began with Petronius, and has contributed so much to the growth of ideas, will not be lost.

RELIGION, SUPERSTITION AND MAGIC

In the last few years a development has been noticeable in Rome, similar to what happened in the imperial age: the city has seen a growing amalgam of languages and cultures, and above all of religions. For since the end of the 1980s Rome has experienced an influx of immigrants from very diverse countries of origin, with their own traditions and forms of worship. The Romans have long ago learnt to adapt to this: in the market in the Piazza Vittorio, for instance, many of the butchers have learnt that Moslems not only refuse to eat pork, but they will only eat beef that has been slaughtered in the approved *halal* manner, that is to say, with its throat cut and drained of all blood. Wherever this service is offered, you can even read notices in Arabic script. Many employers have also found

Above: Bocca della Verità, Mouth of Truth
Right: Is the future not looking too good?

out that their Moslem employees are obliged to call on the name of Allah at prescribed times and to kneel down facing Mecca.

The great mosque, which has arisen on the Monte Antenne, is a widely visible sign of the substantial Moslem presence in Rome. There are well over 50,000 of them, who in recent years have arrived from North Africa, Pakistan, Somalia and elsewhere.

By contrast, the large Jewish community in Rome has roots that go back a very long way. The first wave of Jews arrived in Rome in the year 70 AD, after the destruction of Jerusalem by the Roman army. The Jews feel themselves to be Roman through and through, and today are completely integrated in the economic and intellectual life of the city. The place where they meet and worship is the synagogue with its easily recognizable dome, standing at the edge of the Ghetto on the Lungotevere Cenci.

Less obvious is the presence of Buddhist communities, which have no center

234

of worship of their own. They are cared for by representatives of their religion, who are sent to Rome from the monasteries of distant Asia.

These days, all big western cities are home to a variety of religious sects. What makes Rome different, however, is its own traditional leaning towards magic and superstition, which the city has preserved throughout its millennia of history, and which is manifested in very ancient as well as modern magical practices. Astonishingly, these have developed entirely within the traditional framework of the Catholic Church, though many ancient or exotic "heathen" practices have been embodied in them.

Many Romans can still remember the actor Maurizio Arena, who was at the peak of his fame in the 1970s. After a life of excessive self-indulgence, he suddenly had an attack of religious zeal, and under the guidance of the Philippine miracle healer Alex Orbito, he began to perform miraculous cures himself. His house at Casalpalocco, south of Rome, became a place of pilgrimage. People who suffered from all manner of afflictions, came to him in the hope of being miraculously healed.

Another pilgrim shrine was the dwelling, or rather the glory-hole below a staircase in the Via Grandi, where a simple woman of the people, known only as "Maestra," received her visitors. Surrounded by an odd assortment of religious objects, both from Catholic ritual as well as from a diversity of other religions, she bestowed her apparently beneficent blessings on supplicants of every social station.

By way of complete contrast, in a modern and very elegant practice in the Largo di Torre Argentina, a magician named Arcella operates in a highly professional manner, making use of a wide range of magic techniques, but above all specializing in the *malocchio*, the Evil Eye. The fee for an examination of this kind, with appropriate prescriptions, is no higher than would be charged by a good specialist in orthodox medicine, and even the magician will agree to a reduction if one baulks at his bill.

Operating on the same professional level is a Greek lady named Patra, who commutes back and forth between her home country and Rome. Whenever she arrives in the Eternal City, there will be a large number of clients waiting for the oracular Greek Cassandra to read their destiny from coffee grounds.

Anyone who is interested in esoteric beliefs, but does not want to abandon the comforting embrace of the Catholic faith, can visit the "Demon Museum " (Museo del Demonio) on the Lungotevere Prati, where you can see evidence of all sorts of strange happenings, which prove the existence of evil.

The African bishop Milingo is quite convinced of the tangible presence of the Devil. At the end of his well-attended church services he performs public exorcisms, thus causing considerable embarrassment to the official church. He is also prepared to struggle with the Spirit of Evil in private, for which purpose he receives those possessed at his appartment in the Via Porta Angelica.

Those who want to widen their knowledge of the esoteric can browse in the numerous specialized booksellers, from *Asek* in the Via di Sant'Eustachio to the *Europa* bookshop in the Via Venier, where one can obtain expert bibliographic advice from the proprietor, Enzo Cipriano.

For the visitor in a hurry, who is looking for immediate results at modest prices, we recommend the magic supermarket, *Skaramantica*, in the Via Merulana, where knowledgeable sales assistants, having listened carefully to your problem, will immediately supply you with the appropriate magic potion, without charging you anything extra for their professional advice.

"What makes a film work? That's easy to explain: it needs a big opening, one which hits the audience like a thunderclap and pins them to their seats, and it must have a breathtaking finale that they won't forget in a hurry. In between you give them any old story!" (Quoted from an Italian film-producer of the 1950s)

ITALIAN CINEMA

Italian film is inseparably bound up with the life and history of Italy. The period from 1945 to the mid-1960s was, to a much greater extent than in any other film-making nation, the Golden Age of the Italian cinema. It was in these years of greatest material austerity and need, that Italy produced films of notable artistic quality.

It is true that in the age of silent films Italian cinema produced some important

Above: Anna Magnani, an unforgettable star of the Italian cinema. Right: Shooting on location in the Piazza Navona.

phenomena, such as the actress Eleonora Duse, idolised as a goddess of beauty, or the muscleman Maciste, but these were isolated examples.

After the Second World War a new artistic movement swept through Italian cinema – Neorealism. Directors who later became world-famous, like Luchino Visconti, Roberto Rosselini, Giuseppe de Santis, Vittorio de Sica and Alberto Lattuada, working in very rough-and-ready conditions and without any financial support, were passionately dedicated to the idea of using their art in a radical way to show life as it really was. When Rosselini made *Rome – Open City*, a film which today ranks among the most important in the history of cinema, he had to use bits of old filmstock left behind by American war reporters. He wrote the screenplay during the final months of the American occupation and shot the film while the US troops were still pulling out. This is why the tanks seen in the film are real tanks, and the stories that he told in the neorealist manner were essentially true – even if they may not have happened exactly as he showed them.

Many of the directors used the artistic techniques of Neorealism to put over Communist ideas. Yet ironically their films were first shown to the public in the movie theaters of New York, and only later became known in Italy. The Italian government wanted to establish at least one non-Communist director and stumbled upon Federico Fellini. In the years that followed he was showered with state funds and soon his films became famous all over the world. To make *La Dolce Vita* (1959), the largest studio in the Cinecittà production complex was put at his disposal for eight months. In it an accurate replica of several hundred yards of the Via Veneto, one of the most famous streets in Rome, was constructed.

Meanwhile other writer-directors were making cinema history: Michelangelo Antonioni's sensitive films, including

L'Avventura, and *Red Desert*, used a severely economical visual language; Pier Paolo Pasolini made his name as a director with *Accatone* (1961) and over the years came to represent the moral conscience of the nation. When Pasolini was murdered in 1975, his pupil Bernardo Bertolucci had already become famous with his *Last Tango in Paris*. Luchino Visconti always remained wedded to the theater, but directed many films which were worldwide successes, starting with *Rocco and his Brothers* (1960), then *The Leopard* (1963), which portrayed life among the Sicilian aristocracy in the 19th century, and ending up in 1971with his film version of Thomas Mann's haunting novella, *Death in Venice*.

Since the 1960s Sergio Leone has been making the very popular "spaghetti Westerns," such as *Play me the Song of Death* (1968), while Francesco Rosi and the Taviani brothers made committed and believable political films. Around the same time Lina Wertmueller and Ettore Scola were trying similar things.

After Neorealism, in the early 1960s, Italian cinema took off in another new direction: into comedy. Though the critics never really took them seriously, these films faithfully reflected the confidence and optimism of those boom years. Comic actors like Alberto Sordi, Vittorio Gassman, Ugo Tognazzi, Nino Manfredi and Totò gave a credible portrayal of the average Italian of these days – but with just enough exaggeration to make him funny. One could say that the Italian comedies of those years, so cheerful and carefree, gave no thought to the longer term future, but perhaps typified a levity and *joie de vivre* which today can no longer be recaptured because harsh reality does not permit us to do so.

It is true that there are a number of very fine young comic actors around today, such as Roberto Benigni, Massimo Troisi and Nanni Moretti; but their style of comedy is very individualistic. It no longer has that flavor of easy-going good humor, which was so typical of classic Italian comedy.

A LOVE-LETTER TO ROME

By a remarkable coincidence the letters which spell *Roma*, when read backwards, give *Amor*, the Latin word for Love. Now if, just for fun, you think for a moment about this odd fact, you might come to the conclusion that Rome is the City of Love, because its name contains the sweetest word in the world. But on the other hand you might say that Rome is the exact opposite of love, because the name of the city reverses the word Amor. This little word-game contains a grain of truth which is very familiar to anyone who has ever stayed in Rome, even if only for a few days: you can love the Eternal City, or you can hate it, with equal intensity – or (as is most often the case), love it and hate it at the same time. One thing is for sure; you cannot remain indifferent to Rome.

Above: Balloon-seller in the Piazza Navona.
Right: Early morning in one of the parks of Rome.

The city on the Seven Hills is today a bad-tempered and often aggressive metropolis, and the main reason for this is, of course, the traffic, which from early morning until late into the night torments the city and eats away its very soul, that soul of beautiful travertine marble from which the baroque churches and palaces are built. And yet not even the presence of a million automobiles can justify such contrariness. Friendly is the one thing Rome has never been.

The novelist Albert Moravia remarked that Romans possess a certain harshness, which, combined with their awareness of living in the capital of the world – *caput mundi* –, leads to a particular form of arrogance, known as *boria*.

This expresses itself in that favorite activity of the Roman, *sfottò*: it amuses him to mock his fellow men with a contemptuous wit and pay him false compliments with an ironic smile. And yet a carefully judged measure of *sfottò* (only the Romans know just the right amount) can also be the greatest proof of friendship –

another strange contradiction in this city which attracts and repels simultaneously, which caresses its lovers and then suddenly (and sometimes brutally) mistreats them.

The love for Rome is not awakened from one day to the next. It is the result of a lengthy seduction, and once you are aware of being smitten, it is already too late to do anything about it. It is like an illness which goes unnoticed during the incubation period and then breaks out suddenly and unexpectedly.

In the long years of its history, the city in which, as it happened, both a Messalina and a Lucrezia Borgia lived and made their mischief, has refined its ancient arts of seduction and acquired many new ones. This city, which has seen both the splendor and cruelty of the Caesars, the piety and corruption of the popes, modern Fascism and democracy – remains a beautiful paradox.

It is sufficient, on a winter's day when the *Tramontana* is blowing down from the mountains, to look down on the city from the Gianicolo, and discover the perfect outlines of its domes, spires and cupolas etched against the background of a cobalt-blue evening sky. It is sufficient to experience those August afternoons when the summer heat of 90°F (35°C) or more hits you in the face – in that absolute silence that hangs between the vault of an almost white sky and the black asphalt of the streets, in which the only things moving are weary tourists and roaming cats. It is sufficient to see Rome just once in all its springtime glory, with the glowing carpet of blooms in the Villa Sciara or the Villa Celimontana, and the wild flowers growing on the pediments and cornices of the old houses.

And one must see Rome at least once in autumn, as you walk on the Gianicolo or the Pincio, past the busts of all those famous Italians, at whose feet the dead leaves gather; or as you stroll on a rainy evening across the loneliest and most ma-

jestic piazza in the city, St Peter's Square, listening to the gentle conversation between the rain and the two fountains, which reminds you of the gossip of old ladies in the drawing-rooms of a bygone age which were illuminated by the same soft light that radiates from the great lamps in the colonnades.

But unfortunately Rome has quite another face. Those same domes and façades are sadly afflicted by a daily stream of traffic that is more the sort of thing you would expect in a Third World megalopolis than in a European city; and its historic parks are often littered with junkies' needles, waste paper and plastic bags.

Yet despite all its sinister and unsavory qualities, the city has preserved its past glory, and even if its present is rather problematic, it is not so bad that no spark of hope remains. And so, let us close with a few lines by Gioacchino Belli: *Si moro e po'arinasco, prego Iddio d'arinasce a Roma mia* – If I should die and then be born again, I pray to God that I will return to earth in my beloved Rome.

239

Nelles Maps ... get you going.

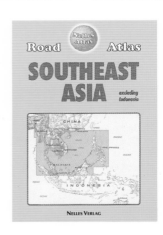

- Afghanistan
- Australia
- Bangkok
- Burma
- Caribbean Islands 1 / Bermuda, Bahamas, Greater Antilles
- Caribbean Islands 2 / Lesser Antilles
- Central America
- China 1 / North-Eastern China
- China 2 / Northern China
- China 3 / Central China
- China 4 / Southern China
- Crete
- Egypt
- Hawaiian Islands
- Hawaiian Islands 1 / Kauai

Nelles Maps

- Hawaiian Islands 2 / Honolulu, Oahu
- Hawaiian Islands 3 / Maui, Molokai, Lanai
- Hawaiian Islands 4 / Hawaii
- Himalaya
- Hong Kong
- Indian Subcontinent
- India 1 / Northern India
- India 2 / Western India
- India 3 / Eastern India
- India 4 / Southern India
- India 5 / North-Eastern India
- Indonesia
- Indonesia 1 / Sumatra
- Indonesia 2 / Java + Nusa Tenggara
- Indonesia 3 / Bali
- Indonesia 4 / Kalimantan

- Indonesia 5 / Java + Bali
- Indonesia 6 / Sulawesi
- Indonesia 7 / Irian Jaya + Maluku
- Jakarta
- Japan
- Kenya
- Korea
- Malaysia
- West Malaysia
- Manila
- Mexico
- Nepal
- New Zealand
- Pakistan
- Philippines
- Singapore
- South East Asia
- Sri Lanka
- Taiwan
- Thailand
- Vietnam, Laos, Cambodia

GUIDELINES

PREPARATIONS

Travel seasons

The mediterranean climate with mild winters, hot summers and relatively light rainfall, (which is limited to spring and autumn, and does not last long) makes a visit to Rome attractive throughout the year. If you want to avoid large crowds of tourists, you should not come at Easter or Whitsun, when pilgrims from all over the world descend on the Holy City. From the middle of September onward, when the weather is not so hot, is the time we would recommend for visiting Rome. However, if you can handle temperatures of up to 40° C (100° Fahrenheit), you can enjoy a relatively traffic-free Rome in July and August, when most of its citizens have escaped to the sea or the mountains. Then, on Sundays, the city seems so dead and deserted that you can even risk exploring the historic center on a rented bicycle. On the other hand, at this time many of the shops and restaurants are closed.

Even in winter a visit to Rome has its attractions. It never gets really cold – the average temperature in the coldest month, January, is 8° C (46° F.) – and this is the season when one meets the fewest foreigners.

Clothing

Even in the hottest summer months you should take care not to be too scantily clad when walking around the city. If you wear a miniskirt or shorts and a shoulderless shirt or blouse, you will not be allowed to enter many churches. In spring and autumn it is advisable to take a lightweight jacket for the evenings; and in winter you will certainly need a thick pullover, since Roman houses are very poorly heated, and the proximity of the sea can make even moderately cool weather seem rather unpleasant. It is very important to have comfortable shoes, since Rome is best explored on foot.

Facts and figures

The city of Rome, or *Comune di Roma* (approx. 3 million inhabitants) is the capital of the Republic of Italy and also of the province of Rome (pop. 4 m) and of the region of Lazio (pop.5.2 m). It is situated on the river Tiber, about 12 miles (20 km) from the sea. The city boundary has a length of approximately 174 miles (280 km) and the city covers an area of about 580 sq. miles (1500 sq. km). It is divided up into 22 traditional *rioni* (inner city districts), 18 *quartieri* (more modern districts), 11 *suburbi* (suburbs) and the outlying *agro Romano* (country area). Since the 1930s new outer suburbs (*borgate*) have been added, where low-paid agricultural workers and unemployed people from southern Italy have settled.

The mayor of the city of Rome has his official seat on the Capitoline Hill, the parliament consists of two chambers, the Chamber of Deputies and the Senate. The State President has his offices in the Quirinal Palace. Local elections take place every five years.

Getting there

By air: The international airport, *Leonardo da Vinci*, is located in Fiumicino, 19 miles (30 km) west of Rome. A bus service (ACOTRAL) connects the airport with the main station, Roma Termini. The bus leaves every 15 minutes and, depending on the traffic conditions, the journey takes between 25 and 45 minutes. There is also a suburban rail connection to the Ostiense station, where you can pick up the Metro (Line B) and various buses. Charter flights land at the *Ciampino* military airport, 9 miles (15 km) outside the city, on the Via Appia Nuova. There are taxis to take you from both airports to the city, and the journey from Fiumicino to the central station costs around 60,000 lire. To be sure that you do not get ripped off, you should only use the official yellow taxis. If there are none to be had, agree the fare in advance!

By train: If you are already in Italy, use the fast and comfortable InterCity trains from Milan, Florence, Venice or Naples, but note that you have to book a few hours, at least, before departure. International and IC train journeys end right in the center of the city at the *Stazione Termini*. As in every large railroad station you must be sure to keep a close eye on your luggage!

Outside the station there is a taxi-rank and numerous bus-routes (yellow ATAC buses); the quickest way to many destinations is by Metro. There is a tourist office in the station building and an ATAC information booth on the left, outside the station, should you need help.

By car: the (toll-paying) motorway from northern Italy, the *Autostrada del Sole*, ends at the *Gran Raccordo Anulare* (GRA for short), a very busy orbital motorway which runs right round Rome and, especially in the holiday season, is hopelessly overcrowded. The many routes into the city are well signposted.

By bus: There is a regular service from London's Victoria Coach Station. The journey takes two days.

Car-sharing: In many cities in Italy and neighboring countries, there are organizations who will arrange for you to travel as a passenger in a private car, at a reasonable price. However, anyone with fragile nerves must realize that Italian motorists tend to have a driving style which would make most people's hair stand on end! In Rome, information can be obtained by calling: 6794935.

Entry requirements

Visitors from Great Britain, the United States and other western countries do not require a visa, only a valid passport.

TRANSPORT

Connections in Rome

The historic center can be explored relatively quickly on foot, and this is the only way to discover all the hidden corners, narrow alleys and courtyards which add so much to the charm of the city.

The quickest way to get from one part of the city to another is by **Metro**: Line A runs from *Ottaviano* (near the Vatican) to *Anagnina*; underneath the central station it crosses Line B, which runs from the north-east of Rome *(Rebibbia)* to *EUR-Fermi* in the south-west. The current price of a Metro ticket to any destination is 700 lire.

Important stops on Line A: Ottaviano (Vatican); Flaminia (Piazza del Popolo); Piazza di Spagna; Piazza Barberini; Piazza della Repubblica; Stazione Termini; Piazza Vittorio Emanuele; S.Giovanni in Laterano.

Important stops on Line B: Cavour (S. Pietro in Vincoli); Colosseo; Circo Massimo; Piramide (from here there is a suburban rail connection to Ostia Antica and Ostia Lido); S. Paolo fuori le Mura.

Disadvantages of the Metro: during the rush-hour the trains are appallingly overcrowded (beware of pickpockets), and they only run until 10.30 pm.

Until about 1am at night the orange colored **buses** of the ATAC keep running, as do the few remaining **tram (streetcar)** routes. At the ATAC kiosk outside the central station you can buy a transport route map showing all the bus, streetcar and Metro routes, which make up a dense and scarcely comprehensible network. Bus and streetcar-drivers are happy to give you information, and any Roman standing beside you at the stop will be glad to answer your questions. With a single ticket costing 800 lire, you can travel for an hour and a half on all public transport other than the Metro. The tickets are sold in kiosks, bars and tobacconists, or at the green ATAC huts found at major bus-stops. They have to be punched on board the bus or streetcar.

Tourists are entitled to buy one-day or one-week tickets at reduced prices (only from ATAC in the Piazza Cinquecento).

For excursions into the country outside Rome you should make use of the blue **long-distance buses** of ACOTRAL. These depart from the Piazza della Repubblica, near the central station.

Taxis are relatively cheap in Rome: the basic fare is 3000 lire, but at nights and weekends there is a supplementary charge. In the city center there are numerous taxi-ranks, yet whenever it rains you will have a problem finding a free cab. But even then you should, if possible, avoid taking a private taxi: they are more expensive than the authorized ones and they carry no insurance.

In principle, we would *not* recommend that you try touring the sights in your **own car**. Private traffic is banned from the center of the city and the frantic driving style of the locals takes some getting used to. If you really do not want to do without your own car, you should park only in well-frequented areas and leave nothing lying inside. In case of theft or break-in go to the nearest police-station. The first thing they will check is whether your car has been towed away.

Car rental (*Autonoleggio*)

Avis: International reservations at local rates: Tel: 01307733. Piazza Esquilino 1/c, Tel: 4701216. Via Sardegna 38/a, Tel: 4750728, 4701229; Fiumicino airport, Tel: 601531. **Europcar**: Internat. reservations at local rates, Tel: 01303151. Piazza Vivona 3, Tel: 591375; Via Lombardia 7, 4750381, 4759103; Fiumicino airport, Tel: 601977. **Hertz**: International reservations at local rates: Tel: 01303151. Hilton Hotel, Via Cadlolo 101, Tel: 343758. EUR, Viale America 133, Tel: 5915544. Fiumicino Airport, Tel: 7240095. Maggiore: Piazza della Repubblica 57/58, Tel: 463715, 4755037.

Scooter hire

The rates are about 50,000 lire per day. No driviers license is needed, but it is better not to be acomplete novice in Rome.

Scoot-a-long, Via Cavour 302, Tel: 6780206. **Scooters for Rent**, Via della Purificazione 66, Tel: 465485.

Bicycle hire

I Bike Rome, Via Veneto 156, Tel: 3225240; **Bicinoleggio Telefonico** (bike hire by telephone), Lungotevere Marzio 3, Tel: 6543394; **Collati**, Via del Pellegrino 82, Tel: 6541084.

Breakdown assistance

If you belong to the AA or RAC in Britain, you can obtain the necessary documentation from them entitling you to free assistance if you break down in Italy. Cars may only be towed on the *autostrade* by breakdown vehicles.

Rescue service of the **ACI**, Via Solferino 32, Tel: 4041051/4041052. **Roadside emergencies**, Tel: 116.

Train stations

Central station **Stazione Termini**: Intercity and international train services, information Tel: 4775; seat and couchette reservations Tel: 110; sleeping-car reservations: Via Boncompagni 25, Tel: 4754941. **Tiburtina Station**: certain trains running between northern and southern Italy only call at this station; information Tel: 4956626. **Trastevere Station**: trains to Pisa and Genoa. **Ostiense Station**: trains to Ostia, Nettuno al Mare, Naples. **Roma-Nord Station**: Trains to Viterbo. **Prenestina Station**: Trains to Pescara. **Tuscolana Station**: Trains to Grosseto, Viterbo. **San Pietro Station**: suburban trains. **Porta S.Paolo Station**: Trains to Viterbo and Ostia Lido.

PRACTICAL TIPS

Accommodation

Rome offers an enormous choice of accommodation in every price category. Information can be obtained from the Rome Tourist Office, EPT. One can also stay very cheaply in pilgrim hostels run by various monastic orders. You can find out about these from your local Catholic church or diocesan office at home.

LUXURY: **Le Grand Hotel**, Via Vittorio Emanuele Orlando, Tel: 4709. **Hassler-Villa Medici**, Piazza Trinità dei Monti 6, Tel: 6792651. **Cavalieri Hilton**, Via Cadlolo 101, Tel:31511. **Excelsior**, Via Veneto 125, Tel: 4708. **Jolly**, Corso d'Italia 1, Tel: 8495. **D'Inghilterra**, Via Bocca di Leone 14, Tel: 672161. **Raffael,** Largo Febo 2, Tel: 650881.

MID-PRICE: **Archimede**, Via dei Mille 19, Tel: 4454600. **Britannia**, Via Napoli 64, Tel: 4883153. **Buenos Aires**, Via Clitunno 9, Tel: 8442404; **Canova**, Via Urbana 10/a, Tel: 4873314. **Celio**, Via SS. Quattro 35/c, Tel: 750759. **Columbus**, Via delle Conciliazione 33, Tel: 6865435. **Degli Aranci**, Via Barnaba Oriani 9-11, Tel: 8085250. **Doria**, Via Merulana 4 and Piazza S.M.Maggiore, Tel: 7316939 and 4465888. **Fontana**, Piazza di Trevi 96, Tel: 6786113. **Gregoriana**, Via Gregoriana 18, Tel: 6794269. **Internazionale**, Via Sistina 79, Tel: 6784686 and 6793047. **Manfredi**, Via Margutta 61, Tel: 3207676. **Marghera,** Via Marghera 29, Tel: 4454237. **Pincio**, Via Capo le Case 50, Tel: 6790758. **Sicilia**, Via Sicilia 24, Tel: 6790758. **Teatro di Pompeo**, Largo del Pallaro 8, Tel: 6872566. **Trevi**, Vicolo del Babuccio 20-21, Tel: 6789563 and 6785894.

BUDGET: **Assisi**, Via dei Mille 27/a, Tel: 4453813 and 4454041. **Campo de' Fiori**, Via del Biscione 6, Tel: 6540865. **Colibri**, Via Boncompagni 79, Tel: 4743218. **Elide,** Via Firenze 50, Tel: 4883977. **Erdarelli**, Via Due Macelli 28, Tel: 6791265. **Forte**, Via Margutta 61, Tel: 3207625. **Giuliana**, Via Palermo 36, Tel: 4881637. **Liberiano,** Via Santa Prassede 25, Tel: 4883804. **Lydia**, Via Sistina 42, Tel: 6791744. **Marchionni**, Via Palermo 28, Tel: 4882746. **Oceania**, Via Firenze 38, Tel: 4824696. **Piccolo**, Via dei Chiavari 32, Tel: 6542560.

Rimini, Via Marghera 17, Tel: 4461991. **Suisse,** Via Gregoriana 56, Tel: 6783649.

YOUTH HOSTELS: (admission only with YH card): Information: **Assoziazione Italiana Alberghi per la Gioventù**, Via Cavour 44 (3rd floor), Tel: 462432. **Ostello del Foro Italico**, Viale Olimpiadi 61, Tel: 3964909, (absolutely essential to book ahead).

CAMPING SITES: **Camping Tiber**, Via Tiberina (1 mile / 1.4 km), Tel: 6912314. **Capitol**, Via Castelfusano 45 (Ostia Antica) Tel: 5662720. **Flaminio**, Via Flaminia Nuova. (5 miles / 8.2 km) Tel: 3279006. **Nomentana**, Via della Cesarina 11, Tel: 6100296. **Roma Camping**, Via Aurelia 831 (5 miles / 8.2 km), Tel: 6223018. **Happy Camping**, Via Prato della Corte 1915, Tel: 6422401. **Camping Seven Hills**, Via Cassia 1216, Tel: 3765571.

Airline offices

Air Canada: Milan, Tel: 2-29523943. **Alitalia**: Via Bissolati 13, Tel: 46881, reservations, Tel: 5455, 5456. **British Airways**: Via Bissolati 76, Tel: 471740. **Quantas**: Via Bissolati 20, Tel: 486561. **Swissair**: Via Po 10, Tel: 8470511/2; reservations, Tel: 8450555. **United**: Tel: 6-48904140.

Banks

Business hours: 8.30am - 1.30pm and approximately 3pm - 4pm. The afternoon times vary from bank to bank. You can change money at a bank, and at weekends at the central station and airport. Italian bank staff like to take their time so be prepared for a long wait. You can also change US dollars into lire in automats, but the rate is very poor. Best places to change money are **Thomas Cook**, Piazza Barberini 21a, open Mon-Sat 8.30am-6pm, and **American Express**, Piazza di Spagna 38, open Mon-Fri 9am-5.30pm and Sat 9am-12.30pm. These days credit cards are accepted in many shops and restaurants in Rome.

City tours

Information about tours of the city can be obtained from the Rome Tourist Office, EPT (see under Information), or from a leading travel agent: **CIT**, Piazza della Repubblica 68, Tel: 47941; **Univers**, Via Marsala 20, Tel: 4450290 or American Express, Piazza di Spagna 38, Tel: 6792658.

You can make a pleasant and inexpensive tour of Rome by streetcar (tram) on route 30. This takes an hour and a half and runs from Piazza Thorvaldson via the Viale Regina Margherita to San Lorenzo and on past the Porta Maggiore, S. Giovanni in Laterano and the Colosseum, to the Piazza Ostiense.

Another good way to see the city is in one of the horse-drawn carriages, affectionately known as *botticelle* (little barrels). You should ask to go through the parks and the old part of the city, around the Pantheon, since these are closed to motor traffic. The charge for an hour's trip is about 100,000 lire, but you should negotiate this with the driver before starting. You will find carriage-ranks in St Peter's Square, the Piazza di Spagna, by the Trevi Fountain, in the Piazza Navona, at the Colosseum and in the Piazza Venezia, Via Veneto and Villa Borghese.

Embassies and consulates

Australia: Embassy, Via Alessandria 215, Tel: 852721; consulate, Corso Trieste 25. **Britain**: Embassy and consulate, Via XX Settembre 80a Tel: 4825551. **Canada**: Embassy, Via G.B. De Rossi 27 Tel: 445981; consulate, Via Zara 30, Tel: 44598421. **New Zealand**: Embassy and consulate, Via Zara 28, Tel: 4402928. **USA**: embassy and consulate, Via Veneto 121, Tel 46741.

Emergencies

Police: Tel 113. **Carabinieri** (militia): Tel: 112. **Ambulance**: Tel: 5100. **First aid and Red Cross**: Tel 5100. **Emergency doctor:** Tel: 4756741-4. **Detoxification center**: Tel: 490663. **Cardiac emergency**: Tel: 47721. **Children's hospital**: Ospedale del Bambini Gesù: Piazza Sant'Onofrio, Tel: 65191. **ACI (Italian Automobile Association)**: breakdown service, Tel: 116. **Radio-taxi**: Tel: 3875, 4994, 4517, 3570.

Festivals and holidays

January 1, New Year's day. All shops are closed. **January 6**, *Befana*. The witch Befana gives presents to good children and punishes bad ones. Big market in the Piazza Navona. **March 8**, International Women's Day (*Festa delle Donne*). Women parade through the streets carrying mimosa. **March 9**, Day of Santa Francesca Romana, the patron saint of motorists. The Pope blesses drivers and their cars in front of the Colosseum. This is the only day when the convent of St Francesca is open to visitors. **March 19**, *San Giuseppe*. Local festival in the Trionfale district. **Palm Sunday**. All the churches are decorated with palm leaves and olive branches. On **Maunday Thursday** the Pope washes the feet of the poor. **Good Friday**: *Via Crucis* – the Pope follows the Stations of the Cross, to the Colosseum. **Easter Saturday**: Midnight Mass in S. Prassede. The high point of the religious celebrations is the Pontifical Mass on **Easter Sunday** (*Pasqua*), and the papal blessing *Urbi et Orbi* in St Peter's Square. On **Easter Monday** (*Pasquetta*) the Romans drive out into the country for the first picnic of the year. On **April 21** Rome celebrates its birthday. Fireworks and torchlight on the Capitoline Hill. **April 25** is the National Holiday. A ceremony of remembrance is held at the Fosse Ardeatine for the 335 hostages shot by the Nazis, and wreaths are laid at the national Vittorio Emanuele II memorial. **May 1**, Labor Day. Demonstration in front of S. Giovanni in Laterano. **Other festivals in May**: the "Antique Furniture Week" in the Via dei Coronari. Rose show in the rose garden on the Aventine. International show-jumping at the Villa Borghese. **June 2**, Republic Day. Military parades at the Villa Borghese. **June 23-24**, *San Giovanni* (Midsummer night), street festival in the San Giovanni district. **Mid-July**, *Festa de'-Noantri*. Sreet festival in Trastevere. **August 5**, *Ferragosto* – Ascension Day. **November 1**, All Saints Day. **December 8**, Feast of the Immaculate Conception. The Pope visits the Column of the Virgin Mary in the Piazza di Spagna. **December 24-25**, *Natale* – Christmas.

Food and drink

The newcomer has to get used to Italian eating habits: the kind of breakfast eaten in Anglo-Saxon countries is only served in the larger hotels; in the morning an Italian drinks an *espresso* or a *capuccino* in the bar on the corner, and at the most a croissant with it. The midday and evening meals are much more important, and both will consist of an *antipasto*, or cold starter, a pasta dish, then a fish or meat dish with vegetables or salad on the side, then cheese and a *dolce* (dessert) to finish with.

Around the family dinner-table, the meals are not always quite so lavish, and many restaurants have adapted themselves to tourism and now accept that not everyone wants to eat in such style twice a day. However, if you go out to eat with Italians, you should be prepared for long, self-indulgent meals. The midday meal (*pranzo*) is usually between 1pm and 3pm, and in the evening, the *cena*, between 8pm and 11pm.

During the day the Italian will drop in several times at his "local" to fortify himself with an espresso and maybe a *tramezzino* (toasted sandwich), a normal sandwich, a *pizzetta* (small pizza) or a *dolce*. You have to pay at the cash-desk first, then take your ticket to the bar and place your order. Most people remain standing at the bar, and if you want to sit down you have to pay extra.

Rome has many famous old-fashioned bars, cafés and restaurants. It is a matter of luck whether you eat cheaply and well, or expensively and badly. The more unpretentious a place looks from the outside, the safer it is to assume that you will be served simple but delicious food at moderate prices. Near big markets and in sidestreets, you will often find little trattorias, which, from the outside, are scarcely recognizable as such, are often family-run, and will serve mainly local dishes – generally a guarantee of excellent food, prepared by Mamma herself. You should avoid the kind of restaurant that announces it accepts all credit-cards, before you are inside the door.

If you start feeling peckish between meals, you can pop into one of the pizzerias and buy a slice of pizza *a taglio*, to take away, or into a *rosticceria*, where you can get grilled food for very little money. And be sure you remember to call in at a *gelateria*, where delicious ice-cream is served. The tastiest is the home-made *gelato artigianale*, which is available from many bars and in the famous ice-cream parlours. The addresses of these, as well as cafés and restaurants in various categories can be found in the Guidepost feature at the end of each chapter.

Glossary of food and drink terms

Although many restaurants nowadays have menus in English, you will find below the most important words you are likely to find on Roman menus.

Foods (*cibi*)

abbacchio	baby lamb
acciughe	anchovies
aceto	vinegar
affettato	cold meats
agnello	lamb
aglio	garlic
alici	anchovies
anatra	duck
anguria	water-melon
arancia	orange

aragosta	lobster
arrosto	roast meat
bistecca (ai ferri)	steak, cutlet (grilled)
brodo	meat broth, consommé
bruschetta	toasted bread with garlic and olive-oil
burro	butter
caprese	tomatoes with mozzarella
carciofi	artichokes
cavolfiore	cauliflower
cervello al burro	calf-brains in Butter
coniglio	rabbit
cinghiale	wild boar
coda alla vacinara	ox-tail
contorno	dish of vegetables
coratella	calf's offal
costata	entrecôte
cozze	mussels
crema	thick soup, cream
crostata	fruit flan
crudo	raw
erbe	herbs
fagiano	pheasant
fagioli	white beans
fagiolini	green beans
fegato	liver
finocchio	fennel
formaggio	cheese
frittata	pancake
fritto misto	mixed fried fish
funghi porcini	boletus mushrooms
gallina	chicken
gambero	crayfish
gnocchi	small dumplings
grano turco	sweet corn
grasso	fat
involtini	stuffed, rolled meat
lampone	raspberries
lingua	ox-tongue
lombata	loin of meat
lumache	snails
maiale	pork
mandorla	almond
manzo	beef
mela	apple
melanzane	aubergine
menta	mint

merluzzo	cod
miele	honey
minestra	soup
noce	nut
orata	golden perch
ossobuco	veal ragout with vegetables
ostriche	oysters
panino	bread roll
panna	cream
pasta e fagioli	thick noodle soup with white beans
patate	potatoes
pepe	pepper
peperone	paprika
pera	pear
pesce	fish
pesce spada	swordfish
pesto	basil sauce
pinoli	pine kernels
piselli	peas
pizzaiola	spicy tomato sauce
pollo arrosto	roast chicken
pollo alla diavola	grilled chicken with a spicy sauce
polpetta	meatballs
pomodoro	tomato
porchetta	sucking-pig
prosciutto	ham
ragù	meat sauce
riso	rice
rognoni	kidneys
rognoncino	calf's kidneys
sale	salt
salmone	salmon
salsa (verde)	(green) sauce
salsiccia	pork sausage
saltimbocca	medallions of veal with sage
scaloppine	veal cutlets
seppia	squid
sogliola	sole
spezzatino	goulash
allo spiedo, spiedino	spit-roasted
spigola	perch
succo	juice
sugo	sauce, gravy
tacchino	turkey
tartufo	truffle (also a cold dessert)
tonno	tuna-fish

tramezzino	sandwich
triglia	mullet
trippa alla romana	tripe cooked in the Roman style
trota	trout
in umido	steamed
uovo	egg
uva	grapes
verdura	vegetables
vitello	veal
vitello tonnato	veal with tuna-fish sauce
vongole	scallops, clams
zucchero	sugar

Drinks (*bevande*)

acqua fresca	drinking water
acqua gasata	carbonated water
amaretto	almond liqueur
amaro	bitter aperitif
aranciata	orangeade
bicchiere	glass
birra (alla spina)	(draught) beer
caffè (espresso)	espresso
caffèlatte	coffee with milk
cappuccino	espresso with foamy milk on top
ghiaccio	ice cube
grappa	spirit made from wine-lees
latte	milk
latte macchiato	milk with a dash of coffee
mezzo, quarto di litro	half, quarter litre
sambuca	aniseed liqueur
spremuta d'arancia, di limone, di pompelmo	freshly squeezed orange, lemon, grapefruit juice
spumante	sparkling wine
tè (al limone, con latte)	tea (with lemon, with milk)
vino abboccato, amabile	mild wine
vin santo	sweet dessert wine
vino secco	dry wine

Information

Rome Tourist Bureau EPT: Via Parigi 11, 00185 Roma, Tel: 461851, 463748, open daily 9am-1pm, 2pm-7pm, closed Sundays. *At the central station:* Tel: 465461, 4750078, open daily 9am-7pm. *At Leonardo da Vinci airport:* Tel: 6011255, 60124471.

Enjoy Rome: Via Varese 39 Tel: 4451843. This is a new agency, staffed by helpful and knowledgeable English-speaking personnel. Good for offbeat ideas and cheap accommodation. Open Mon-Fri 8.30am-1pm and 3.30-6pm; Saturdays 8.30am-1pm. Telephone service until 10pm.

Vatican Information Bureau: switchboard Tel: 6982. Ufficio Informazioni Pellegrini e Turisti, on the south side of St Peter's Square. Tel: 6984866, 6984466.

ENIT (Italian National Tourist Organization) Via Marghera 2, Tel: 49711. The best place to go for information on Lazio and the rest of Italy. Open Mon-Fri 9am-1pm, also Mon, Wed, Fri, 4pm-6pm.

ENIT has offices in England, 1 Princes St, *London* W1, Tel: (071) 408 1254; in the USA: Suite 1565, Rockefeller Center, *New York* NY10111, Tel: (212) 245 4822; 500 N. Michigan Ave., *Chicago* IL 60611, Tel: (312) 644 0990; and 12400 Wilshire Blvd., Suite 550, *Los Angeles* CA 90025, Tel: (310) 820 0622; and in Canada, 1 Pl. Ville Marie, Suite 1914, *Montréal*, Québec H3B 3M9, Tel: (514) 866 7667.

Lost and found

City Lost Property Office (*Servizio Oggetti Rinvenuti*) Via V. Bettoni 1, (Trastevere), Tel: 5810583, open Mon-Sat 9am-11am. **ATAC** (City Transport Services) Via Volturno 65, Tel: 4695, open Mon-Sat, 9am-12 noon. **Railway Lost Property** (*Ufficio Oggetti Rinvenuti delle FFSS*) Via Marsala 53, Tel: 47306682, open daily 7am till midnight.

Markets

Porta Portese (Trastevere); Sunday mornings. **Via Sannio** (near Porta S. Giovanni), every morning except Sunday. **Piazza Fontanella Borghese**, daily except Sunday. **Piazza Vittorio**, every morning except Sunday.

Medical help

In case of emergency you should go to the first aid station (*Pronto Soccorso*) at one of the hospitals. You will be treated free of charge, even without international medical insurance. A selection of hospitals with first aid stations: **Ospedale Fatebenefratelli**, on the Tiber Island, Tel: 58731. **Policlinico Umberto I**, Viale Policlinico 255, Tel: 49971. **Ospedale S. Giacomo**, Via Canova, Tel: 67261. **Ospedale S. Giovanni,** Via Amba Aradam, Tel 77051. **Policlinico Gemelli**, Largo Gemelli 8, Tel 33051. **Rome-American Hospital**, Via Emilio Longoni 69, Tel: 225571. Always an English-speaking doctor on duty.

For a house-call or consultation with an English-speaking doctor, call **International Medical Center**, Via Amendola 7 Tel: 4882371 (after hours and on Suns 4882371). The fees charged are not excessive. Failing all else, the British, American and Commonwealth embassies keep lists of English-speaking doctors.

Opening hours

Food shops: **Summer**: Mon-Sat 8am-1.30pm and 5.45-7.30pm. Closed Sat afternoons from July to September. **Winter**: Mon-Sat 8am-1.30pm and 5-7.30pm. Closed Thur afternoons. Other shops: Mon-Sat 9am-1pm and 4-7.30pm. In the main shopping streets they often stay open all day. However, they all close on Saturday afternoons in summer and on Monday mornings in winter. Many shops are closed right through August.

Pharmacies

Pharmacies or chemists (*farmacia*) sell more or less the same products as you find at home, but often under different brand names. Their opening hours are the same as for other shops, but in every district there is one pharmacy that stays open 24 hours. The list of all-night pharmacies is published in the daily newspapers or can be got by ringing 110 or 1921. **International 24-hour pharmacies**: Via Cavour 2, Tel: 4600 19. Piazza Barberini 49, Tel: 462996, 4755456. Other all-night pharmacies in the city center: **Farmacia allo Statuto**, Via dello Statuto 35. **Cristo re dei Ferrovieri**, Stazione Termini. **Jucci**, Piazza dei Cinquecento. **Piram**, Via Nazionale 49.

Post Offices

The Post Offices are open Mon-Fri 8.15am-2pm and Sat 8.30am-12 noon. Head Post Office: Piazza S. Silvestro. The Vatican City has its own Post Office (in St Peter's Square near the colonnades), which operates faster and more reliably than the Italian postal service.

The letter-boxes in the Vatican are blue, and in the rest of Italy red. Postage stamps can be bought at *tabacchi* shops.

Telephone

The are a large number of telephone booths in which you can use coins, tokens (*gettoni*) or phone-cards. A local call costs 200 lire. The Italian telephone service, SIP, has no connection with the Post Office. The SIP headquarters in the city center is in the Piazza S. Silvestro, and there are other offices in the central station and the Via Santa Maria. You can buy phone-cards here and in many tobacconists. In the SIP offices you can make long-distance calls by paying cash at the counter. The international prefix codes are:

Australia	0061
Ireland	00353
New Zealand	0064
United Kingdom	0044
USA, Canada	001

Tipping

A service-charge is included in your hotel or restaurant bill, but a further 5% or 10% is expected, as a *mancia* or gratuity. In bars, service is not included, so you should leave around 15% on the tray as a tip. In contrast to most countries, the usherette in the cinema also expects to be tipped. The usual sum is 500 lire.

AUTHORS

Ulrike Bossert, Project Editor of this book, studied German literature and Romance languages and literature, with Italian literature as her special subject. After several courses of study in Italy she now works in Munich as a freelance television and radio journalist and translator.

Luciano Arcella is a Neapolitan by birth. For some years he has been teaching anthropology and comparative religion at the Aquila University in Rome.

Nello Avella also comes from Naples but has lived for many years in Rome. He is another faculty member of Aquila University, where he lectures on the language and literature of Brazil.

Corrado Conforti was born and brought up in Rome, where he ran a language school. He is currently teaching Italian language and literature at the University of Eichstätt, in Germany.

Esther Dorn grew up in Rome, where she attended the German School. She then studied languages and literature in Munich and today works as an interpreter and translator in Munich and Rome.

Paolo Gatti is from the family of archaeologists in Rome. After working for several years in bookselling, he is now involved in adult education and organizing Italian cultural events in Munich.

Sabina Magnani-von Petersdorff was born in Rome and attended the Swiss School in the city. After studying history of art she moved to Berlin, where she has been working since 1982.

Andreas Miekisch comes from Munich but studied at the Film Academy in Rome. At the moment he is working in Munich and Rome as a freelance editor and screen writer.

Beatrice Rangoni-Machiavelli is a direct descendent of the Renaissance author of *The Prince*, Nicolò Machia-

velli. As a journalist she edited the weekly *La Tribuna* for many years, and since 1982 she has worked on international political committees.

Sabine Seeger-Baier studied to be a teacher at the College of Education in Heidelberg. After working in schools for several years, she went to Rome in 1986 and now works there as a correspondent for German and Swiss daily papers.

Gudrun Wendler is a painter, born in Hessen. After spells in New York, Moscow, Dublin, Paris and Tel Aviv she has lived in Rome and Bonn since 1992.

PHOTOGRAPHERS